FILM TALK

Directors at Work

WHEELER WINSTON DIXON

RUTGERS UNIVERSITY PRESS

NEW BRUNSWICK, NEW JERSEY, AND LONDON

Library of Congress Cataloging-in-Publication Data

Dixon, Wheeler W., 1950–
Film talk : directors at work / Wheeler Winston Dixon.
p. cm.
Includes index.
ISBN-13: 978–0-8135–4077–1 (hardcover : alk. paper)
ISBN-13: 978–0-8135–4078–8 (pbk. : alk. paper)
1. Motion pictures—Production and direction. 2. Motion picture
producers and directors—Interviews. I. Title.
PN1995.9.P7D548 2007
791.43023'30922—dc22

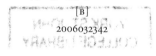

[B]
2006032342

A British Cataloging-in-Publication record for this book
is available from the British Library.

Manufactured in the United States of America

FOR GWENDOLYN,
always . . .

CONTENTS

INTRODUCTION

Film Talk is a series of interviews with contemporary film directors from all aspects of the film medium: pop culture directors, documentary directors, feminist filmmakers, social satirists, and Hollywood mavericks. For the sake of convenience, I have organized this material into three distinct sections. "The Old Masters" include Ronald Neame and the late Val Guest, who created some of the most important and influential films of the Golden Age of British cinema, from Neame's *The Horse's Mouth* and *Tunes of Glory,* to Guest's science fiction classic *The Day the Earth Caught Fire.* Also included in this group are the late Budd Boetticher, who most notably directed a group of Westerns with Randolph Scott that influenced Sam Peckinpah's best works, and Albert Maysles, who along with his late brother, David, created some of the most important documentaries of the 1960s, including *Salesman* and *What's Happening! The Beatles in the U.S.A.*

The second section, "Cult Visions," presents talks with Jack Hill, a Hollywood filmmaker whose 1970s action films have influenced Quentin Tarantino; Monte Hellman, the auteur of the minimalist masterpiece *Two-Lane Blacktop;* and Robert Downey Sr., whose social satires *Putney Swope* and *Greaser's Palace* paved the way for a generation of filmmakers to come. The final section, "New Voices," features conversations with Takashi Shimizu, director of the huge box office hit *The Grudge* and a master of contemporary Japanese horror; Jamie Babbit, an outspoken lesbian director, whose *But I'm a Cheerleader* was done on a tiny budget and became a mainstream crossover hit; Bennett Miller, who made the low-budget digital film *The Cruise* before embarking on *Capote,* the film that put the director and his star, Philip Seymour Hoffman, firmly on the map; and Kasi Lemmons, whose *Eve's Bayou* is a classic of the contemporary African American cinema.

Here, these directors speak frankly about their work in conversations that are both intimate and revealing, offering valuable insights for the aspiring filmmaker as well as the general reader. Each director, naturally, had his or her own vision of what was personally valuable in the cinema. Ronald Neame and Val Guest, both stalwart members of the British film industry, are the oldest figures in the book, and both had long and varied careers in the industry. Neame has worked with distinction as a cameraman and director, and has enjoyed a considerable amount of critical and commercial success. Among his most famous films is *The Poseidon Adventure,* a film that did not particularly engage him on a personal level, but one that nevertheless made a fortune for its producers. Whereas Neame has worked with equal success in both Britain and Hollywood, the late Val Guest was content to remain in the United Kingdom and create some of the most ambitious science fiction films of the 1960s, in particular *The Day the Earth Caught Fire,* one of the finest dystopian visions, with the theme of nuclear proliferation gone mad. Both men are matter-of-fact about their successes and near misses in the industry, which in Neame's case stretch back to the silent film era and an apprenticeship with Alfred Hitchcock, all of which is covered here in considerable detail.

I was privileged to speak with Budd Boetticher just before his death, for what I believe is the last interview he ever gave. Boetticher was one of the great directors of Westerns in twentieth-century cinema, possessed of a vision that is as brutal as that of Howard Hawks and devoid of the sentimentality that one finds in many of John Ford's films. Boetticher began his career as an avid devotee of bull fighting and drifted into films as a technical advisor on the 1941 version of *Blood and Sand* with Tyrone Power. Always the individualist, Boetticher at one point was content to rot in a Mexican jail rather than return to Hollywood and work with John Wayne as director of *The Comancheros* (Michael Curtiz took over the project, which became his last film, with a directorial assist from the uncredited Wayne), simply because he was involved in a project that he believed in so passionately that neither divorce, nor bankruptcy, nor prison could bend his will. It's all a fascinating story, and I'm glad I got a chance to talk to the cantankerous old master before he passed on; his conversation was witty and knowing, and he took the time to flesh out even the most minor parts of his career with relish.

Documentary filmmaker Albert Maysles, in contrast, has been entirely his own man from the beginning of his career, as he made abundantly clear in our long interview from his New York studio. Working with his brother David as well as other respected documentarians, such as D. A. Pennebaker, Maysles helped to create the medium's first lightweight portable sync-sound 16mm camera and used it to shoot *Primary,* a documentary on the 1960 presidential election, as well as films on the Beatles, Marlon Brando, and showman Joseph E. Levine, all of which are discussed in detail in our interview. During the 1960s, the Maysles brothers were the "go to" guys for off-the-cuff documentary filmmaking, working either for themselves or for hire, but insisting that any project they worked on had to be of interest to them personally. *Salesman,* perhaps their most famous film, follows a group of itinerant Bible salesman making their rounds in some of the most economically depressed territories imaginable and remains one of the touchstones of the documentary film, a deeply effective and personal document of the American class system in the 1960s. Maysles is clearly fond of his older films, but at the same time keeps his vision focused firmly on the future; he has embraced digital technology in his new films with the sculptor Christo, many of which are made directly for television.

For Jack Hill and Monte Hellman, who worked on low-budget exploitation films with a deeply personal slant, film was primarily a medium of personal expression, albeit one that was continually mediated by commercial considerations, forced upon them by the vicissitudes of the marketplace, producers, and economic circumstance. Hill and Hellman both had brushes with the major studios, and both have worked on big-budget films with varying degrees of success. Each man learned his craft working for legendary producer/director Roger Corman, a tight man with a dollar, and realized early on that personal filmmaking was fine, but that, above all, film was, and remains, a deeply financially dependent medium; if your film doesn't make a profit, in the long run, opportunities to make future films will evaporate. Both Hill and Hellman have successfully navigated the shoals of the commercial film world while staying true to their personal visions, and they bring vitality and honesty to their conversations here, offering a refreshing "reality check" for those who have dreams of making it in the world of commercial cinema.

I have known Robert Downey Sr. since the 1960s, when he made his most influential films, *Putney Swope* and *Greaser's Palace,* and I welcomed the chance to talk with him about his work because I know and love it so well. Downey's films during that era were strictly take-no-prisoners affairs, with minimal budgets and outrageous satire, effectively pushing forward the countercultural agenda of the day and bitingly showcasing the inherent hypocrisy of human interaction. Whether satirizing the advertising industry in *Putney Swope* or sending up the Western genre in the lavish and underappreciated *Greaser's Palace,* Downey made films only for himself; he was lucky enough to work in a time and place that embraced his vision and gave him free rein to bite the hand that funded his films, which he did unremittingly.

Takashi Shimizu is one of the new breed of Japanese horror directors who mimic the evocative strategies of 1940s producer Val Lewton, preferring to suggest menace and violence rather than directly depict it. Shimizu is extremely fond of the work of director Steven Spielberg and, somewhat surprisingly (at least to this observer), cites *E.T.* as one of the key influences on his work in film. Shimizu was forced to start his career in video because of economic constraints; but when his first version of *The Grudge* became a big hit on the straight-to-video market, he was able to mount several versions of the film in 35mm format, including an English-language remake (shot in Japan) with Bill Pullman and Sarah Michelle Gellar. Shimizu resists being typecast as a horror filmmaker and hopes to branch out in other genres as his career progresses; one nevertheless gets the distinct feeling that the "dreamy" edge he brings to his horror films, reminiscent of the surrealist works of David Lynch and other outré auteurs, is ideally suited to the subject matter he chooses.

Jamie Babbit is a social satirist of more recent vintage. Her lesbian comedy *But I'm a Cheerleader* was a commercial and critical success when first released and has become a cult film on DVD in subsequent years. Babbit talks about her start in the industry, working on big-budget films in a variety of menial capacities, and details how she finally broke into feature films, after much toil in television, with a film that was true to her own spirit and commercially viable as well. In recent years, she has been busy working in television and most recently brought out a new feature film, *The Quiet*. Another feature is in the works for release in 2007.

Bennett Miller and I first met when we were part of a National Public Radio roundtable discussion on the future of digital filmmaking, and we hit it off immediately. Miller had just finished *The Cruise*, a handheld digital feature film documenting the hard life of a New York City tour bus guide. It was a surprise hit and opened up numerous doors for Miller as a commercial filmmaker, but he turned down project after project until he was able to get the biopic *Capote* off the ground. Working with two longtime friends, Philip Seymour Hoffman (as Capote) and Dan Futterman (who wrote the screenplay from Gerald Clarke's book), Miller created a brilliant evocation of literary New York in the 1960s and a stunning feature film debut. As a filmmaker of the twenty-first century, the second century of cinema, Miller has embraced both digital and conventional cinema, and proven himself a master at both.

Kasi Lemmons is an African American woman director who has worked on numerous projects, battling against the ingrained sexism and racism of the film industry with style and grace. From her early work as an actor on the television series *Murder, She Wrote, The Cosby Show,* and the daytime serial *Another World,* Lemmons moved on to featured roles in the films *Candyman* and *The Five Heartbeats,* to name just two of her many feature film credits, before striking out on her own as a director with *Eve's Bayou, The Caveman's Valentine,* and *Talk to Me,* all of which are deeply resonant personal statements made within an industry that doesn't often allow such films to go before the camera. Lemmons's work is an ongoing testament to the creative possibilities of film, and her career is just beginning; it will be interesting to see what she attempts as her next project.

These interviews originally appeared in a number of film journals, and I am pleased to thank the editors and publications for their permission to reprint these materials; in most cases, the interviews printed here are much longer than could be accommodated in the journals. "Filmmaking 'for the fun of it': An Interview with Jack Hill," originally appeared in *Film Criticism* 29.3 (Spring 2005), as did "Budd Boetticher: The Last Interview," *Film Criticism* 26.3 (Spring 2002); both are reprinted by kind permission of Lloyd Michaels, editor. "An Interview with Monte Hellman" first appeared in *Quarterly Review of Film and Video* 22.3 (2005), as did "An Interview with Takashi Shimizu" (with Shoichi Gregory Kamei, translator), *Quarterly Review of Film and Video* 22.1 (2005), and "A Conversation with Albert Maysles," *Quarterly Review of Film and Video* 20.3 (2003); my thanks to Taylor and Francis for permission to reprint these materials here. "An Interview with Bennett Miller" was first published in *Post Script* 26.1 (Fall 2006), 3–12, as were "The Golden Years: An Interview with Ronald Neame," *Post Script* 23.2 (Winter/Spring 2004), 3–18, "No More Excuses: An Interview with Robert Downey Sr.," *Post Script* 21.1 (Fall 2001), 3–13, and "An Interview with Jamie Babbit," *Post Script* 21.1 (Fall 2001), 14–23; my thanks to Gerald Duchovnay, editor, for permission to reprint these complete interviews here. Finally, "The Man Who Set the Earth on Fire: An Interview with Val Guest," was first published in *Classic Images* 333 (March 2003); my thanks to Bob King for permission to use this interview here. The Kasi Lemmons interview appears here for the first time in print.

Dana Miller, as always, assisted in the typing of the final manuscript, and Jay Goldstein supervised the transcription of the tapes for most of these texts. Carol Inskip prepared the meticulous index. Dennis Coleman and Jack Gourlay provided me with contact information for a number of these directors; without their help, many of these discussions would have been impossible. In addition, I wish to thank Joy Ritchie, chair of the Department of English at the University of Nebraska, Lincoln, and Richard Hoffmann, Dean of the College of Arts and Sciences, for their unstinting support of my work, as well as my colleagues, who made invaluable contributions to this volume through discussion and suggestions, especially Oyekan Owomoyela, Stephen Hilliard, Stephen C. Behrendt, Maureen Honey, Linda Pratt, and many others. As with all my works, Gwendolyn Audrey Foster remains, thankfully, the one central point in a rapidly changing landscape; her love, devotion, and faith in my work keeps me anchored in the real, as opposed to the reel, world. To these many people, then, both the directors and those who facilitated the process, my sincere thanks. I hope readers will find as much pleasure in perusing this volume as I did in creating it. The cinema is still young and vibrant, and the directors showcased here demonstrate why it retains such resilience and vitality as it moves into the second hundred years of its existence, a cultural touchstone of unequaled social and cultural impact.

The Old Masters

RONALD NEAME

Ronald Neame is one of the last surviving members of the British film industry during what he himself terms its "golden years." An intimate of Alfred Hitchcock, J. Arthur Rank, Noel Coward, David Lean, and numerous other luminaries, Neame began his career as a camera assistant in 1933. He photographed some of the most memorable classics of the British cinema, including Gabriel Pascal's *Major Barbara* (1941), Noel Coward and David Lean's *In Which We Serve* (1942), and David Lean's *Blithe Spirit* (1945), before moving on as a producer of Lean's *Brief Encounter* (1945), *Great Expectations* (1946), and *Oliver Twist* (1948). Finally, he created a third career for himself as a director on such superb films as *The Horse's Mouth* (1958), *Tunes of Glory* (1960), and *I Could Go on Singing* (1963), although the film that remains (somewhat to his dismay) his most resounding commercial success is *The Poseidon Adventure* (1972). Speaking from his house in Los Angeles, Neame was candid and nostalgic as he remembered working with Coward, Lean, and other of his late compatriots, and simultaneously shrewd in his assessment of the current state of the British and American film industry. This interview took place on January 29, 2004.

WHEELER WINSTON DIXON: Tell me a little about your early life and how you got involved in the industry.

RONALD NEAME: I was born on April 23, 1911, in London. My mother and father, of course, were very involved in film. My father was the photographer Elwin Neame, who was very famous in his day, and my mother was the actress Ivy Close. My brother Derek scripted several films, but he had a rather rough life, to say the least. He was an unhappy character, I'm afraid.

WWD: How did your father and mother meet?

RN: Well, you see, the *Daily Mirror* ran a world beauty competition. There'd never been anything like it before; it was designed to find the most beautiful

3

girl in the world, like the first Miss World except that, of course, it was just done by photographs of lovely girls. There was none of this bathing costume stuff or any of that. So my father was a very young but highly successful photographer in London, and he got the job of shooting all the finalists for the contest. He really was very famous for his time. In fact, on the Underground in London, if you were on the platform and you looked at the wall opposite, at every station there would be an enormous photograph of a lovely girl, and underneath was the caption, "If it's a Neame, it's you at your best."

So my grandfather, my mother's father, felt that his daughter was beautiful, which, indeed, she was. So really, just for a joke more than anything else, they sent a picture that he had taken of her to the *Daily Mirror*. And she was ultimately picked to go to London, and she was among the twenty-five top finalists of the first world beauty competition. My father was approached and asked if he would photograph the twenty-five finalists, being paid a handsome sum for his work, of course. He was very happy to do this, as a result of which he met my mother, as a result of which she won the world beauty competition.

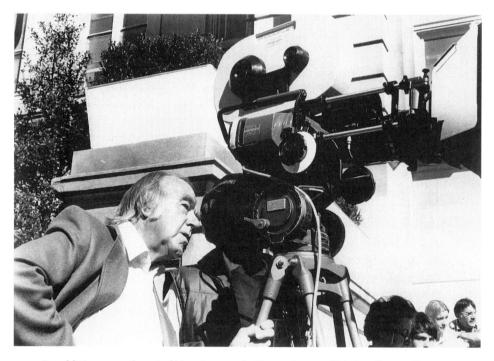

Ronald Neame on the set of his 1980 comedy *Hopscotch*, one of his last films as director. Courtesy Jerry Ohlinger Archives.

WWD: That's a really romantic story.

RN: And surprise, surprise, they got married.

WWD: That's great.

RN: She immediately became a film star, because they were both really the toast of the town. The pictures that I have of my mother in the *Daily Mirror* days, it's astonishing how famous they became. This was round about 1908 or 1909.

WWD: So your family was pretty connected to the film industry, but how did you break in?

RN: Well, I started in the industry as a gofer, a messenger boy, a call boy, or everything you like to name boy. I had to; my father was killed in a motor accident when I was twelve. So at the age of fifteen, I had to go to work, because there was no money left. You see, he died in 1923, by which time my mother had sort of given up the screen. Her last big picture was with the famous director Abel Gance, *La Roue* [1923]. My mother is the young star in that. So she used her influence to get me this job at Elstree Studios.

WWD: Do you recall what you were paid for your first job?

RN: Two pounds ten shillings a week.

WWD: Would they give you a car home if they worked you late?

RN: Oh, we always worked late. We always worked till the director told us to go home—particularly with Hitchcock—but there were no unions then. If you worked past the last train, which we almost always did, then they took us home by car; but there would be about four or five of us in each car, and the car had to stop and let everyone off along the way.

WWD: What attracted you to being a cameraperson, above all other things?

RN: Well, that was where there was a possibility of me having a job, and it was essential for me to support myself. And the moment that I could, I supported the family. I was very, very young, and this was 1927. So I was sixteen and pretty much the sole support of the family.

WWD: What was it like working with Alfred Hitchcock on *Blackmail* [1929], one of the first British talkies, on which you're an uncredited assistant cameraman? It seems you were promoted pretty rapidly.

RN: I was there a year before I worked with Hitchcock. But then it wasn't too difficult to work your way up the ladder, because there were people that came and went. And so an assistant's job on the camera at that time was, you know, fairly easy. Michael Powell worked on that film as well, in the same capacity. Hitchcock, of course, storyboarded everything and was totally meticulous in his approach to shooting his films. But he loved to play rather, I think, sadistic practical jokes on people.

WWD: Were you ever the object of one?

RN: No, I wasn't. But on the set of *Blackmail* there was a little property man called Harry. And Harry was the person that Hitchcock would always play his tricks on. For example, we had a set where there was a tobacconist's shop, and there was a flame on the counter to light cigars with. One day, Hitchcock got a pair of pliers. He was holding a half crown in the flame, and he heated it up till it was white hot and then dropped it on the floor. Then he said to Harry, who hadn't seen what was going on, "Harry, there's a half crown on the floor. Pick it up." And Harry would pick it up, and, of course, it would be white hot, and it gave him a terrible burn.

WWD: That's not funny at all.

RN: Well, you see, Harry became the sort of the clown of the set. But you're right; it was cruel.

WWD: Did you learn a lot from Hitchcock?

RN: Oh, Lord, yes. He really was better than just about everybody else who was working at that time—miles ahead of everyone. You see, a studio in those days when I first started was very, very different from what it is today. For the first six to eight months, I turned the camera by hand. Two turns of the camera every second to expose sixteen pictures a second. When I first went into a studio, there were four films being made. It was a big studio, divided in half with a thin wall down the center. And on one side, there were three productions.

One starred Madeleine Carroll, whom you probably know; she worked with Hitchcock later. Then there was a second one and a third one, but there were no dividing walls between them, because it was silent. Most films during this period had a little three-piece orchestra that played music to keep people in the mood. And on the other side of the thin wall down the center, occupying all three areas, was a film directed by the boy genius, the rather plump Alfred Hitchcock. The first time I saw him was the second day that I was in the studio, when I was asked if I would go and get a skyhook. I was told that there was only one skyhook in the studio, and it was an important piece of equipment.

WWD: I know that one: there *is* no skyhook.

RN: That's right, there is no skyhook. That was one of his jokes. But that was how things went on a Hitchcock set. This was during the making of a film called *The Farmer's Wife* [Hitchcock, 1928]. I went onto the set to ask for the skyhook. But the cameraman, Jack Cox, who was a very nice man, said, "Look, Ronnie, I have to tell you something. They're pulling your leg. There is no such a thing as a skyhook. So why don't you go back to your set and tell them that they've sold the skyhook because nobody was using it." And that was the first time I met Jack Cox, who was Hitch's main cameraman.

WWD: Now, didn't *Blackmail* start as a silent film and then become a talkie?

RN: We made it as a silent film, and about three-quarters of the way through it, sound suddenly happened. A picture came over from America, *The Jazz*

Singer [Alan Crosland, 1927], and that was the end of that. Silents were finished. Elstree decided that they wanted to get in on the act quickly, and what better person to go to than Hitchcock, because Hitch—and I'll always call him Hitch—was the obvious choice. He was much more talented than almost anybody in any of the studios there.

In the film, we had a little actress called Anny Ondra; she was Czech, very pretty. She eventually married Max Schmeling, the boxer. But she had this thick Czech accent, and she was supposed to be the daughter of a London newspaper editor. Of course, there was no such thing as dubbing or looping or anything. The problems with the early days of sound could fill a volume. So, what to do?

Hitchcock finally figured out that he could do it if he had a woman standing outside of camera range, speaking Anny Ondra's lines at the same time that she did, sort of on-set lip syncing. We used a lot of the silent film in the sound version, so there aren't two whole films. It was just that we were practically through with the silent version when it was decided to put some sound in. So additional scenes were written, and the original playwright [Charles Bennett] was brought down to the set. And we then remade a lot of the sequences with dialogue.

Hitchcock engaged an actress named Joan Barry, who would stand on the side of the set. She would rehearse in the evenings with Anny Ondra. Then she would come on the set and stand right underneath the microphone, out of camera range. She did the dialogue, and Anny Ondra mimed it on the set. Anny Ondra couldn't make a sound, because if she would have done, it would have fucked the whole thing up. It was a real last-minute experiment, but it worked. I learned a lot of things from Hitchcock; he really was a genius with camera placement, cutting, then sound. He could do it all.

WWD: You worked on lots of films as an assistant camera operator, including Herbert Brenon's *Honours Easy* [1935], Paul Merzbach's *Invitation to the Waltz* [1935], Harry Hughes's *Joy Ride* [1935], Thomas Bentley, Alexander Esway, Walter Summers, and Arthur B. Woods's *Music Hath Charms* [1935], Woods's *Once in a Million* [1935], Marcel Varnel's *Girls Will Be Boys* [1934], Woods's *Give Her a Ring* [1934], and Frederic Zelnik's *Happy* [1933]. But I'd like to jump to your first film as a full-fledged director of photography, Woods's *Drake of England* [1935]. This seems like a rather ambitious film. How did you make the jump?

RN: Well, it was a big jump, obviously. There's a period in here we haven't discussed, where I left the studios [after *Blackmail*] and tried to run my father's still photography business, which was a failure because I was too young. So I went crawling back to the studio about two years later. I was the assistant on a whole lot of films with a cameraman named Claude Friese-Greene, who was the son of William Friese-Greene, whom we [the British] claim invented the motion picture camera.

WWD: Right, everybody seems to have been working on it the same time.

RN: Yes, that's right. It was the Lumière brothers in France, and Augustin Le Prince in England as well, and Edison over here. Everyone made a contribution.

WWD: So how did you make the jump to *Drake of England*?

RN: Well, Claude Friese-Greene was a heavy drinker. He was also ill, but he kept on working, until one day he collapsed on the stage and was rushed to hospital. The head of the studio, which in this case was Wardour Films, was a very tight-fisted man named Stapleton, who didn't like spending a penny on anything extra if he didn't need to. He asked me to come and see him at lunchtime and said, "Ronnie, if you think you can do it, would you take over from Friese?"

   Well, the director of that film, Arthur Woods, was a nice guy, and I'd become very friendly with him. He said, "You can do it, Ronnie, you know you can." What I didn't know about lighting then would have filled volumes! However, you know, fools step in—the confidence of youth and everything. So I took over, and I came through all right. But it was quite a big picture for the time.

WWD: Now, I wanted to ask you about *Invitation to the Waltz* [1935], which was directed by Paul Merzbach. Wendy Toye acted in that film as Signora Picci—

RN: And also she did the choreography.

WWD: This was my question. I've interviewed Wendy Toye, and she claims that the choreographer kind of fell apart, and Paul Merzbach told her to step in.

RN: She really did the choreography on the whole thing.

WWD: What were your impressions of Wendy Toye?

RN: Well, she was a very beautiful young woman, very young, and a beautiful little dancer. She was just a teenager, really, but she knew exactly what she was doing.

WWD: Did you see her later films as a director, such as *The Stranger Left No Card* [1952]?

RN: I think I saw *The Stranger Left No Card*, and we were very friendly during the shooting of [*Invitation to the Waltz*]. We were both very young. I didn't know her all that well, but I knew her well enough never to forget her, because she really was a sweetheart.

WWD: You were also the director of photography on George King's *The Crimes of Stephen Hawke* [1936] with Tod Slaughter, the top 1930s British horror star. Any memories of Mr. Slaughter?

RN: Well, he was a very nice man. I remember that he was a rather big man, and, of course, all his films were firmly tongue-in-cheek. We made them as serious films, but we knew they were comedies, rather like the first Bond picture, *Dr. No* [Terence Young, 1962].

wwd: What were the budgets on these films and the schedules?

rn: Well, these were the days of the quota quickies, which is a whole other subject. In an effort to save the British film industry, which was always in dire financial straits, the government brought in legislation that demanded that 25 percent of all screen time throughout Britain should be given to British films. And, of course, we all thought, "Golly, this is wonderful," you know.

But what happened, of course, was that all the American companies immediately formed British companies—there was Warner British, Paramount British, MGM British—simply for the purpose of cranking out low-budget "British" films. The American companies would go to a low-budget British producer, and they would give him £6,000 for a five-thousand-foot film, roughly a fifty-, sixty-minute film. But the producer—and there were a lot of them—made the film for £5,000 and pocketed the other £1,000. And the film was made in one week! We made them. We started early Monday morning, and sometimes we had to work on Sundays, but we worked right through the week.

wwd: So was *The Crimes of Stephen Hawke* a quota quickie?

rn: Absolutely.

wwd: Six days, £5,000, that's it?

rn: That's it. Now, what happened, which is the funny part, looking back, was that the Americans were showing their films in all the British theaters, including all the theaters in the West End of London. So when they got this finished product from us, they put the film on at eight o'clock in the morning for the cleaners and ran it twice, I think! And then they put it in the back of the projection booth and ran their own film. But they had to "obey" the law, and that's how they got around it.

wwd: Ingenious, if utterly criminal. Is this how you got involved in the George Formby movies, such as Anthony Kimmins's *Keep Fit* [1937]?

rn: Well, the Formby movies were a step above. They weren't quota quickies. Formby was highly popular with audiences, and his films were really British films and had better budgets and schedules. I don't really know what these films cost, because at that time I wasn't interested in cost. They were all modestly budgeted, yet quite well done. On each film, he would have a different leading lady, all of whom I got to know. Formby's wife would always come to the set to keep an eye on George; he had quite a bit of a roving eye.

wwd: Googie Withers was one of them, yes. It seems to me that Formby's modern equivalent is Adam Sandler, essentially an average guy who gets the girl, plays a few songs badly on a guitar—a not particularly handsome everyman whom audiences seem to identify with.

rn: I'd agree with you. I mean, it's a very good formula.

wwd: It really is. All of the Formby films had the exact same plot, right?

RN: Oh, yes! In fact, not only the same plot, but practically the same songs! But there were some very good things in the Formby films. One of the best was a film called *It's in the Air* [Anthony Kimmins, 1938], where George flies upside down through an airplane hangar, and it includes a lot of rather clever sight gags. But these were a definite step up from the quota quickies.

WWD: You worked with Edmond T. Gréville on *Brief Ecstasy* [1937]; he later went on to direct the British juvenile delinquent classic *Beat Girl* [1960].

RN: He was a Frenchman, and it was a love story starring Paul Lukas. It was an average film for the period, nothing special. I enjoyed working on it, but it was just another film at the time.

WWD: Then you shot *The Gaunt Stranger* [1938], from an Edgar Wallace play. Walter Forde directed that. Wallace was the top British author of thrillers during this period, incredibly prolific, writing plays, novels, short stories, the lot.

RN: That's right. Walter directed several pictures that I shot, including *The Four Just Men* [1939], which was also from an Edgar Wallace book and starred Anna Lee, whom I saw just three days ago. I know her very well because I photographed her in several pictures directed by Robert Stevenson, her first husband, including *Return to Yesterday* [1940] and several other projects.

WWD: So, with all of these films, *The Gaunt Stranger, Four Just Men*, you were pretty much moving toward A status?

RN: Well, they did very well in England and got their money back, mostly because they were made so cheaply. So they were practically guaranteed to make their production costs back, especially the Formby films. The Wallace films also had a pretty much ready-made audience, because his books were so successful.

WWD: Then you photographed *Major Barbara* [1941] for Gabriel Pascal, with a screenplay by George Bernard Shaw, based on his play. You describe Pascal in your autobiography as rather a con man. What was he like as a director, and how did you make the jump from *Let George Do It* [Marcel Varnel, 1940], another Formby comedy, to *Major Barbara*?

RN: Well, I was going to do a film called *Convoy* [Pen Tennyson, 1940; the directors of photography were Roy Kellino for the exterior work and Günther Krampf for the studio shots], but I was very unhappy with the new black-and-white Kodak negative film stocks that were being made during the period. It was very, very empty in the shadow areas; there was nothing there; it had no depth. They shouldn't have put it on the market.

So I ran into terrible trouble with the film; it just wasn't working out. I was in a real state of nervous exhaustion, so I went to [the film's producer] Mickey Balcon, and I said, "Look, I think I've made too many films in the last couple of years. Would you let me leave this film and have a holiday?" He was very, very nice and said, "Well, of course, Ronnie." So my wife, Beryl, and I went on a holiday, and that's when I first tried to learn golf and failed miserably.

Whilst I was there, my agent at that time, Christopher Mann, phoned me and said, "You're not doing a film. Would you like to do the makeup tests on Shaw's *Major Barbara*, which is going to star Wendy Hiller? They want tests of Wendy, and the film has already started shooting in Cornwall. A young editor named David Lean will be directing the tests."

So I went along, and I made Wendy look very, very good indeed. In those days, cameramen hitched their wagon to a star, because the star would always use them. Mary Pickford wouldn't make a film without Charles Rosher. So I made Wendy look very good, and David immediately liked me, and I immediately liked him. Freddie Young was then photographing the picture, but Freddie fell out with Gabby [Pascal] on location in Cornwall and decided that he didn't want to work with Gabby. So somebody else had to take over. And that someone was, after some negotiation, me. This was a whole step up for me. The film had an amazing cast, including Rex Harrison, Robert Morley, Robert Newton, Sybil Thorndike, and, of course, Wendy.

WWD: Was Pascal just the consummate promoter?

RN: He was a pirate, and I admire those pirates. He could charm anyone into doing anything.

WWD: He talked Shaw into giving him the rights to the play for nothing.

RN: Yes, he went to Shaw and came away with the rights on "a figure to be decided," which was really rather astonishing.

WWD: What was shooting *Major Barbara* like? Did Pascal have any sense of how to use the camera?

RN: He had no sense of camera at all. Gabby was the so-called director, but he had two helpers, so to speak, on either side of him. One was David Lean, and the other was Harold French. French looked after the dialogue, because he was a stage director, and David Lean looked after the visuals with me. Gabby just got in the way. Gabby would ask us to do impossible things, but he got the money. And as I say, he was a pirate, and we could do with a few more of them in the industry, if they want to make quality films like *that*! David wound up editing the film with Charles Frend, and William Walton did the music, so this was absolutely an A film.

WWD: Your next project, *One of Our Aircraft Is Missing* [1942], is a Michael Powell and Emeric Pressburger film for the Archers.

RN: Yes, they were our partners in Independent Producers. You see, Arthur Rank got together with a bunch of us and formed this company called Independent Producers. David [Lean] and I with Tony Havelock-Allan formed Cineguild, and then there were Frank Launder and Sidney Gilliat, whose company was called Individual Pictures. Mickey [Powell] and Emeric created the Archers. Together, we were the Independent Producers. Arthur put up the money but gave us total creative freedom; it was a marvelous arrangement. *One of Our Aircraft Is Missing* was a wonderful picture. It had a great cast: Googie Withers, Eric Portman, and Peter Ustinov, among others. It was about a British bomber crew shot down over Holland and how they make their way back to safety with some help from the Dutch underground. Very much a wartime picture.

WWD: Your next film as a director of photography was Noel Coward and David Lean's *In Which We Serve* [1942], which was a superb picture on all counts. How did you meet Noel Coward, and what were your impressions of him at the time?

RN: Well, Noel Coward had agreed with [producer] Filippo Del Giudice to make a war effort film. The reason we weren't called up into the army was that they wanted films that reflected the British war effort; some were good, like *In Which We Serve*, and some not so good, like *The Lion Has Wings* [1939], which was cobbled together by Adrian Brunel, Brian Desmond Hurst, Mickey [Powell], and Alexander Korda.

The reason I came on *In Which We Serve* was that Noel Coward, before he decided to make any film, had to look at a lot of films to get a better idea of what he was doing. He particularly liked *Major Barbara* and one or two others that I photographed. He also liked David Lean as an editor. Tony Havelock-Allan was our executive producer; the three of us were friends. Tony, who later became Sir Anthony, of course, introduced us to Noel Coward.

WWD: How did the co-direction of the film work with Noel and David Lean?

RN: Noel contributed an enormous amount, including dialogue, and he starred in the film. But it's funny. Noel was so talented, but he wasn't that great an actor for the screen. Very limited, very brittle. Mannered. But the funny part is, one always wants to play Hamlet, you know? He always wanted to do the things that he was perhaps less good at. So he was determined to play the leading role [of Captain Edward V. Kinross], and Lord Louis Mountbatten supported him.

In Which We Serve is based on the real-life sinking of the HMS *Kelly* [HMS *Torrin* in the film], which was [commanded by Mountbatten and] sunk in the Mediterranean. Noel gets credit for the screenplay, but all three of us worked together on it. Right from the beginning, when I worked with David, I worked not just as a cameraman. We worked as a team, and we planned the whole thing out. So the three of us really got on very well, although [press baron] Lord Beaverbrook tried to stop the picture. He was head of one of the war ministries at that time. He *hated* Noel Coward.

WWD: Noel Coward was openly gay, although at the time, of course, very few people were "out." Was this one of the reasons that he was being attacked?

RN: No, that wasn't it; they were attacking the film. Beaverbrook was against the whole project and asked, "How can this matinee idol possibly play the commander of a destroyer in wartime?" So it was a big battle between us and the British government, which felt that, and maybe up to a point quite rightly, "in wartime, in this war with Germany, we don't want to show a British ship being sunk. We want to show a German ship being sunk!" They thought the whole film was counterproductive to the war effort, and they fought against it tooth and nail. But Lord Mountbatten, who was a great friend of Noel's, fought for us, and he won the day. It was the biggest picture being made in England at the time. It was a smash success, and after that, everyone forgot all their initial objections.

But as you say, Noel was completely "out" in his sexuality; he really didn't care what anyone else thought about it. When we were doing the screenplay of *This Happy Breed*, we went to the Miter Hotel to see Noel, and we were going to have a chat with him and then have lunch with him. I don't know if it's there anymore, but in the Miter Hotel then, they didn't have numbers

Noel Coward (center) and members of his crew face disaster at sea in the celebrated *In Which We Serve* (1942). Directed by Noel Coward and David Lean; photographed by Ronald Neame. Courtesy Jerry Ohlinger Archives.

on the any of the rooms. They had names on the doors. There was the Duke's Room. There was the Baron's Room and the Knight's Room. Each room had its own name. Noel had a big room at the top of the stairs, so we all went up to see him. And there above the door was the plaque, the Queen's Room. We went in, and there was Noel in a large four-poster bed. And the first thing he said was, "You see the room they've given me, my dears."

WWD: That's perfect. Next, you photographed *This Happy Breed* [1944] for David Lean, for which Noel Coward wrote the script. I've always liked this film a lot. It's basically shot on one set, but I thought it was quite striking, particularly the muted use of color.

RN: Well, I find that it's become dated, whereas a lot of the films we made at that time didn't. We tried to use color, but, of course, the prints you see now are dreadful. We tried to use color in a different way. This was my first film in color, three-strip Technicolor, and we wanted to make it look unlike a Hollywood film—more muted, more real. But it's about a certain time and place, and I think that's the reason it became dated. It was very much a stage play. We tried to open it up as much as possible; we would open it up with episodes of the period, like the Wembley Exhibition, and there's also the scene at the end in Hyde Park, at Speakers Corner. Again, Noel wrote the play, and Tony did the adaptation. And we had a typically superb cast: Robert Newton, Celia Johnson, John Mills, and Stanley Holloway were the leads. But today, I just don't think it stands up.

WWD: After that, you photographed *Blithe Spirit* [David Lean, 1945] and made some contributions as well to the screenplay. This is another Coward stage play; it seems as if you were becoming Coward specialists.

RN: You're right. After *In Which We Serve*, Noel liked it so much that he wanted us just to go on making his plays, and it was very convenient for us. By that time, we had gotten to know Noel very well, and we did quite a lot of writing with him. In fact, David and I one day were with Noel, discussing the screenplay of one of our films together, and he suddenly said to both of us, "And which of my little darlings wrote this brilliant Coward dialogue?" He accepted our scenes; we were really working together as a team. But Noel was away whilst we were making *Blithe Spirit*, and when he saw the film, he didn't like the result at all. And there's no doubt that David's strength, quite frankly, is not in comedy. Margaret Rutherford's great in the film as Madame Arcati, the medium, and Rex Harrison did as much as he could in the lead; but it was still a photographed stage play.

WWD: You did some uncredited screenplay chores on *Brief Encounter* [David Lean, 1945], then you did the screenplay for Lean's *Great Expectations* [1946], and finally topped this off by producing *Oliver Twist* [David Lean, 1948], on which you also made some contributions to the screenplay, all for Cineguild. Was *Great Expectations* your first meeting with Alec Guinness?

RN: Yes, and it was my first film as a producer.

WWD: And what was your relationship with Alec Guinness like? It seems to have been, shall we say, respectful but wary on both sides.

RN: Well, I must say, he was wonderful in *Great Expectations*. But at that time, I didn't know how wonderful he *was*, obviously, because he'd never done a film before. *Great Expectations*, I think, was his first film, or certainly his first important film. [Guinness's very first film role was as an uncredited extra in Victor Saville's *Evensong* (1934).] I got him extended leave from the navy, but we had to have him for the length of the film. We couldn't cast him if there was any chance that he'd be called back. And so, as the producer, I had to make sure that he was available. But he did a superb job in the role. I knew immediately he was going to be a major star.

WWD: I wanted to ask you why you moved to production from being a director of photography. It would seem to entail more headaches, more hassles.

RN: Well, in 1944, after *In Which We Serve*, Arthur Rank asked me to go to Hollywood and look and see what we needed in British studios in the way of equipment, to bring us up to date with Hollywood. So I spent a wonderful six weeks here and went around to all the studios. I was treated like a lord, not because I was Ronald Neame, but because I represented Arthur Rank, who booked the films from all the big American companies and had somewhere around eight hundred theaters in Britain at the time. Whilst I was over here, I thought, "I think I can make a film that American audiences might like." And so, when I went back to England, I went to Arthur Rank (I called him Uncle Arthur, because he was so benevolent, constructive, and helpful), and I said, "Arthur, would you let me produce a picture?" "I don't see why not, Ron," he replied. "What do you want to make?" And I said, "Well, I'm not quite sure, but I would hope that David Lean will direct it." So he said, "Well, go make a choice and then come back and see me." And that was how we made *Great Expectations*. Alec had played [the role of Herbert Pocket] on the stage, so it was really matter of just adjusting his performance to film.

When *Great Expectations* was a hit, we realized that Dickens was a good idea, so we decided that we would make *Oliver Twist*. Alec came to me and said, "I would like to play Fagin." And I said, "Come on, Alec, you're not Fagin. You're too young and this just isn't going to work." But Alec said, "Just give me a screen test, and you'll see." So he got together with Stuart Freebourne, the makeup man that we had employed at that time, and we gave him his test. He came on the set, and there was Fagin. From that moment on, I knew that Alec could play anything that he wanted to.

wwd: You switched to directing for the first time with *Take My Life* [1947], which was a rather standard murder mystery, would you agree?

rn: Yes, it was a very, very small nothing little picture.

wwd: Why did you do that?

rn: Well, having been for many years in the film studio, I just hated being behind a desk. When you're producing a film, you're basically spending all your time in the office, keeping an eye on the budget and keeping the film moving. I hated having to say to David, "David, you've gotta get off that set tonight, because otherwise we're in trouble." I hated budgets and schedules and all of that. I was much more interested in making certain that David got all he needed to make a great film. So I took much more part in the making of the film than normally a producer does. Finally, I decided that it was just not my scene. I didn't want to be a producer. I could have gone back to being a cameraman, but I thought that that was retrogressive in a way. So I thought, "Well, I'll never be a David Lean, but why don't I have a go at directing a

Alec Guinness as Fagin in David Lean's *Oliver Twist* (1948). Produced by Ronald Neame and Anthony Havelock-Allan. Courtesy Jerry Ohlinger Archives.

picture? I've been around the studios enough to know the pitfalls." So Tony Havelock-Allan found *Take My Life* by Winston Graham for me, and it was never meant to be anything more than it was.

WWD: It was just a curtain raiser, so to speak.

RN: Just a little film.

WWD: Now on your way up the ladder, you ran into somebody whom I know, Freddie Francis [the Academy Award-winning director of cinematography on numerous classic films, and a director in his own right]. Freddie was the camera operator on your next film as a director, *The Golden Salamander* [1950]. Didn't he walk out on the picture while you were working on it?

RN: "Walking out" is perhaps an overly strong term. However, what happened whilst we were on location in North Africa on *The Golden Salamander*, which wasn't a very good film, by the way, was that it was Ossie [Oswald] Morris's first picture as a lighting cameraman, and his operator was Freddie Francis. Suddenly, in the middle of the picture, Freddie announced to me that he wanted to go back to England, because he had a job that was more important with Michael Powell, if I recall. And he left! Since then, I've become very good friends with Freddie, and we laugh about this together now, but I was rather surprised when it happened. You just didn't walk out on a film in the middle of production, you know!

WWD: What do you think of the films that Sidney Gilliat and Frank Launder made when they went off as a team by themselves, particularly the St. Trinian's films? Are you fond of them at all?

RN: Yes, they made the St. Trinian's comedies, didn't they? I was very, very fond of both Frank and Sidney. They were very close personal friends. They didn't make great films, in my opinion, but they made good films that did well, like *Green for Danger* [1946]. They were very much a part of the industry, and they did very well financially.

WWD: What was it like directing *The Million Pound Note* [1953; released in the United States as *Man with a Million* (1954)], with your first certifiable American star, Gregory Peck?

RN: That was a slightly awesome experience, I have to tell you, because it was from a short story by Mark Twain, and therefore, there had to be a great deal of original writing to fill the film out. [Writer-director Jill Craigie was responsible for the film's screenplay.] John Bryan, who by that time was my producer, was the art director for *Oliver Twist*, and in order to get him away from David, I said, "Why don't you come and work with me, and you can be the producer?" So John took over as producer, but really went on designing all the sets. He was a wonderful designer, but he was also a very good producer, and he found this short story.

I loved the central conceit of the story. [In the film, Peck plays a penniless

American sailor who is given a £1 million bank note by two eccentric British millionaires. Whenever Peck tries to pay for something by presenting the bank note, he is given the item for nothing.] It's an excellent idea; you can get by with no money if you have the *appearance* of having money. It worked pretty well; but it was slow going, and we didn't think, quite frankly, that we would get an American star. But Greg Peck happened to be in Paris at that time, and he happened to have just met the lady who was to become his wife, and he wanted to stay in Europe. So on the basis of, you know, "all he can do is turn it down," we sent him a screenplay of *The Million Pound Note*. He was very impressed with all of us in our little group at that time, because we were making some good pictures. I call them the golden years.

WWD: I agree. Are there any particular directors from this period, or directors of photography [DPs], whom you really admired?

RN: Well, most of the British DPs at that time trained under me. Guy Greene worked for me as an assistant on *This Happy Breed* and *In Which We Serve*. Ossie Morris worked for me as an assistant on *Oliver Twist*. Arthur Ibbetsen photographed my film with Alec Guinness, *The Horse's Mouth* [1958]. Jack Hildyard was working at Soper's in London, on Bond Street; his job was in the shirt department, and he was twenty-six or twenty-seven at the time. He came to me and said, "I want to be in the film industry." I told him, "Well, you know how: you've got to work your way up from the bottom, like every-one else." He said, "I just want to get my foot in the door." I reminded him, "You'll have to go back and start at the beginning. Would you really want that?" He said, "Yes, I would really want it." So all these people started in with me, in various capacities.

WWD: *The Horse's Mouth* is one of the films that you're most associated with. Alec Guinness wrote the script for that from Joyce Cary's novel?

RN: Yes. I had been sent the book a couple of years earlier by Claude Rains, of all people, who said, "I think this would make a wonderful film, Ronnie, and I'd like to play Gulley Jimson [a rebellious British painter]." I read the book, but I just didn't think there was a film there. I got back to Claude, whom I was very friendly with, and said, "Claude, I think it's a fascinating book, but I just don't see where there's a film." So we dropped it. Then a couple of years later, Alec phoned me and said, "Ronnie, I've just read a book. I think it would make a great film; it's called *The Horse's Mouth*." I said, "Well, Alec, it is a great book, but I don't see a film there." He said, "Oh, you're wrong." I said, "Well, what do you suggest?" So he asked, "Would you let me try having a go at writing a script?" I said, "By all means, be my guest." And so he, with John Bryan and myself seeing him every few days, put the script together. His contribution to *The Horse's Mouth* is enormous, and the character of Gulley Jimson was designed for him. I don't know quite what Joyce Cary thought about it. I liked Joyce very much, but he had bone cancer, and he was dying. He died before we started the picture.

WWD: Was it your favorite picture of all your work?

RN: No, *Tunes of Glory* [1960] is my favorite. First of all, I think it's a story that really commands your attention: the military man [Guinness's Jock Sinclair] who is passed over for promotion by a younger rival and the bitter contest between them because of this. But also I think there are two—I'll use the word "impeccable"—performances: one from Guinness and one from John Mills. I'll tell you why I used the word "impeccable." A few weeks after the film was released, I had a telegram from Noel Coward, who was abroad, and it just said, "*Tunes of Glory* is impeccably acted and impeccably directed. Congratulations. Love, Father." Noel always used to call himself "Father." I just thought it was a really solid script, with remarkable performances, and it had great depth and resonance.

WWD: Shortly after that, you directed Dirk Bogarde and Judy Garland in *I Could Go on Singing* [1963], which was, from all I can gather, a harrowing experience.

John Mills and Alec Guinness in Ronald Neame's favorite of all his films as a director, *Tunes of Glory* (1960). Courtesy Jerry Ohlinger Archives. Copyright © 1980 by United Artists Corporation.

RN: Yes, but I had great sympathy at the end of the film for Judy Garland, despite the fact that the shooting was a nightmare. There was a love/hate relationship there. Dirk helped me out enormously, because Judy had been friends with him. Judy cared about Dirk very, very much, which was a tremendous help for me, because I think perhaps I didn't quite understand how insecure Judy was. But Dirk could be very, very sympathetic. He had a lot of patience with her. Mind you, Judy got very angry with him on occasion. I think we were on location in Canterbury, on the grounds of the school, and I was having problems with the dean, who was trying to chuck us off. Judy was very angry that morning, because she'd come down the previous evening to stay in a hotel, and she'd asked Dirk to go down also, and he didn't. He came down in the morning. Judy was very angry, and she threw her breakfast tray at him. So it was a difficult shoot, but we got through it, and I think Judy gave a really superb performance. Dirk went off after that and made a bunch of great films with Joseph Losey, especially *The Servant* [1963] and *Accident* [1967].

The tempestuous Judy Garland and "mediator" Dirk Bogarde during production of Ronald Neame's *I Could Go on Singing* (1963), a film that was marked by numerous production problems. Courtesy Jerry Ohlinger Archives.

wwd: Did you ever have any interaction with Losey?

rn: No, I met him, but that was it.

wwd: Speaking of Losey, did you have any personal interactions with the House Un-American Activities Committee in the United States? Did this affect you in any way?

rn: Well, I knew [screenwriter and producer] Carl Foreman quite well. Carl wrote the first script on a film I directed called *Windom's Way* [1958]. He wrote the first screenplay, but it wasn't used; Jill Craigie took over from him, and we shot her version. It still wasn't a very good film.

wwd: What were your feelings about the blacklist?

rn: Oh, well, I thought it was just ridiculous. At that time, over here [in the United States], the very mention of the word "communist" made them all go mad. I had a splendid secretary. She must have been with me for, I don't know, fifteen years. She was a communist. She *believed* in communism. When I came over here for the very first time, I said, "I have a secretary in London who's a communist," and they said, "What? You have a communist working for you?" I mean, it was astonishing. The whole thing was over the top.

wwd: Why did you decide to make the move to Hollywood?

rn: I decided that I was fifty-two, and I thought, "Well, I probably won't make all that many more pictures." Little did I know! But at that time, quite frankly, I couldn't afford to retire in England, because the tax rate in my bracket was something like 80 percent. I had some very good friends who lived in Italy, just over the border from France. And I thought, "Why don't I retire in Italy?" I built a villa overlooking the Mediterranean, and we all moved to Italy.

Then, instead of my not getting more pictures, I found that I was continually coming over to Hollywood. Although I made practically all of my films in England, they were all made with American finance, *The Horse's Mouth* being one, *Tunes of Glory* another, and *The Prime of Miss Jean Brodie* [1969] as well. They were always made in England, but they were U.S./U.K. co-productions financially. The Americans put up the money because in Britain, suddenly, nobody would put up any money for films. So I bought a little pied-à-terre in the States because I was coming over so often. Over the years, I've built on to this little house, and it's now quite a big house. I've been living here for thirty years. As I sit here talking to you, I can see the ocean on one side and all the mountains and the valley on the other side. It's a beautiful spot.

wwd: When did you move to the States?

rn: Well, I didn't move to the States permanently, because I operated from Italy. I used to commute during the editing period. I can leave my home in Italy, drive to Nice, and get on a plane to London. I had a car at the airport in London; I mean my own car. I would drive to Pinewood Studios and be in the

cutting room before the editor arrived. I could get there by 8:30 in the morning from Italy. So the Italian house became quite important. It was much,
much later that I settled in America. I made *The Poseidon Adventure* [1972]
here and *Gambit* [1966] before that, for Universal.

WWD: Making *The Poseidon Adventure* was somewhat difficult, I imagine, working with Irwin Allen, who was really a frustrated director. But that made
potfuls of money, right?

RN: It made a lot of money. I didn't make the kind of money that others made
who didn't really have anything to do with it. The two men who made the
most money, because they had 50 percent of the picture, walked away with
at least $20 million each, and they never even came near the studio.

WWD: Nice work if you can get it! I guess my last question has to do with today's
films and their emphasis on digital technology, special effects, and technical
wizardry to keep audiences entertained, often at the expense of plot, char-
acterization, and other considerations. Do you keep up with what's going
on today?

RN: Quite frankly, I'm not all that interested in them. I'm much more interested in the small picture, which sadly has now become the picture you see
on the little screen, your television screen, if at all. I liked *The Quiet American* [Philip Noyce, 2002] very much, but this year . . . I'm just trying to think.
I think the only thing I've enjoyed this year is *Something's Gotta Give* [Nancy
Meyer, 2003], with Jack Nicholson and Diane Keaton. I enjoyed that film
except for the last five minutes, because they didn't quite know how to finish
it. It's the kind of film I like, because it's about people, you see, and the thing
I don't like is that films today don't really need a director. All they need is
the special effects supervisor. It's all special effects or animation. And at least
with *Poseidon*, which was slaughtered by the press, there were very few special effects in the technical sense; it was all done on the floor. That cast went
through all that hell, which gave the film a kind of special feeling, a sense of
reality. That's really missing from the newer films. You can't go back, of course,
but I think that the films we made back then had a special feeling because
they were personal; we really made them for ourselves. That's why I call
them the golden years; we were making films we believed in, and we had a
lot of fun doing it. And, along the way, we made some damned good films!

VAL GUEST

The late British filmmaker Val Guest will forever be remembered as the director of three science fiction horror classics from Hammer Films: *The Quatermass Xperiment* (1955), known as *The Creeping Unknown* in the United States and given its odd title spelling for the "X" certificate the film received from the British censor for its horrific content; *Quatermass II* (1957), also known as *Enemy from Space*; and *The Day the Earth Caught Fire* (1961), an apocalyptic nuclear disarmament thriller. His work ranges from bizarre comedy (*Expresso Bongo*, 1960) to crime films (*Hell Is a City*, 1960) to classic British comedy (*The Runaway Bus*, 1954) and big-budget spectacles (*Casino Royale*, 1967). Guest gave Peter Sellers his first big break in films and later performed the same service for Woody Allen. In addition to directing some fifty-four feature films, Guest also worked extensively as a journalist for the film trade papers in the 1930s. He wrote the scripts for most of the films he directed, took on scripting chores for other filmmakers, and even composed the songs for some of his musical films. At first typed as a director of domestic British comedies, Guest stumbled into his association with Hammer in the early 1950s with two comedy films; then, despite his initial resistance, he agreed to direct the film that put Hammer on the map as an international studio. Val Guest was married for many years to the actress Yolande Donlan, who figured prominently in his career as a filmmaker. I interviewed Val Guest on July 22, 2001, shortly before *The Day the Earth Caught Fire* and *The Quatermass Xperiment* were screened as part of a retrospective of his work at the American Cinematheque in Los Angeles. Val Guest died on May 10, 2006.

WHEELER WINSTON DIXON: The first thing that struck me in looking through all your credits is that, while you have a cult reputation as a horror and science fiction director, it's really not true.

VAL GUEST: No.

Producer Charles K. Feldman with director Val Guest on the set of *Casino Royale* (1967), the big-budget spoof of James Bond films that failed to click with audiences or critics, despite an impressive cast. Courtesy Jerry Ohlinger Archives.

WWD: It's a small aspect of your work; you're really a general all-arounder.

VG: Yes, very much so. In fact, I don't consider any of my films to be horror pictures. I looked upon them as science fiction, with the possible exception of *The Abominable Snowman* [1957].

WWD: Could you tell me a little bit about your early life, what your mother did, what your father did, and how you broke into the industry? You were born in London in 1911.

VG: That's right. I grew up with my father. All I knew about my mother was what he told me, that she had died. He never told me much more than that. When I got to be ten years old, somehow or other he allowed me to go and see my grandparents, my mother's parents. I got quite friendly with them. As a ten-year-old I used to go on the bus and see them. Then one day there was a lady there who spoke to me—we were all having tea or something—and after she'd gone, my grandmother said to me, "Did you like that lady?" and I said, "Well, yes, she's nice." She said, "Well, I'm so glad, dear, because that was your mother." That's how I first met my mother. And then after that, my grandparents made me swear on my scout's honor that I would never tell my father that I'd met my mother.

WWD: Why did your father keep it a secret?

VG: I have no idea, and I never asked him. I was never close to my father, I'm afraid. I think he thought, "How do you explain divorce to a three-year-old? It's easier to say she's dead."

WWD: What did your father do for a living?

VG: My father was a jute and gunny broker. I was born in London and went with him to Calcutta. I spent my very early years in Calcutta. Eventually I came back to London and started striking out on my own.

WWD: How did you get into the industry?

VG: Well, oddly enough, I got into the entertainment business through my mother. She was a stage actress, a principal in many of the London pantomimes. Her name was Anna Thayer. I was in a terrible job in the City that my father put me into, at the Asiatic Petroleum Company. First I was in the accounts department, and I couldn't add up four and five. Then one day the boss of the department saw a copy of *Stage* on my desk and said, "Do you know anything about theater?" I said, "Well, my mother is on the stage." So just like that, he put me in charge of a charity concert the company was sponsoring. They did a lot of charity affairs at the Alhambra Theatre in Leicester Square.

I went back to my mother and asked, "How do I go about this?" So she helped me enormously, and I got the show together with some big star names like Ivor Novello and people like that. After that, I continued on by getting myself a small part in a play because it wasn't that difficult then. There were rep companies all over the place.

WWD: Not that much later on, you were single-handedly running the London bureau of the *Hollywood Reporter*.

VG: Well, it's very funny. I was writing on the side because I wasn't earning much as an actor, so I had to earn enough money to be able to eat. I was writing for various film magazines. A friend of mine read some of my stuff for these small magazines and said, "Why don't you write for American papers? Why don't you get a column going, like Walter Winchell?" Then Billy Wilkerson, who was the founder and publisher of the *Hollywood Reporter*, came to London, and I went to interview him. Billy said, "Come and have some lunch," and over lunch he made a proposition to me: "Would you like to do a column for me from London?" So that's how I became the *Hollywood Reporter*'s London columnist.

WWD: And this gave you enormous access to the studios, because you were talking to directors, writers, and producers on a daily basis. I understand it was Marcel Varnel, the director, who gave you your first real chance in films.

VG: You're quite right, it was through the *Hollywood Reporter* that we got together. I was doing all the book reviews and film reviews, everything. There was a picture that came out called *Chandu the Magician* [1932], which Marcel directed with William Cameron Menzies. In the brashness of youth, I wrote a scathing review of the film, in which I said that if I couldn't write a better picture than this with one hand tied behind my back, I'd give up the business.

WWD: Oh, my God.

VG: So Marcel Varnel called Billy at the *Reporter* offices in Hollywood, and he was furious. Then Billy called me in London and said, "Look, you threw down the gauntlet here, so it's up to you to put matters right. Go and see Varnel." So I went to Elstree Studios and saw Varnel. I said, "Look, I apologize." I had my hat in my hand. "Of course I couldn't write a picture." But he really surprised me by saying, "Well, I think you could. I've been reading your column." And he said, "I think that with the help of somebody else you could do a great screenplay." So I wrote a film called *Public Nuisance Number One* [1936]. Then one day, coming out of the rushes, Marcel said to me, "How would you like me to put you under contract?" I thought the walls had fallen in. And when Gainsborough Studios asked Marcel to direct a Will Hay comedy, Marcel took me with him. So that's how I got to become a contract writer at Gainsborough Studios. And then I started directing with *Miss London Ltd.* [1943], and directed four or five films after that in the same vein.

WWD: You wrote so many of the films you directed.

VG: I did a lot of work, yes. I would cook up an idea myself and then go around trying to sell it to people, but it wasn't easy. It was very hard for me to get out of comedy. I wanted to do something more, but I was typecast, after a fashion.

WWD: But then you directed *Murder at the Windmill* [1949], which is sort of a murder mystery, isn't it?

VG: Yes. It's a drama, a musical mystery. I did the score for that, too. I wrote a lot of music for the theater in the late 1930s and was very active as a composer for the stage.

WWD: Now, where did you get the idea to direct *Mr. Drake's Duck* [1951], which centered on radioactively contaminated ducks who lay eggs with uranium yolks? Douglas Fairbanks Jr. was in that film, along with Wilfred Hyde White.

VG: *Mr. Drake's Duck* was originally a playlet on the BBC radio. [Gainsborough] bought the idea, and then I enlarged it to make it a feature. It's a very short film; it's only about seventy-five minutes. These are all pretty modest films, but then I got the chance to do *Penny Princess* [1952] with Dirk Bogarde. That was for our own production company, Conquest Productions, and we shot it in color. Geoffrey Unsworth was the cinematographer.

WWD: What was it like working with Dirk Bogarde? Could you tell that he was going to be a major star?

VG: Well, he was already pretty well known. He was doing dramas. He was wonderful at drama, but everybody was a little unsure whether or not he could do a light comedy. *Penny Princess* was the first light comedy he'd ever done, but then he went into the *Doctor* series, which went on and on for years; he became a light comedy star. Oddly enough, Dirk wasn't our first choice. We asked Robert Cummings, and Bob wanted to do it, but he had his television series and it would have clashed completely. I even sent a script to Montgomery Clift, but that didn't work out.

WWD: Then you directed *The Runaway Bus* [1954], which had a remarkable cast. It starred Frankie Howerd, a rather famous knockabout comedian; Petula Clark, who became a pop star in the 1960s with the song "Downtown"; and Margaret Rutherford, who went on to do the Miss Marple films for MGM in the 1960s. It was quite a hit for you. So really, at this point, everybody thinks of you as a comedy director?

VG: That's right.

WWD: So how did you get to direct *Men of Sherwood Forest* [1954], starring Don Taylor as Robin Hood?

VG: That was for Hammer Films, of course, and I got involved with Hammer through another comedy, *Life with the Lyons* [1954], which was based on a popular BBC radio series. Then we did a second one, *The Lyons in Paris* [1955]. They were both substantial hits, and from then on, Hammer kept saying to me, "Well, would you like to do this?" So that's how I got to direct *Men of Sherwood Forest* and finally began to break away from comedy.

WWD: So then you're given the chance to do the film that transforms Hammer into an international institution, *The Quatermass Xperiment* [1955], which was a worldwide hit and released in the United States as *The Creeping Unknown*. This was based on a popular BBC television serial by Nigel Kneale and became the first really big international hit Hammer ever had. How did that come about? Was this just another assignment at the time?

VG: No, it wasn't, actually. In fact, the reason I did *Quatermass* was entirely my wife's doing, because without Yolande, I wouldn't have done it. At the time, it was the thing that all England stayed in to watch on television.

WWD: Yes, it was the top serial on the BBC, absolutely. It dealt with the continuing adventures of a Professor Bernard Quatermass, who continually seems to come in contact with hostile alien forces. It was pretty much the *X-Files* of its era.

VG: Absolutely. I was probably the only person in England who hadn't seen it, because I wasn't into science fiction at that time. Tony Hinds at Hammer asked me to direct a feature film from the serial and gave me a bunch of the television scripts to read. Yolande and I were just about to go on holiday to

A tense scene with Brian Donlevy as Professor Bernard Quatermass and doomed space traveler Richard Wordsworth in Val Guest's *The Quatermass Xperiment* (1955). Courtesy Jerry Ohlinger Archives. Copyright © 1956 by United Artists Corporation.

Tangier, so Tony met us at the airport with a whole lot of these scripts and said, "Read them and let me know." So I took them to Tangier and put them beside the bed. After the first week, Yolande saw them there and said, "Well, aren't you going to read them?" And I said, "Well, you know, it's science fiction. It's not really my cup of tea." But fortunately, she insisted, and I took one down on the beach and read it. I was riveted by it. The only problem I saw was how to condense it. I don't know how many weeks it was on television, so how was I going to get all this down into one film? But we figured it out, and Hammer went ahead with it. Brian Donlevy came over as the token American star to get the funding for the film, and we added Jack Warner, Gordon Jackson, and Lionel Jeffries to the cast from my rep days. It was a great group. I thought the script was very plausible, and I was very pleased with the result.

WWD: What was it like working with the Hammer people?

VG: Wonderful. They were very efficient, very cost conscious. It was like a family down there. Because, you know, they didn't really have any studios. They just had a big manor house at Bray, and we shot the whole thing there and on location. We used to shoot in the living room! If you wanted a long shot, the camera operator had to get his bottom in the fireplace.

WWD: Then came *The Abominable Snowman*, with Forrest Tucker and Peter Cushing. Was that your first time working with Peter Cushing?

VG: Yes, first and only time. Peter was wonderful, and he was a joy to work with; Forrest Tucker was a more down-to-earth guy, but great fun to work with. He was the American star again, whom we needed to get financing for the film and U.S. distribution.

WWD: Why did you agree to direct *The Camp on Blood Island* [1958], which is sort of an early "splatter" film?

VG: That was also for Hammer.

WWD: Right. But did you just say, "Hey, I'm just going to do it"?

VG: Yeah.

WWD: What was the schedule on something like that?

VG: Oh, my God. I would think four or five weeks at the most.

WWD: And the budget would maybe be in the £100,000 range?

VG: *Way* under that. These were very carefully budgeted films.

WWD: Are you happy with your next major project, *Hell Is a City* [1960]?

VG: Yes, that's one of my favorites; and I've done far too many of them.

WWD: You are prolific; there's no getting around it.

VG: I always say my favorites are *The Day the Earth Caught Fire* [1961], *Expresso Bongo* [1960], *Yesterday's Enemy* [1959], and *Hell Is a City*. On all those pictures, I tried to keep it real. I said to Hammer, starting with the *Quatermass* film, "Look, if I shoot this, I want to shoot it for real. I want to shoot cinema verité. I want to use handheld cameras. I want it to look as though it was a newsreel of an actual event, rather than something we'd staged." And Tony Hinds and Hammer let me do it. From then on, all those other pictures, I tried to shoot almost newsreel style. I wanted to shoot them in black and white because most of television and newsreels were in black and white in those days.

WWD: It looks so much better in black and white than in color.

VG: Yes, indeed it does.

WWD: And on *Expresso Bongo*, what was the genesis of this project?

VG: It started out as a play. Yolande went with a girlfriend and saw the stage version, and came home saying, "You've got to see this. I'm sure it would make a movie." So she took me to the play, and I must honestly say I wasn't all that impressed. I thought, "Yes, but does anybody really want to see the rise and fall of a rock star and all that?" But my wife, being the schemer that she is, arranged a party to which she invited a lot of people, including the play's author, Wolf Mankowitz. The more I talked to Wolf at the party, the more I got excited about *Expresso Bongo*. So I signed him up, and we did it.

WWD: What was Laurence Harvey like to work with?

VG: Great.

WWD: Some people say he was rather difficult, but you didn't have any problems?

VG: He certainly wasn't difficult with us, no. He was very down-to-earth and everything. It's very funny, because on that picture Larry said to me, "Well, what kind of person is Johnny Jackson, the manager? I mean, what sort of an accent do you see him having?" And I suddenly thought, "He's like Wolf Mankowitz!" And so Larry Harvey made a couple of dates with Wolf and listened to him talk very carefully, and then said, "I think I've got it, I've got the accent absolutely." So he did a Wolf Mankowitz imitation, and it worked. But halfway through the film Larry said, "I'm losing it." So from the set of the studio he called up Wolf to talk to him about something or other, to get it back. And then he got it down cold, and we went back and shot it.

WWD: You also directed *Quatermass II* [1957], known in the United States as *Enemy from Space*, once again starring Brian Donlevy as Professor Quatermass, fighting off an alien invasion.

VG: Yes. That was a great film, I thought. If I had five pictures to mention, I'd mention that as well. I did the sort of newsreel approach I'd used on my other films, and we shot much of that on location in Brighton.

WWD: What do you think of *80,000 Suspects* [1963], which is about an epidemic breaking out in London?

VG: I like it. It's not one of my favorites, but yes, I do like it.

WWD: You wrote, produced, and directed it. How do you feel when you're wearing that many hats at once?

VG: Actually, it's a lot easier for me, because I know what the writer has been through, and I know what the director is going through. You know, one way or the other, I find it a lot *easier* to write, direct, and produce, because when you're directing somebody else's script, as a director you're always liable to say, "What can I do to help the script?" and you start making changes. And if the picture doesn't go down well, the writer is just as liable to say, "Well, look what the director did with it." So one way or another, it's nice to have control—if you know when to put the other hat on.

WWD: Speaking of *The Day the Earth Caught Fire*, that's one of my favorites of yours. It's just a beautiful film. You co-wrote that with Wolf Mankowitz, is that correct?

VG: Well, it was my original idea, and then Yolande said, "Why don't you bring in Wolf?" Wolf added a lot of bite to the screenplay; he had a brilliant talent. Michael Caine is in that, in a very brief bit as a policeman. It's one of my favorites, about the end of the world, brought about by a profusion of

Brian Donlevy holds a mysterious projectile from outer space in the highly successful sequel to *The Quatermass Xperiment*, Val Guest's *Quatermass II* (1957). Courtesy Jerry Ohlinger Archives.

nuclear tests. And the whole film takes place pretty much in a newspaper office, as the reporters scramble to keep up with the story and blow the lid off a government cover-up.

WWD: Janet Munro, Edward Judd, and Leo McKern are the leads in the film, but you used a real editor as the editor of the fictional London newspaper in the film.

VG: Yes, Arthur Christiansen, a Fleet Street icon. He was editor of the *Daily Express* for twenty-five years or something like that. He was a historic figure, and I happened to know Arthur personally, so I signed him up on the picture to be my technical advisor, because it was all about newspapers and things. Then I talked him into playing a small part. He also played a small part for me again as an editor on *80,000 Suspects*.

WWD: Yes, but he's got more than a small part in *The Day the Earth Caught Fire*. I mean, he's the editor-in-chief of the newspaper, isn't he?

VG: Yes, he is, but it is quite a small part. There's a lot of footage of him sitting behind the desk saying, "Look, we've got to do this and we've got to do that,"

Edward Judd and Janet Munro in Val Guest's masterful vision of the end of the world, *The Day the Earth Caught Fire* (1961). Courtesy Jerry Ohlinger Archives.

to his fictional staff, and it looks like a large part because you keep coming back to it.

WWD: How did he feel working with all those other actors who were really professionals?

VG: Very, very worried. And in the end, the public response was mixed. Some people say, "Oh, he was great," and other people say, "Wasn't he awful?" Arthur had terrible trouble with his lines all through the film, and I had to keep cutting away, when he blew a line, to a close-up of one of his staff listening attentively. But I thought he came off all right.

WWD: How on earth did you get hooked into *Casino Royale* [1967]? That's a film that seems like a foredoomed project.

VG: Yes, but it made a *fortune*. It's become a cult movie.

WWD: Yes, I guess so. I can't see it myself.

VG: In fact, a few weeks ago in Los Angeles, they had a psychedelic film festival, and they picked *Casino Royale* as one of the films for the series. Yolande and I went to the screening, and I must say, the house rocked with laughter right through.

WWD: So how did you get involved with that?

VG: I got involved because one day the phone rang and my agent at the William Morris office said, "[The producer] Charlie Feldman is in town, and how would you feel about making a picture back-to-back with John Huston?" I said, "What do you mean, back-to-back?" And he said, "Feldman wants to do a picture with various segments done by four different directors, and he's signed John, and he wants to know if you're interested." And I said, "Yes, of course, I'd be happy to work with John." So that's how I got in. So Charlie Feldman called me and said, "Look, it's one film with four different stories, and you can write your own story." What had happened is, he had bought the rights, the only rights still available, to the novel *Casino Royale*, the one [James Bond] novel that wasn't scooped up by Eon Productions. But Charlie had found that all he had bought really was the *title*, because the other Bond pictures had ripped out everything in the book. So Charlie signed Ben Hecht to write the screenplay. And Ben Hecht died before he finished it, so we pretty much had to take it from there.

WWD: So, what sections of this did you direct?

VG: Well, there are a bunch of directors on the movie: myself, Ken Hughes, John Huston, Joseph McGrath, and Robert Parrish. And quite a bunch of writers, too: myself, Wolf Mankowitz, John Law, Michael Sayers, Woody Allen, Ben Hecht, Joseph Heller, Terry Southern, Billy Wilder, and Peter Sellers! Some of them got credit on the final film, and some of them didn't. They got fired one by one, or their contracts ran out, or something. Peter Sellers had one of the directors fired, I know. Then toward the end of the picture, watching the "dailies" one day, I was in there with John watching some stuff from the film. As we came out, John said, "This could turn into a load of crap, couldn't it?" And I said, "Yes, it could. But that's why they sign up people like you, John, to see that it doesn't." He said, "Don't you put it all on me, for Christ's sake!" Then one day John told me, "Look, I'm through with this. My contract is up, and I want to go to Ireland and play poker. You can do the rest

Woody Allen in *Casino Royale* (1967), which Val Guest directed, along with Ken Hughes, John Huston, Joseph McGrath, and Robert Parrish, to no one's satisfaction. Courtesy Jerry Ohlinger Archives.

of my stuff." So I had to take over his section, and originally I was signed to do the last segment, the Woody Allen section. So I did all the Woody Allen stuff. Then, when the editor put all this together, Charlie Feldman and I took a look at it, and he said to me, "This needs some sort of a story going for it, doesn't it?" [*Laughs.*]

wwD: Yeah, always a good idea. Holds the picture together. [*Laughs.*].

vG: I said, "Yes, it does need a story, Charlie." He said, "Well, write one." So I had to write a linking story right through it. I did it only on the condition that he let me keep working with David Niven and Ursula Andress, who were both in the picture, because they were great gigglers and we could laugh at all our problems. So I then tried to do a linking thing all through it and finish up all the bits of pieces everybody left. At the end of it, Charlie took me to dinner one night with Bill Holden and a few people and said, "I've got a surprise for you. I'm going to give you an extra title on the film: 'coordinating director.'"

wwD: Oh, my Lord.

vG: I said, "Charlie, if you do that, I'll sue you. People are going to look at this and say this was coordinated by *me*? No thank *you*!" But Charlie had the last laugh. When the picture finally opened, Charlie called me up at four o'clock in the morning from New York in London and said, "Want to hear the box office take?" And he gave me the figures, which were incredible. So, somehow, we pulled it off.

wwD: What about working with Peter Sellers? Was he utterly impossible or not?

vG: No, because I started Peter's career in films. I wrote a film for him called *Up the Creek* [1958] and also directed it. Peter was on *The Goon Show* and things like that. I thought he was very funny. So I wrote this thing for him, *Up the Creek*, and I took it to Jimmy Carreras at Hammer. And Jimmy said, "Peter Sellers doesn't mean a damn thing in the box office. But if you give me a name, I'll do it." So I finally got him David Tomlinson, who was a big name then, and we shot the film.

wwD: Nobody remembers Peter Sellers's early black-and-whites from the 1960s, before he got involved in the *Pink Panther* films, which were just absolutely brilliant. What about working with Woody Allen? Was he telling you already he wanted to go on and direct his own stuff?

vG: Yes, but I'll tell you what happened. Woody had just written the story of *Take the Money and Run* [1969]. And he said, "Oh, I'd love to direct, but they'll never let me direct this. I've given the story to Charlie Feldman, and he's got an option on it, but nothing's happening." And then finally Woody and his manager asked me if I would direct it for Woody in New York. And I said, "Sure, fine, if you're all available at the same time." In fact, Woody actually writes that in his autobiography. But when it came time to do it in New York, surprise, surprise, they said that he could do it. And that was the beginning of his career.

WWD: Now what about *When Dinosaurs Ruled the Earth* [1970], which is one of your odder films, it seems to me?

VG: That's one of my *un*favorites. And it gets played on television more than anything else I've done. But it's become a cult film. That's the terrifying thing about these things. You have no control. You send them out in the world, and look what happens.

WWD: What about *Toomorrow* [1970], a science fiction musical with Olivia Newton-John?

VG: Oh, well, that was a *disaster*! It was one of the great fiascoes. I wrote and directed it, against my better judgment, for Don Kirshner and Harry Saltzman. None of us got paid, and I finally had to stop it from being shown.

Victoria Vetri and Robin Hawdon in one of Val Guest's "unfavorite" films as a director, *When Dinosaurs Ruled the Earth* (1970). Courtesy Jerry Ohlinger Archives. Copyright © 1970 by Warner Bros. Inc.

Don and Harry Saltzman did not get on together. Kirshner didn't like any-thing about Saltzman or the story. He didn't like anything except Olivia Newton-John.

WWD: What about *The Au Pair Girls* [1972]?

VG: Oh, that was a little giggle we did. My goodness. I didn't know that anybody still remembered it.

WWD: What strikes me as interesting is that as we come to the end of your ca-reer, we wind up with two sweet, small-scale comedies: *Dangerous Davies—The Last Detective* [1981] and *The Boys in Blue* [1982].

VG: Well, *The Boys in Blue* is another *un*favorite. I never wanted to make that.

WWD: Isn't that a remake of *Ask a Policeman* [1939], an early Will Hay comedy that you scripted?

VG: You're absolutely right. They came to me and said, "Would you like to re-make this?" And I wound up doing it, to make a long story short, but my heart wasn't in it.

WWD: How do you feel about the episodes that you did for the teleseries *Ham-mer House of Horror*: "Child's Play" [1985], "In Possession" [1984], and "Mark of the Devil" [1984]?

VG: That was fun doing. I did that for old time's sake, to work once again for Hammer. Roy Skeggs, who was running Hammer then, called me up and asked me to do it. I had practically retired, and I came back to do that. It was great working with a lot of the old gang. So I enjoyed doing it.

WWD: Who are your favorite directors, people you admired?

VG: Jules Dassin, particularly for his work on *Naked City* [1948], which was one of the first American films to use the newsreel technique we've been talking about. David Lean I liked a lot, and Noel Coward, as an actor and director.

WWD: Do you watch any contemporary movies now? Do you have any direc-tors whom you particularly like who are working these days?

VG: Yes, Christopher Guest. I loved his film *Best in Show* [2000]. I thought that the direction, the writing, and the acting in that film were beautifully done. It could so easily have gone over the top. He's very, very restrained. He does a really good job.

WWD: How does it feel being remembered primarily as a science fiction direc-tor for Hammer, when you've done so much other work besides?

VG: Well, I'm nearly ninety years old, and I've done a lot of work, and I'm glad to be remembered for what I consider to be some of my best work. There are other films of mine that I wish were better known, but as I said, my favorites include *The Day the Earth Caught Fire*. And so I'm very pleased to have been a part of that and to have worked in an industry I love for such a long time.

BUDD BOETTICHER

Budd Boetticher (pronounced "bettiker") was primarily known for his work as a director in the Western genre, but I didn't want to tell him that. Boetticher refused to be pinned down with any labels and described any attempts to pigeonhole his talents as "laziness on the part of all those critics!" Born Oscar Boetticher Jr. on July 29, 1916, in Chicago, Boetticher attended Culver Military Academy and later Ohio State University. During college, he went to Mexico to recover from a football injury and saw his first bullfight. Entranced by the drama of the ring, Boetticher wanted to make a career for himself as a matador. He returned to Hollywood only at the behest of his mother, who got him a job working as a horse wrangler on the second unit of Lewis Milestone's *Of Mice and Men* (1939). (In our talk, Boetticher disputed this story, stating emphatically, "I was never a horse wrangler! I was the second assistant director.") This experience led to work as a technical advisor on Rouben Mamoulian's *Blood and Sand* (1941), for which Boetticher coached Tyrone Power on the fine art of bullfighting and served as choreographer for the "El Torero" dance number, though without receiving formal credit.

From 20th Century Fox, Boetticher drifted over to Columbia, where he formed an unlikely alliance with Harry Cohn, the mercurial head of the studio, and he was soon working as an assistant director on such films as *The More the Merrier* (1943), *Destroyer* (1943), *The Desperadoes* (1943), and the big-budget Rita Hayworth vehicle *Cover Girl* (1944). Simultaneously, Cohn allowed Boetticher to finish up directorial chores on two films credited to Columbia B director Lew Landers (*Submarine Raider* [1942] and *U-Boat Prisoner* [1944]) before giving Boetticher his first chance to direct an entire film, *One Mysterious Night* (1944; credited to Oscar Boetticher). From then on, Boetticher made a name for himself as a reliable and inventive director in a variety of genres until he left Hollywood in 1960 for what should have been a brief trip to Mexico to make a documentary feature on the life and career of matador Carlos Arruza, one of Boetticher's idols.

The project, entitled simply *Arruza,* turned into an epic, seven-year-long disaster. Obsessed with completing the film, Boetticher turned down numerous directorial assignments, finally ran out of money, got divorced, and wound up spending one week in an insane asylum and another in a Mexican jail. To make matters worse, Arruza was killed in an automobile accident on May 20, 1966, forcing Boetticher to complete the film with the materials at hand. Finally, after numerous other production and financing problems, the film was released in 1972 to rapturous reviews, and it remains one of the classics of the documentary

Director Budd Boetticher in the 1950s. Courtesy Jerry Ohlinger Archives.

film. Boetticher made one other film, *My Kingdom For . . .* (1985), and wrote an autobiography, *When in Disgrace* (1989).

Throughout our interview, Boetticher was frank and blunt in his assessment of his own work, as well as that of his associates, and refreshingly candid in his opinions. Entirely his own man, Boetticher was utterly unreconstructed and unapologetically macho during our long talk, occasionally shouting at me if he thought I didn't understand the point he was trying to make, and then apologizing a bit sheepishly afterward. There were a number of surprises for me during our conversation (Boetticher's intense love/hate relationship with John Wayne and John Ford; his frank admiration for the German propagandist Leni Riefenstahl), but Boetticher tells the story much better himself. This interview took place on June 5, 2001, just a few days after the death of actor Anthony Quinn, one of Boetticher's best friends, and he was still quite shaken by Quinn's passing. Ironically, it was the last interview that Boetticher himself gave before his death on November 29, 2001.

BUDD BOETTICHER: Well, where do you want to start? If you want to start with *The Missing Juror* [1944], then you want to go pretty far back. That's only my second picture!

WHEELER WINSTON DIXON: Actually I want to start before that, with *Of Mice and Men* [1939]. You worked as a horse wrangler on that film, I believe . . .

BB: Well, you know, I didn't really start out wanting to direct pictures. When I was young, I did a lot of things. For a while, I thought my whole life was football, but then I had a knee injury, and I went to Mexico to spend a year away from school, but not lose my eligibility as a football player. And that's where I saw my first bullfight. It was like the opening of a whole new world. Actually, my favorite sport was not football and not boxing; it was track. My favorite was the hundred-yard dash, because if you lose, it's your fault; you don't need ten men to block for you. And when I looked down in the bullring, this first week I was in Mexico, I was eighteen and here's a fella in a gold suit who later became my mentor. And I thought, "Boy, talk about individualism, he's *really* in a lot of trouble out there."

WWD: Was your goal then to become a professional matador?

BB: I became an apprentice, sort of like an intern becoming a doctor. I was honored when I was forty years old, fighting with Arruza, when they made me a formal matador. It was during a charity bullfight, and I hadn't killed a bull for seventeen years! By that time, I'd been a director for many years, but it was a great honor. Half of the people were there to see me get killed, but I came through all right.

WWD: They had a lot of faith in you, huh?

BB (*laughs*): Yeah! It was wonderful, though. I made Carlos take the tour of the ring with me after the bullfight, and I still have the ear of the bull I killed that day, and it's the only trophy I have in my whole house that I ever put up. It's down in the den.

WWD: Well, how did you get from this to working on *Of Mice and Men*?

BB: Well, God, first off, I was never a horse wrangler! I was the second assistant director on that picture, working under Lewis Milestone. Great picture.

WWD: But how did you get from Mexico to Hollywood? You were set on a career as a matador. What happened?

BB: I didn't drift back to Hollywood. My mother discovered what I was doing from the papers, that her son had become a bullfighter, and she couldn't have that. It wasn't that she was worried about me getting killed; it just wasn't culturally acceptable for a Boetticher to be a bullfighter. So she called Hal Roach, and Mr. Roach got me the job working on *Of Mice and Men*. That film was made at the Hal Roach studios. And after that, Roach called up Darryl Zanuck, and that's how I got the job as a technical advisor on *Blood and Sand*.

WWD: How did you wind up at Columbia after working at 20th?

BB: They wanted me there! George Stevens was working over at Columbia, and you know, being a bullfighter was a pretty romantic thing in Hollywood. Everyone wanted me to visit with them. I went to Columbia as a messenger boy, 'cause I didn't have any talent for anything else; I had no career ahead of me. But I would take letters to the different offices as a mail carrier, and I would sit down with the great directors, like George Stevens, who is my favorite director in all the world. And then we would talk about bullfighting, and the mail would never get delivered! So from there, they made me a reader, and I would read things and suggest that the studio buy them, and eventually I worked my way up.

WWD: How did your involvement with *Submarine Raider* [1942] come about? You directed sections of that film, apparently, but it was credited to Lew Landers.

BB: Well, Harry Cohn was a very dear friend of mine.

WWD: You don't hear many people say that!

BB (*laughs*): No, you sure don't, but what can I tell you. He was a great guy, and we got along great. I liked him a lot, and he liked me for what I had been. You know, it's a great thing; even when you've been a novice bullfighter, the bulls are just as big for you as they are for the real pros, and you get a lot of dignity. Nothing really frightens you.

WWD: Yeah, I get the impression that if you let Harry Cohn walk all over you, he would, but if you stood up to him, you were in.

BB: That's it exactly! We met when Cohn walked on the set while George Stevens was making *The More the Merrier* [1943] with Joel McCrea and Jean Arthur.

I was the assistant director. When Cohn walked onto the soundstage, I tossed George Stevens a tennis ball. George had a backboard built on the set, and he started to play handball by himself with the tennis ball until Harry Cohn left, which didn't take too long, because every moment that Stevens was playing handball was costing Columbia about $100 a second! So when Cohn came on the set again, and I tossed the ball to George, Cohn turned to me, pointed at George Stevens, and said, "Tell that son-of-a-bitch I want to talk to him." And I said, "That son-of-a-bitch you're referring to is probably the best son-of-a-bitching director in all of Hollywood. I'm sorry, but he's busy." Cohn was furious and started in on me. He said, "Hey listen, you son-of-a-bitch . . . ," and that got me mad. I said, "Whoa, wait a minute! Nobody calls me a son-of-a-bitch, and you better not say that again." Cohn said, "And if I do?" And I said, "If you do, I'm going to knock you on your ass." He said, "Do you know who I am?" I said, "Yes, Mr. Cohn, I certainly do, but compared to those black bulls that come out of the chute at the bullring you look like the Virgin Mary." That's word for word. And so Cohn stared at me for a long time and then said, "Look, you be in my office at six o'clock. I want to talk to you." And I thought to myself, "Brother, here you are, twenty-six years old, and you better get a lot of pencils and a lot of apples, because you're sure as hell not in the picture business anymore. I'm going be out on the corner selling pencils or something."

So I went to his office, and he told me that he needed a young director to finish up a picture. So he put me on the last two days of *Submarine Raider*, which was a twelve-day picture. And my God, I studied! I prepared every angle, I went over the script line by line. I prepared for those two days as if I were directing *Gone With the Wind*, because I didn't have any talent for it. But they gave me an assistant director who was a deadly enemy of mine, and I knew I had to show him who was boss. So when he came over to me on my first day on the set and said, "Excuse me, sir, but would you mind telling me what your first setup is?" I said, "Yeah, I will, as soon as I have a cup of coffee." And I turned away and said to myself, "Son-of-a-bitch, you're *really* a director now." And it worked; he never gave me any trouble after that. So I directed the two days, and then I went back to working as an assistant on the bigger films. Two years later, Cohn put me on another Lew Landers picture, *U-Boat Prisoner* [1944], which was an *eight*-day picture. Well, Lew Landers was really a no-talent guy. They called him the "D director" there at Columbia; he just wasn't any good. Whenever they had a picture they didn't really care about, they'd give it to Landers.

WWD: While we're in the 1940s at Columbia, I'm going to throw some other names at you and get your reactions. What about [director] Ray Nazarro?

BB: Well, Ray Nazarro is a very interesting figure in my life. Ray was a ten-day picture guy, and they assigned me to his company for two days' work as an assistant director. We had lunch together, and I told him the story of my life in Mexico, because he wanted to know about my life as a bullfighter, which, as I said, everyone always thought was fascinating. And he said "Budd, if you put this down on paper in longhand, I'll type it up. There's this fellow I know named Dore Schary at MGM; he's a producer, and I can get this picture made." And then years later, when I finally made the picture, *Bullfighter and the Lady* [1951], which originally was called *Torero*, Mr. Nazarro got credit for my screenplay [along with Boetticher], and I was nominated for an Academy Award. And if I go down in the den and look it up, I have a certificate that states that *Bullfighter and the Lady* is "an original screenplay by Ray Nazarro and Budd Boetticher." Can you believe it? But there was no such thing as arbitration then . . . there was nothing you could do.

WWD: What about William Castle?

BB: Oh, Bill Castle was a hell of a nice guy. He directed all those *Whistler* pictures for Columbia, which were great mystery films. We didn't hang around together, though; there was no sort of relationship. Directors are worse than bullfighters, believe me; they all want to be stars. But he was a good guy, and he ended up doing some really good horror pictures [such as *House on Haunted Hill* (1958)].

WWD: The next credit I have for you is *The Girl in the Case* [1944], and once again you're helping out on someone else's film, in this case director William Berke.

BB: Well, what happened there was that they fired the director and I got the job, and I finished the picture. It was another short schedule picture. My first real film as a director was *One Mysterious Night* [1944], as Oscar Boetticher, which was a Boston Blackie picture with Chester Morris. Once again, it was a very short schedule, twelve days. All these pictures were made for under $100,000: they cost so much, they made so much, and that was it.

WWD: Did you do any pre-planning on these films? Did you start off with the master and then go for the close-ups, or how did you break it down?

BB: No, I didn't do anything like that. I just figured I was the director and I'd go on the set and direct the picture. Listen, you don't learn to be a director; you either are or you aren't. And you better damn well be able to deal with people. I would look at the scene and rehearse the scene with the actors, and then shoot it. Today they don't really know what they're doing, so they use a lot of different angles to protect themselves in the cutting room. On the *Buchanan* pictures, they averaged a running time of about an hour and seventeen minutes. There wasn't a lot of wasted footage because we didn't have any film to waste! I cut the picture on the set, in the camera, so they couldn't cut it any other way, and then I'd go off between pictures to Mexico and shoot another two or three bullfights. Then I'd come back and make another eighteen-day picture, then back to Mexico for more bullfights. I did all of this stuff intuitively, and I can't really analyze them because I didn't shoot 'em that way. If you tell me a story, and you're a good storyteller, I pay attention. You've got a beginning, you've got a middle, and you've got an ending. That's the way I made pictures. And I did that very well, and suddenly I was a *good* director, after about fifteen pictures. [*Laughs.*] But I didn't design anything; I just went on the set. I was the boss, and I did it.

WWD: On your second feature, the mystery programmer *The Missing Juror* [1944], you're working with George Macready [a memorable screen villain]. What was that like?

BB: Oh, he was great! And that was his first really big performance [as a man falsely convicted of a crime he didn't commit, who then "snaps" and exacts his own brand of justice upon the members of the jury who convicted him]. From that picture, he went on to be one of the top character actors in Hollywood. He had a scar on his cheek that was real; I don't know if it was from a car accident, or a dueling accident, or what, but it really added to his personality on screen, and I liked him very much.

WWD: From there, you went on to direct several program pictures for Columbia—*Escape in the Fog* [1945], *A Guy, a Gal and a Pal* [1945], and *Youth on Trial* [1945]—all as Oscar Boetticher. These were very small pictures, right?

BB: Oh, they were *nothing* pictures! But they gave me a chance to work with some great people—Nina Foch, Otto Kruger, people like that. Nina is a great actress; she went on to do some really good stuff.

WWD: Why did you decide to drop "Oscar" and become simply "Budd" Boetticher?

BB: I dropped it when I did *Bullfighter and the Lady*. I came from a very, very wealthy family, and I've survived in spite of it. And I didn't find out until I was thirty that I was adopted. My father named me Oscar Boetticher Jr. because he wanted me to follow in his footsteps and go into the hardware business. When I was fifteen, he said, "Budd, what do you want to be when you grow up?" I said, "Dad, I don't know, probably a football coach if I'm lucky." He looked disgusted and said, "Oscar, you see that telephone right there?" and I said, "Yes, sir." "Well," he said, "I can pick up that telephone, and I can call Chicago and buy a million dollars' worth of kegs of nails. I'll buy them at $16 a keg, and I call Los Angeles and I sell them for $17 a keg, and I've made a huge profit in five minutes." And I said, "Yes sir, but you've made it in Evansville, Indiana." He was furious. He didn't speak to me after that for many, many weeks.

WWD: What did your mother do?

BB: She didn't have to do anything.

WWD: She was a homemaker?

BB (*laughs*): A homemaker? She was never a homemaker! She was the countess of whatever you want to call it; she was something very special to me.

WWD: Now we come to *Behind Locked Doors* [1948], which was one of three pictures that you made for Eagle-Lion, which was formerly PRC [Producers Releasing Corporation], perhaps the cheapest studio in Hollywood.

BB: That was the first picture I made after the war. Three weeks after I got out of the navy, my agent called me and said, "Budd, I've got you a three-picture deal at Eagle-Lion Studios." I said, "What the hell is that?" He said "Well, it's a studio right next to Warner Brothers. Brynie [Bryan] Foy is the head of it. It's a new organization, and I talked them into giving you a contract." I said, "How the hell did you do that? I don't know anybody there." And he said, "Well, I told them you were the Gentile Sammy Fuller," and I said, "Jesus, I'd rather be the Jewish John Ford!" But I was stuck with the deal. It was a small studio, and they didn't have much money, but the pictures were all right. Richard Carlson starred in *Behind Locked Doors*, and it was fun to work with him and Doug Fowley, Lucille Bremer, Tor Johnson, and the rest of the cast. The others were *Black Midnight* [1949] and *Assigned to Danger* [1948]; they were all right, but nothing special.

WWD: Then you went to Monogram for *The Wolf Hunters* [1949].

BB: Monogram! That was *really* second rate! *Wolf Hunters* was an outdoor picture, kind of an "in the snow" thing, and I put all my friends in it who were out of work—Jan Clayton, Kirby Grant, everyone I knew who was out of a job. It was twelve days, just terrible.

WWD: *Killer Shark* [1950]?

BB: That was a small picture with Roddy McDowall as the star, and I just loved him. He always had his mother and father with him on the set, but he was just about to have his twenty-first birthday. So we went out on location on purpose, so that he could get out from underneath their jurisdiction and see some girls here and there. So we made the picture in Baja, California, and Roddy was no virgin after that.

WWD: Now we come to *Bullfighter and the Lady*, which is one of your most famous pictures.

BB: Well, *Bullfighter and the Lady* was my life story. Bob Stack was in that, still a very good friend of mine. But I've lost two very good friends in just the last couple of months: Burt Kennedy and Tony Quinn. Burt was a great writer and director; he wrote most of the Randolph Scott Westerns I directed in the fifties. And Tony Quinn . . . well, I don't have to tell you, he was one of the greatest actors in the business. *Bullfighter and the Lady* was a Republic picture, but we never went in the studio. John Wayne produced it. Duke heard my life story and wanted to meet me, and I went over and met him. And that was the beginning of the war between Budd Boetticher and John Wayne that went on and on and on. I've done five forewords for books about the Duke, and they all have to say exactly the same thing, and this is the way that we felt about each other. I always say, "Anybody who knows me well knows that I truly love John Wayne; but anybody who *really* knows me well knows that I also hate his guts."

WWD: What was going on?

BB: Well, Duke was Duke, and he was wrong about a lot of things, I thought, and I was the only one around who ever told him so. He was a tough, wonderful son-of-a-bitch, but he was wrong about a lot of things. We didn't agree on anything, politically or otherwise. Politically myself, I'm right down the middle.

WWD: So, then, how did he wind up producing the film?

BB: He liked the story; it was as simple as that. And so we did it.

WWD: Were you at loggerheads all during the shooting?

BB: No, he never bothered me at all; he was wonderful. Duke produced the two best pictures I ever made: *Seven Men from Now* [1956] and *Bullfighter and the Lady*. But then he and John Ford cut 42 minutes out of *Bullfighter and the Lady*, so that it would be less than 90 minutes, a B picture. It took me forty years to get it back the way I wanted it, and that's the way it is now in the full 124-minute cut. After I put together the first rough cut, no one would look at the picture, much less release it. I called up John Ford, and he said, "You know how I love Mexico, goddammit. Call the studio and tell them to let me see the picture." So he ran the picture on a Monday, but nothing happened until Friday. He called me up at five o'clock on Friday afternoon and said, "Budd, I saw your picture." And I said, for the only time in my life, "Is it any good?" He said, "Nope, it's *great*! You *know* it is. Come in and see me and we'll talk about it." So I got in my car and drove straight to Republic. There was a drive-on pass for me, and I parked my car in the lot and walked into Mr. Ford's office. He said, "Sit down, kid." So I sat down and asked him again, "You really thought the picture was great?" and he said, "It sure as hell is! 'Course, it's got 42 minutes of real *shit* in it."

WWD: Unbelievable.

BB: Isn't that awful? He said, "You've got to cut it down to an hour and a half, so it'll come out as a B picture." I finally restored it just a couple of years ago, but it was a helluva blow, I tell you.

WWD: Your next picture was *The Sword of D'Artagnan* [1951], which is a very small film for Hal Roach. How did you get involved with that?

BB: Ah, that's a *very* interesting story. Hal Roach called me up and said, "Budd, I need your help." So I went in to see him, and he said, "Budd, we're going to make *The Three Musketeers* as an hour picture for television," for Westing-house, I think. I said, "OK, what's the shooting schedule?" He said, "Three days."

WWD (*laughs*): One day for each musketeer, right?

BB (*laughs*): Yeah. I said, "Three days??!! Just how much do I get, for my own information?" He said, "Five hundred dollars." I said, "I get five hundred dollars to direct a three-day picture?" He said, "Yep." So I went in, and I did it in three and a *half* days! A year went by, and my ex-wife and I were at Grauman's Chinese Theater, and the second feature came on, and it was *The Sword of D'Artagnan*, my three-and-a-half-day picture. I thought, "Great, just when I'm getting somewhere, here comes this three-and-a-half-day tel-evision film to screw the whole thing up." The next morning I called up my good friend Hal and said, "Hal, you owe me $34,500." He said, "What are you talking about?" and I said, "I made you a feature picture, and you only paid me $500; my current fee is $35,000 a picture, so you owe me $34,500." And he shot back, "A deal's a deal," and that was that. You know, we never saw each other again. That's all I needed.

WWD: You made a Western after that, *The Cimarron Kid* [1951], with Audie Mur-phy; a war picture, *Red Ball Express* [1952], with Alex Nicol; and then you really seem to get into your Western phase with *Horizons West* in 1952.

BB: These were all for Universal. I got a seven-year contract there and wound up directing a lot of pictures for them. But let me tell you something: I don't make Westerns. I make *movies.* That's just laziness on the part of all those critics! I've made fifty-two pictures, counting the one that I made during the war for the navy [*The Fleet That Came to Stay* (1946)], and out of that I've made twelve Westerns. And they say, "He's a Western director." I made three bullfight pictures, and they say, "He's a bullfight director." And I made one gangster picture, *Legs Diamond* [*The Rise and Fall of Legs Diamond*, 1960], and they say, "He's a gangster director." So it's a lot of nonsense. I'm a direc-tor. I don't make Westerns.

WWD: But do you have a fondness for the Western genre?

BB: Oh, I love it, because it's outside and you can do a lot with people and there's a lot of action. I'll tell you a story. When we were getting ready to do *Seven Men from Now* [the first film in the *Buchanan* series, comprising seven films between 1956 and 1960], we walked into Duke's office one day, Burt [Kennedy] and me, because Duke was producing the first show. Duke said, "Hey, who do you want to play the lead in *Seven Men from Now*?" And I said, "I don't know, Duke, who do you want?" And he said, "Let's use Randolph Scott. He's through."

WWD: That's brutal.

BB: And we shoved Randolph Scott up Duke's ass! We made five pictures in the series, and then they wanted to make two more. But Columbia wanted to fire Harry Joe Brown [who produced the series], can you believe it? He made a hundred pictures for that crappy organization.

WWD: Why did they want to fire him?

BB: They figured that Randy and Burt and I could do it by ourselves; they figured we didn't need him. Save some money. So we just said, "If you fire Harry Joe, we'll go to Warner Brothers." And they backed down. So we did *Ride Lonesome* [1959] and *Comanche Station* [1960], the last two films in the series.

WWD: Let me back up a bit to *The Magnificent Matador* [1955]. That's Anthony Quinn.

BB: That's Anthony Quinn all right, and he'd won two Academy Awards, and he couldn't get a job. So I wrote a script, and the studio changed the title to *The Magnificent Matador*, which is about the worst title you can imagine. He was typed; he couldn't get work, so I wrote a script in which he was the star. Maureen O'Hara played the opposite lead; she was great, the greatest lady I ever worked with. The picture was OK, but I was happier about what it did for Anthony Quinn. We put him in a gold suit, and he was a star! He wasn't a star in *Viva Zapata!* [1952]; he was a character actor. And *The Magnificent Matador* made him a star of the first magnitude.

WWD: *The Killer Is Loose* is a noir film from 1956 that has been rather overlooked by critics.

BB: I did that with Lucien Ballard, the best cinematographer there ever was. We shot *The Magnificent Matador* together, and when we got through with that, all the producers said, "Don't let these two guys make a picture together ever again. They're tough as hell; they don't care about the money; they're going to break the studio." I discovered that there was an eighteen-day picture called *The Killer Is Loose* at Warner Brothers; so Lucien and I went there, and we made it in fifteen days. And that put that rumor to rest. Joseph Cotten was the star, a complete professional, always knew his lines. Of course, he'd worked with Orson Welles on *Citizen Kane* [1941]; he was a member of the Mercury Theatre group, so he was great to work with.

WWD: Did you know Orson Welles?

BB: I knew him *very* well. I met him when I was working on *Blood and Sand* when I first came to Hollywood; he and I sat around the set between takes, talking about bullfighting, and we became very good friends.

WWD: *The Killer Is Loose* led into the *Buchanan* films.

BB: Yes, we made five great ones and two mediocre ones. *Decision at Sundown* [1957] was already written when I did it, and they wanted me to do another picture. Actually, when Burt and Randy and I got together, we *all* wanted to do another picture. So we did *Decision at Sundown* from the existing script, and we tried to salvage it, and we did the best we could. Then Randy called me one night and said, "I have a terrible thing to tell you," and he was really serious. "I've got to do another Randolph Scott picture at Warner Brothers," he said, and I said, "Oh, Jesus Christ!" So I called the studio, and by this time I was riding high, very expensive. I went over to Warners, found the producer, a guy named Henry Blanke (I'd never met him, and I've never seen him since), and said, "I want to direct *Westbound* [1958]." He said, "Have you read the script?" I said, "I don't have to see the script. I want to make the picture." So Randy and I made the picture, which was pretty good for an eighteen-day picture. But those were the two weakest ones; the rest were really great.

WWD: A lot of these films are in CinemaScope. Did you like working in 'scope?

BB: I liked it very much. I didn't think most of the directors knew what to do with 'scope. They thought with 'scope that you put your leading lady camera right and your leading man camera left, and that's the way you fill your screen. I filled the left part of the screen with trees. But the real reason we used 'scope was because it was a war, to try to combat this horrible thing

Wendell Corey (center, in raincoat) as a deranged prison escapee in Budd Boetticher's suspense drama *The Killer Is Loose* (1956). Courtesy Jerry Ohlinger Archives.
Copyright © 1956 by United Artists Corporation.

called television that was raising its filthy head. But I loved 'scope; I thought it was great, if you knew how to use the camera.

WWD: Did you ever see *Forty Guns* [1957], Sam Fuller's 'scope Western?

BB: No, but I love Sam. I liked him immensely; we became very good friends. But you know, you don't have the time to see too many other people's movies when you're active in the industry. You're too busy making your own!

Randolph Scott in one of the Westerns for which Budd Boetticher became famous, *Buchanan Rides Alone* (1958). Courtesy Jerry Ohlinger Archives.

WWD: A lot of people have commented that the *Buchanan* films are very tough and unsentimental, and very different from the kinds of Westerns that John Wayne and John Ford were making. Do you agree?

BB (*laughs*): Well, I don't think that John Ford and I had the same sentimentality! Jack Ford—the last time I saw him was two weeks before he died [on August 31, 1973], and he was dying year after year in Palm Desert, California. My wife and I had horses stabled from Portugal to Mexico City to Tijuana, and once a month we would go to see Jack. And during this last period of his life, he and I became very, very intimate friends. And the last thing he said to me—we would kind of do a *Of Mice and Men*, George-and-Lenny routine, you know, "Tell me about the rabbits, George"—and I would say to Jack, "Tell me about your next picture, Jack," which was going to be about the black soldiers in the Civil War, the Buffalo soldiers, and he would tell me what we was going to do. Two weeks before he died, I was sitting on the corner of his bed, and I started to leave. I said, "Jack, before I go, tell me what else you've thought of for your new picture." He said, "Budd, you know I'm never gonna make another picture." And then he reached up, and he held my hand like my wife does, and he said, "Listen, kid. If you ever want to be known as the best director in the world, always remember that everybody else is a son-of-a-bitch." And that's the John Ford I knew.

WWD: Next we come to *The Rise and Fall of Legs Diamond*, starring Ray Danton, your only gangster picture. What are your thoughts on that?

BB: Well, the only two actors *ever* that I really hated—I don't know that word, I'm a very happy guy—one was Ray Danton [1931–1992], and the other was Gilbert Roland [1905–1994, in *The Bullfighter and the Lady*]. Those two gave the best performances of their lives. I hated those two bastards so much—what total pains in the ass! Ray Danton was married to Julie Adams, and Julie Adams was the only lady in Hollywood who was a star that I really cared about. Right before the show started, I read in Louella Parsons's column that [Ray Danton] was divorcing Julie Adams. I hadn't seen her in years, but she was doing a *Maverick* [episode of the television series starring James Garner], and I said, "Honey, is this true that he's divorcing you?" and she said, "Yes, I guess so." I said, "Why?" She said, "I don't know." I said, "Do you think it's possibly because you're a star and Ray Danton is a bit player?" She said, "Maybe." I said, "How would you like him to play Legs Diamond?" She said, "No, I've read the script." I said, "No, I'm talking about the *leading* man; Ray will play Legs Diamond." She said, "Don't do that for me." I said, "He's gonna to be the leading man."

So I tested seven fellows, and I shot them over [leading lady] Karen Steele's shoulder, so that you couldn't see them. And then I brought in Ray Danton, and I sent all the other guys home. Then I shot Ray straight on, so you couldn't miss him. When we got in the cutting room, I ran all the tests for Jack Warner [head of production at Warner Brothers]. I could do no wrong at that time at Warner Brothers, because I was doing a gangster picture, which was what put Warner Brothers in the public eye in the first place. So we ran all the tests, and the only guy you could see was Ray, and Jack said, "Budd, that's the only son-of-a-bitch who knows what he's doing!" because that's the only son-of-a-bitch he *saw*.

When I was doing research for that picture, I went out to Chicago, Detroit, and Cleveland, and I met all the hoods. They would meet me in restaurants, and they would say, "Mr. Boetticher"—pronouncing my name correctly— "May we sit down?" Always two guys, very well dressed, Brooks Brothers suits, and they would sit down and say, "We understand you're gonna make a picture about Jack Diamond." I said, "Well, I'm gonna try." They said, "What kind of picture is it gonna be?" I responded, "Well, the greatest picture I ever saw was made by a woman, Leni Riefenstahl, *Triumph of the Will* [1934], about

Ray Danton (left) is up to absolutely no good in the title role of Budd Boetticher's period gangster thriller *The Rise and Fall of Legs Diamond* (1960). Courtesy Jerry Ohlinger Archives. Copyright © 1959 Warner Bros. Pictures Distributing Corporation.

one of the most despicable men of all time, Adolf Hitler. So I want to make a picture about a miserable, no-good son-of-a-bitch that when you walk out of the theater, you say, 'God, wasn't he *great!*' And then you take two steps, and you say, '*Wait a minute*, he was a miserable son-of-a-bitch!'"

WWD: That's amazing.

BB: You know, there's nothing like *Triumph of the Will* ever. That film not only made Nazism look good; it made *Hitler* look good! That's a neat trick if you can do it. I first saw the film in a theater in the Navy Department, with Richard Carlson and Gene Kelly, and we ran the complete uncut version of Riefenstahl's picture. And when the lights came on, we really peeked around to see that nobody was there, and then we said to each other, "Heil Hitler!" The thing is, no matter how you try to recut that film to make Hitler look bad, you can't do it. You start with him flying through the clouds in an airplane, and then he descends from the heavens, and he looks like Christ. So the hoods said, "Are you really gonna do that?" and I said, "Yeah." And they said, "You know something? That's a great idea. Everybody thinks Jack Diamond was a great guy, but he was really a no-good bum." So then they told me everything—who had really murdered who and so on. And when I went back to Warners and told them everything I'd learned, they wouldn't let me make the picture! So we had to clean it up a bit. We had twenty-four days on that; it was a good picture.

WWD: I'd like to ask you a bit about your television work. You directed episodes of *Public Defender* [1954], *Maverick* [1957], *The Count of Monte Cristo* [1955], *Zane Grey Theater* [1956], *Alias Mike Hercules* [1956], *The Rifleman* [1958], *77 Sunset Strip* [1958], and *Hong Kong* [1960]. That's a lot of television shows.

BB: All I did in television was make a lot of pilots. I made the pilot for *Maverick* and then the first four shows after that. I did some shows for *Zane Grey Theater* because I liked Dick Powell so much. Other than that, I only did pilots and the episodes of *Zane Grey*. I did the pilot for *77 Sunset Strip*; I did the pilot for *The Rifleman*.

WWD: Did you know that nowadays, if you direct the pilot, you get a piece of the whole series?

BB: Oh, you get all kinds of things. Back then, I think I made $1,500 to do the pilots.

WWD: What about *Hong Kong*?

BB: *Hong Kong* was going to be let go. They weren't gonna do any more with it; they were gonna cut it out. And they called me and asked me to do the last one, and I did. And then they liked that so much, they let it go for another three years!

WWD: Now we come to *Arruza*, which you deal with extensively in your autobiography, *When in Disgrace*.

BB: You've read it?

WWD: Indeed I have.

BB: Well, it's all true. I left Hollywood in my Rolls-Royce and went down to Mexico to shoot a documentary on Arruza, and it should have been just a short project, but it turned into a seven-year nightmare. Everything in my book is true: there really *was* a prison, there really *was* a sanitarium.

WWD: Why did you leave Hollywood right after *Legs Diamond*, at the top of your career, for such a manifestly uncommercial project?

BB: I left Hollywood because I wanted to do something nobody else in the world could do. I thought, "I'll make a picture about bullfighting, and I'll use Carlos playing himself." That's why I left Hollywood. I had to do that picture. I tossed the whole Hollywood thing over because I couldn't see any other time *ever* when the best bullfighter in the world, the best friend of a well-known motion picture director, could make a picture with him.

WWD: But it didn't turn out to be that easy, did it?

Carlos Arruza demonstrates his skill in the ring in Budd Boetticher's documentary *Arruza* (1972), which the director completed only after a period of great personal and professional difficulty. Courtesy Jerry Ohlinger Archives. Copyright © 1967, Avco Embassy Pictures Corp.

BB: What are you talking about? It turned out *great*, in the end. I mean, what else do you count?

WWD: Yes, but you ran out of money . . .

BB: That's true.

WWD: Went through a divorce . . .

BB: That's no problem.

WWD: Spent five days in an insane asylum . . .

BB: Yeah, well, they wanted me to come home and do *The Comancheros* [Michael Curtiz, 1961] with the Duke. And I turned them down.

WWD: You're stuck in an insane asylum, and you turned them down?

BB: Well, of course!

WWD: *Why?*

BB: Because I didn't want to quit Arruza, the man or the picture. I had a quarter of a million dollars of my own money in it, I had my life in it, and I wanted to finish the picture. I think that if you quit something, it's kind of like stealing; and I think once you steal something, you eventually become a thief. And I was damned if I was gonna get licked by Mexico and the fact that I couldn't finish my picture. So I stayed there. And if I hadn't done *exactly* what I did, I wouldn't be married to Mary. We've been married now thirty years, and I wake up every morning and say, "Thank you, God." And I put a lot more than a quarter of a million dollars in it. When you figure I made three or four hundred thousand dollars a year, and I was gone for seven years, and you add all that up . . . well, *Arruza* was a very expensive picture. And then, of course, Carlos was killed in a car crash in 1966. I had finished everything except a party scene at the end of the picture. Carlos and I were going to go out to a local ranch and ride, but I didn't go, and he was killed on the way home. If I'd been in the car with him, we'd have been sitting in the back seat together, and he wouldn't have been killed. But he sat in the front, and that was the end of that.

WWD: *Arruza* didn't come out until 1972.

BB: I wasn't satisfied with it. I didn't want it to come out until I was completely happy with it. It's still a picture I can go and look at now and say, "Boy, I'm glad I made that." [Roger Greenspun in] the *New York Times* said, "*Arruza* may belong among the last great examples of classical filmmaking." You can't do better than that.

WWD: What about *A Time for Dying* [1971], your second film with Audie Murphy? Lucien Ballard shot that; Audie Murphy produced it; you wrote and directed the film.

BB: Well, I'd known Audie for a long time. I went to the Hunt Gymnasium on the way home every day from the Hal Roach studios, and there was a little guy there who weighed about 150 pounds, and he wanted to box every day.

So we would box a few rounds every day, and he would try to kill me every time! I was a pretty good fighter and weighed about 185 pounds, and so I'd have to belt him once in a while. This went on, and then we were in the steam room one day, and he pulled off his towel to wipe his face, and I saw this horrible scar where he had no hip. I said, "What the hell is that?" and he said, "Well, it's shrapnel." I said, "Really, you were in the war?" And he looked at me with astonishment and said, "Well, yeah." [Murphy was the most decorated combat soldier in World War II.] So I went and asked one of the other guys, "Who's that kid I box with every day?" and he said, "You mean you don't know? That's Audie Murphy." Then when I was working at Universal in 1951, I made a small picture there called *The Cimarron Kid*, and Audie was in it. So that's how we made our first picture together. He was just a kid then. But when we made *A Time for Dying*, Audie got in *real* trouble with some people in Las Vegas, and he needed a director to make a picture, and he would be the producer. He was a friend, and he was in trouble; so I made the picture for him. But then Audie was killed in a plane crash [on May 28, 1971] shortly after the film was finished, so the whole thing was just tragic.

WWD: During the filming of *Arruza*, you wrote the story for *Two Mules for Sister Sara* [Don Siegel, 1969]?

BB: Not what you saw! I wrote a script called *Two Mules for Sister Sara*, which was a love story, and they wouldn't make it the way I wrote it. They wanted me to come home and work on it, but I wouldn't quit *Arruza*. So I stayed down there, and they made that abortion with my good friend, whom I really like, Clint [Eastwood]. I thought it was a just a *horrible* picture, even though Don Siegel was a great director and a very good friend of mine. And when Clint walked down to put out the stick of dynamite at the end of the film— it was a stick of *dynamite*, for God's sake—I was sitting in the theater at the premiere, and I just said, "Jesus Christ!" Don Siegel called me up the next day and said, "Budd, thanks for not walking out on the show last night." I said, "Don, how could you make a piece of crap like that?" He said, "Budd, it's kind of a wonderful thing to wake up every morning and know that there's a check in the mail." I just let this fall on dead silence, and he said, "Well, I guess I'm talking to the wrong guy, aren't I?" "Yeah," I said, "it's better to wake up every morning and not be ashamed of what you see in the mirror."

WWD: Robert Towne gave you a small part as an actor in *Tequila Sunrise*, a film Towne wrote and directed in 1988, starring Mel Gibson and Michelle Pfeiffer. You played Judge Nizetitch.

BB: Bob just wanted me in the picture. So Mary and I went down, and we did one day, and I looked at what they were doing, and I said, "Oh, my God, this is my industry?" And we went home.

WWD: What projects are you working on now?

BB: Well, I want to do a movie based on my autobiography, *When in Disgrace*. I've got a script written, but it's 180 pages, which is way too long. But I'm not going to direct the film, so I'll let the director cut it. We should be able to do that next year.

WWD: Who would play you in the film?

BB: I have *no* idea, *no* idea at all. Robert Redford would have been good about thirty years ago; I was in my forties when most of this stuff happened, and he would have been good. But I don't know anyone today who could handle the role. I mean, who the hell could play *me*?

ALBERT MAYSLES

Two of America's foremost nonfiction feature filmmakers, Albert Maysles and his brother David (1932–87), are recognized as pioneers of "direct cinema," the distinctly American version of the French *cinéma vérité*. They earned their distinguished reputations by being among the first to make films in which the drama of human life unfolds as is, without scripts, sets, or costumes. I have long admired the Maysles' work, especially their 1969 film *Salesman*, and I had the good fortune to meet Albert Maysles at a conference in Arizona. We struck up a pleasant conversation, which led to this interview a few days later, on May 19, 2001, at his home in New York City.

WHEELER WINSTON DIXON: You were born on November 26, 1926, in Dorchester, Massachusetts?

ALBERT MAYSLES: Right.

WWD: And your brother David was born a few years later, in 1932?

AM: Right. As for my college education, I got my bachelor's from Syracuse and then a master's from Boston University.

WWD: How did you drift into filmmaking? Tell me about the first time you realized that you were interested in film, because you started out studying psychology, correct?

AM: Yes.

WWD: You taught for several years at Boston University, didn't you?

AM: I taught psychology for three years at the introductory level.

WWD: And so how did you first get interested in filmmaking? Where did you first have that gestalt—"Here's a camera, I'm going to use it"—moment?

AM: Well, it happened kind of by accident. In 1954, when I was twenty-seven years old, I had a motorcycle. I put it on a ship and went off to Europe and traveled around Europe for that whole summer. And then the next year I thought I'd do something like that again; but by that time, it was 1955, and it interested me a great deal to go to Russia. So I put in for a one-month tourist visa, and I got it. And I thought, "Well, wow, I can make some use of this time." All I had was $1,700 or so—and it took $1,000 for the air transportation. So I made several hitchhiking trips to New York with the idea that maybe I could get some support there to do a story on mental hospitals in Russia, if I could get in. On one of those trips, I went to *Life* magazine and said that if I got into mental hospitals in Russia, I'd like to take some pictures. *Life* said, "We aren't allowed to get you an assignment, but we'd be interested in seeing the photographs when you come back." So I was walking around New York after this interview, and I saw a sign that said CBS, and I thought, "Maybe I should go there, and if they could lend me a movie camera, I would take a movie camera into the mental hospitals and do a story."

Well, I met the head of the news department, and they gave me a movie camera, on loan, with a hundred-foot roll of 16mm film. The guy said, "I understand that you're going back to Boston, then coming back through New York on your way to Helsinki and then Russia. So when you stop off in New York on your way out, shoot a little bit on this roll of film, we'll process it and take a look at it and give you a critique." That was my total filmic training. It was a Keystone 16mm camera, just a wind-up model, a really basic camera.

Left to right: Edith Bouvier Beale, David Maysles, Albert Maysles, and Edie Beale during the shooting of *Grey Gardens* (1975). Courtesy Albert Maysles.

So CBS processed what I shot, about fifty feet or so, and they liked it. And they said, "OK, keep the camera and go to Russia."

When I came back I went to [educational television station] WGBH—I was still in Boston at that time—and said, "I've got this footage that I shot in Russian mental hospitals. Are you interested?" CBS got the first look at it, but all they wanted was fourteen feet of film. Can you believe it? They paid me one dollar for every foot of film they used. I shot about two thousand feet, but they used only fourteen, and so they paid me only $14. But the deal was that they would process the stuff and hand everything back to me so I could do whatever I wanted with it. So I brought it to WGBH in Boston, and I said, "I've got all this footage. I want to put it together, using your editing equipment. And you can show it for nothing on your station." They thought that was fine. While I was putting it together, somebody from a pharmaceutical company visited WGBH, and they were told I was making this film on psychiatry. That kind of interested them. So they said, "When you put it together, we'd like to pay you $2,000 so that we can have prints made—fifty prints to show around the country to psychiatrists who might be interested." So that's how I got started. I shot about fifty minutes, and the final piece was fifteen minutes long. I called it *Psychiatry in Russia* [1955].

WWD: And then it was televised on *The Today Show* with Dave Garroway?

AM: Some of it, yeah.

WWD: What was the footage like? It was silent, right?

AM: Yeah, that was a problem for me, because when I thought of making the movie, I thought that it would be in sound. I didn't realize that portable sound equipment didn't exist at that time. So I went for the images of the people in the hospital and let the faces and actions tell the story. It was very simple in structure. My main interest was—I was, as so many people were then, fed up with Russia from the fifties American political point of view.

WWD: As an "evil empire"?

AM: Right. I wanted at least to picture what people looked like, you know, even in mental hospitals. But it was still a person-to-person sort of approach. And so those images were really quite strong of those people.

WWD: You went back in 1957 with your brother to do *Youth in Poland* [1957], right?

AM: That's right. We got a motorcycle in Munich; it was very cheap, only $300 for a great big BMW motorcycle. We had a passport that was good for entering Russia. And going into any of the satellite countries wasn't that difficult because we could always say, you know, "We have to go through your country in order to get to Russia," which is on our visas. But still, when we were in Vienna, we couldn't get into Hungary. Hungary had just gone through its revolution in 1956.

So we figured we'd go down to Yugoslavia and go to the Hungarian embassy in Belgrade. We didn't think they'd refuse us, because then we would have had to go all the way around Hungary to get to Czechoslovakia and then to Russia. And sure enough, they gave us a transit visa to get into Hungary. But instead of the forty-eight hours that we were allowed, we spent a week in Hungary traveling around on our motorcycles. So then we went into Russia on motorcycles, and we tried to do a sort of *Easy Rider*, but we couldn't get the permission to move around anywhere. And we ended up going into Poland, and there we could travel on our motorcycles. When we were there in 1957, there was a student protest against the banning of their newspaper. So we got that stuff.

WWD: And this is all still silent, right?

AM: It was silent, but we did have a little tape recorder that we used to record some wild sound, and then we ran it over the footage later in the cutting room. And then NBC bought our footage for a half-hour edition of the Huntley-Brinkley show, and they paid $4,000 for that, which is chicken feed.

WWD: Then you shot *Primary* [1960]. And for this project, you helped to build the first sync-sound 16mm camera.

AM: The basic movement was an Auricon, but with a separate Nagra tape recorder for the sound. I did the camera work, and David did the sound boom work. Part of the money to make the film and develop the camera came from Bob Drew, who got it from *Time/Life*. I shot that with Bob Drew, Ricky Leacock, Terrence McCartney Filgate, and D. A. Pennebaker. We split up in separate crews, one covering [Hubert] Humphrey, one covering [John F.] Kennedy. I covered Humphrey, but it overlapped. I also did some shooting with Kennedy. Remember the shot of Kennedy coming into the big auditorium with the camera shooting over the back of his head? That's one of my shots. Then I shot the scene where Humphrey is addressing the farmers, and the shot of the back of Jackie with her white gloves.

WWD: How do you feel about Pennebaker's work? You worked on some later projects of his, but wouldn't you say he split off into his own kind of thing after a while?

AM: Yeah, but I wouldn't say it was so different from what I was doing. See, the thing is that I split off from those guys because I knew the importance of having control. My brother and I both felt that way. I stopped working with Bob Drew because he always felt the importance of filming a crisis situation. And usually that meant, you know, some issue or something of a political nature. We wanted to film everyday life, simpler things.

WWD: You really have been at the epicenter of a lot of the twentieth century's history. Do you look at yourself as kind of a cultural anthropologist in a way?

AM: Yeah, that's a good way to put it. I suppose it's a reflection of my psychological training. And my brother also majored in psychology. So we were interested in ordinary people.

WWD: Now, how did you hook up with Joseph E. Levine for the making of *Showman* [1963]?

AM: That was the first film that my brother and I made together. When I left
Bob Drew, I built my own camera, for myself. And so we used that camera
and shot that in 1962. We got into that in an odd way. David Wolper called
us up one day and said, "I'm doing a series of portraits of interesting people.
If you guys come up with something, it can be any kind of person in some
profession or whatever, let me know." My brother had a friend who was in
the entertainment business and knew something about Joseph E. Levine, and
thought that he might be a good subject. So when we brought it up to Wolper,
he said, "Oh, no, no, we've got too many Jews."

WWD: That's an interesting response.

AM: And he's Jewish himself! And, with that, we said, "No, we've got to go ahead
and do it on our own." It was an interesting time in Levine's life, in that he

David Maysles (gesturing with thumb) and Albert Maysles (extreme right) during the
shooting of *Showman* (1963), featuring producer Joseph E. Levine (center). Courtesy
Albert Maysles.

had been importing these cheap Italian *Hercules* films and dubbing them into English, and then releasing them and making millions of dollars.

But when we met up with him, there was a chance that Sophia Loren would get the Academy Award for Vittorio de Sica's *Two Women* [1961], which Levine distributed in America. And, of course, Sophia Loren did win the Oscar for Best Actress for that picture, and Levine was suddenly in a very different ballgame. So all that happened during the course of the filming, and it was an interesting aspect of the whole film.

WWD: And how did you get him to give you open-door access?

AM: Well, we're good friends, that's all.

WWD: Did he see the finished film?

AM: Yes, he saw the finished film. It's interesting, because we showed it to him and his wife; and when the screening was over, his wife came over to us and quietly said, "I'm so pleased that you didn't have a Jewish voice."

WWD: This seems to be a recurring theme.

AM: That's right. And, in fact, once the film got finished and people saw it—we submitted it for an Academy Award—and when the Academy Award people screened it, five minutes into the projection of the film they said, "No, we can't show this. We can't even consider this. It's anti-Semitic."

WWD: How did your film with the Beatles come about, *What's Happening! The Beatles in the U.S.A.* [1964]?

AM: We got a call one day from Granada Television in England. I happened to answer the phone, and they said, "The Beatles are coming to New York. They'll be arriving in two hours at Idyllwild Airport, and would you like to make a film of them?" At that point I put my hand over the phone and said to my brother, "Who are the Beatles? Are they any good?" And he said, "Yeah, they're good." So we both got on the phone and made a deal on the phone with Granada and rushed out to the airport. We got to the airport in good enough time so that we saw the plane just coming down, so we filmed that. And then we went up to them, introduced ourselves, told them that we were from Granada Television, and then we latched onto them for the next three or four days, day and night.

WWD: And what was it like hanging out with them at that point? Were they sort of amazed by the whole phenomenon?

AM: They were kids, you know. They didn't know—nobody knew—when they got to the airport whether there would be five people or five thousand. Well, there were five thousand people there. And so we got into the limousine with them and filmed them as they were looking out the window at all the people trying to see them, to get in the car, anything. It was unbelievable.

WWD: So you were there with them just for a week, and, basically, you just kept putting film into the camera and shooting it?

AM: Yeah, four-hundred-foot loads, about ten minutes each. Because I built the camera myself, I had it shaped so that it would slip onto my shoulder. In fact, if you look at the Betacam video camera nowadays, that camera is almost a copy of mine. The camera was totally balanced on my shoulder, and I could shoot for hours and hours and never get tired.

WWD: Would you pretty much shoot the whole four hundred feet?

AM: Well, we had to be very careful about the film, because we were always spending our own money.

WWD: Even in this case, though, with Granada?

AM: Yeah, because we were putting up the money. And also, I had to be careful, because ten minutes is not a lot of time, and you were always afraid of running out right in the middle of a great scene, just when something good was happening.

Ringo Starr, George Harrison, John Lennon, and Paul McCartney in the bloom of first success in Albert and David Maysles's *What's Happening! The Beatles in the U.S.A.* (1964). Courtesy Albert Maysles.

WWD: Do you use a clapper for sync?

AM: No, but we always did tail sync, because otherwise we'd draw attention to ourselves. So at the end of the shot I'd turn the camera to my brother and with his hand he would hit the microphone. That was just as good as a clapper board.

WWD: Was this your biggest commercial success up to that point?

AM: Well, we had a little problem with the film. Because we were making this film for Granada, we didn't even ask for a release; we just shot the stuff, and we didn't bother to get a release from the Beatles or anyone else. So when we finished the film, we couldn't get a release because United Artists said, "We're making our own film, *A Hard Day's Night* [Richard Lester, 1964], and this is pretty much what we're going to do, a film about the band touring. So we really can't help you." And that was pretty much that. The only thing that we did with the film was that, I think maybe a year or so later, Carol Burnett had a television show on CBS, and she was running low on ratings, so she showed the film with her narration over it. Which, of course, was against all of our rules, but what are you going to do? We needed the money.

But we never made any money on it after that. Then fifteen years went by, and Apple, which is the Beatles' organization, came to us and said, "We'd like to buy you out, and we'll try to do something with the footage." They were willing to work on getting a release from Granada for the material. And so they paid us a quarter of a million dollars, which was fairly good money. And then a year or so later, they came back to us and said, "We want to change the film and make it more commercial, and substitute some of the songs from the *Ed Sullivan Show*, for example." Now, in our original film there wasn't anything of Ed Sullivan. We did much better than that. When they were on the *Ed Sullivan Show*, we couldn't follow them into CBS. We knew we wouldn't be able to shoot the stuff because of all the unions and so forth in the studio. So, instead, we walked down the street, walked into the first tenement building we saw, and when we heard the Beatles' music through one of the apartment doors, we knocked on the door, and there was a whole family watching the show. So we asked if we could film it, and we filmed the family watching the Beatles on television. It was a hell of a lot better than just standing on the stage with Ed Sullivan.

WWD: So how did you hook up with Truman Capote, the subject of your next project, *A Visit with Truman Capote* [1966]?

AM: Well, we got a call one day from PBS. They were doing a series of half-hour films on writers, and they said, "We've already got Vladimir Nabokov signed up and Saul Bellow, so would you like to do one?" We said, "Well, yeah." So we called up Norman Mailer, whom we knew, and he normally would be cooperative, but he said, "I've just been doing too much advertising for myself.

I'd rather not do it." So we respected that. And we had heard that Truman Capote was just about to publish *In Cold Blood*, and that excited us, not only because of Capote, but this was going to be the first nonfiction novel. So we got along just great with him, and we made this film, which was quite nice. We didn't want to do any interviews with him; that was against our policy. But we were lucky because Capote went up to his summer home in the Hamptons, and a woman from *Newsweek* came to interview him. So we filmed her doing this interview with him, and that seemed to be OK, because that's the way it happened, without anybody setting it up. And then when the film was finished, we showed it to him, and he came out of the screening room crying. He thought it was the best thing he had ever seen done of that sort.

And it's funny, because this led to our next project, *Salesman* [1969]. When I phoned Truman to ask him if he would like to make the film, he said, "Well, you should speak to my editor at Random House." And so we called the editor up, and he said, "Oh, I've heard of you guys. Of course I'll recommend it." And so that's how we got access to Truman. When we finished it, my brother had lunch with Truman's editor and said, "We've been thinking of making a nonfiction feature," just as Truman had done a nonfiction novel.

Truman Capote, David Maysles, and Albert Maysles (with camera) shooting *A Visit with Truman Capote* (1966). Courtesy Albert Maysles.

The editor suggested a nonfiction *Moby-Dick*, going down to the South Pacific and filming a whaling expedition. But that didn't quite appeal to us because of the language problem; at that point there were just Norwegian and Japanese and Russian whalers.

But then he said, "Well, what about door-to-door salesmen?" And that sounded good to my brother. And then, when we both talked it over, we said, "Yeah, that's a great subject, but we've got to have the right product being sold." So we put a researcher on it. Both my brother and I had done some selling in high school ourselves. When I got out of college, I sold the *Encyclopedia Americana*, and I sold Fuller brushes in high school. My brother sold Avon door-to-door. We knew that it could be fascinating for these guys going into it just as we had. It was all about the romance of the road, so to speak, and of the expectations—who knows who is going to answer the door, and whether you're going to be able to sell it? So, that kind of serendipitous sort of journey would be interesting. But it wasn't until several months later that we discovered there were four thousand guys throughout the United States selling the Bible. And we thought, "Oh, my God, this is perfect . . . it's the 'big white whale' of books." But the next thing was to find the right guys. And then we discovered that there were four Irish guys covering the New England territory for the Mid-American Bible Company in Chicago. So all that remained was to meet these guys and see if they wanted to do it, and if we wanted to film them. And we went out with each one of them on some sales calls, and we thought, "Yeah, this is it." So we started filming.

WWD: So what did these guys think of the project?

AM: Well, they didn't know quite what to make of it, because they couldn't quite see themselves as subjects for a movie, because movies have always been of actors and famous people, the Hollywood sort of thing. But they finally said, "OK, we'll do it," and the Mid-American Bible Company went along with it, too. And this time we got releases from everybody [*laughs*] so we wouldn't have the same problem we had with the Beatles film. So we followed them around for six weeks; and then, during that time, they were transferred to Florida, so we just went along to see how they did.

WWD: The thing that I took away from that film was that everyone was exploited. The Bible salesmen were desperately trying to get $2.50 out of these poor people, and the people themselves were so completely hard up that they could barely afford to eat. And meanwhile, their boss keeps telling them, "There's no bum territory, there's only bums." It was just horrible. I felt so sorry for them.

AM: Ah, I don't know. I wouldn't say that the management was abusive or exploitational. You know, that was the nature of the business. I mean, a guy could still do pretty well. They certainly didn't do anywhere near as well as

David Maysles (with microphone) and Albert Maysles (with camera) during the shooting of *Salesman* (1969). Courtesy Albert Maysles.

they were hyped up to do when they had the sales meetings. There's one scene where a guy jumps up and says that he'll do $50,000 the next year, and that's just wishful thinking. At sales meetings for any company, everybody gets on the bandwagon and tries to whip the people up, so they'll go out and sell the product. It's just business.

WWD: What was your perception on this as the contours of the project emerged? How did you feel when you were shaping the material?

AM: Well, Charlotte Zwerin, who cut it, really gets the credit for editing it and putting it together. She's the one who shaped the material. And my brother supervised the editing. She was excellent.

WWD: So she didn't do any shooting? She was a cutter?

AM: Absolutely. Not only did she not do any shooting, she never even was there on the scene. So she brought a fresh eye to the material. And she's the one who saw that [the salesman] Paul was emerging as the tragic hero of the film, although we noticed it, too, and gave him more screen time; but she really brought that out.

WWD: So did you pretty much give her the footage and say, "This is the way we see it going, and give us a rough cut"?

AM: Absolutely. Just take a look at it, and you'll see that she's very, very important in making the film.

WWD: You spoke of those moments in *Salesman* that other people might edit out, but that it's really important to leave them in. The moment when Paul is staring off into space in the restaurant, for example, as he sees his business crumbling around him. His whole life is in his eyes.

AM: Our only fear was that the camera would run out of film, but fortunately it didn't. I kept shooting and shooting, and then, finally, as you may remember, he picks up his cards to leave and raps them against the table and goes off as though he's calling himself to his own fate.

WWD: And he was totally unaware of the camera during all of this?

AM: Completely. He was in his own space. There was nothing in their behavior where you could say, "Well, they're acting for the camera."

WWD: Since you don't speak to the protagonists during the filming, what sort of a relationship do you have?

AM: Well, the way you watch, the way you listen, you're in on everything. You're constantly maintaining good access to people because you're using your love for the people and your respect for them, the empathy that you have for them and the way you look at them, to maintain not a control over them, but a rapport. And that rapport is essential, because if you don't have that rapport, if you're just sort of hanging around all the time without any real connection with them, then that's a problem for the people you're filming. And we shot a lot of film on that one. I think we ended up with a ratio of 40:1. And the whole thing was shot with just one camera and just one cameraman: me. We shot it in 16mm Plus-X negative, which is the best black-and-white stock, I think, and then blew it up to 35mm. It was all our money, although it was partially financed by a Guggenheim Fellowship for $10,000.

WWD: And how much did this film cost to actually make?

AM: I think we estimated something like $200,000 or $300,000.

WWD: And so then you opened it up at the 68th Street Playhouse?

AM: Right.

WWD: Did you "four-wall" it during its initial run [rent the theater for a flat fee and then exhibit the film as self-distributors]?

AM: Yeah, we had to. We didn't have a distributor. In trying to get some money together to "four-wall" it, we had lots of backers' screenings. At each screening there would be a hundred people in the theater, and after the screening, as they left the theater, they'd congratulate us and so forth. But at one of those screenings I happened to peek through a crack in the door, and I noticed that everybody had left the screening room, but there was still one person left, sitting in the front row. And as she got up and turned in our direction, I saw that she had been crying. And as she got closer to us, I elbowed my brother and said, "She's for me." That's how I met my wife, Gillian.

WWD: Are you still married?

AM: Oh, yes. We've got three kids, and just two days ago I attended the graduation of one of them from college.

WWD: But *Salesman* really broke through for you, finally?

AM: Well, I wouldn't say it was a huge success, you know, it only played in several theaters. It was a critical success. It played at the New York Film Festival, but then you don't make any money.

WWD: Next we come to *Gimme Shelter* [1970]. How did you get involved in that?

AM: Well, as you're discovering, it's a different thing that brings us to making each of these films. On this one, we got a call one day from Haskell Wexler, the cinematographer and director. He said that he had been talking to the [Rolling] Stones, who were already in California on the early part of their tour. And he said, "You guys may want to meet them. Maybe there's a film there for you. They're going to be at the Plaza Hotel tomorrow, so you might want to look them up." We showed up, and we were interested enough so that we thought, "OK, we'll go with them the next day to one of their shows in Baltimore." So we went to Baltimore, shot the performance, and we thought, "OK, these guys are great." We filmed them at Madison Square Garden very soon after that. We spent a day or two there, and then we took a chance that if we stuck with them on their tour, that it would make more than just a concert film. What would happen, we didn't know, but we had that kind of confidence. And that's what we did: we stuck with them.

WWD: Weren't the Stones trying to do something at that point that they thought would be the greatest open-air concert of all time?

AM: Something like that. It was also going to be a free concert, and that's what happened at Altamont, which was, of course, a disaster. A guy got knifed to death; it was just terrible. We thought it was going to be great, but it turned out to be a nightmare.

WWD: How did you feel when you were on the stage and all hell was breaking loose? You were one of the photographers, right?

AM: Oh, yes.

WWD: Were you in fear of your life?

AM: No—and this is kind of strange, but you've got to understand the Hell's Angels [who served as security guards for the Altamont concert]. They're sort of, of two minds, you know. They are nice guys, in a way; and whether I liked it or not, they were going to help me out. They were to carry my bags, magazines, equipment, and so on. So, from that point of view, they were very helpful for me.

Mick Jagger and the Rolling Stones during the disastrous concert at the Altamont Speedway in *Gimme Shelter* (1970). Courtesy Jerry Ohlinger Archives.

wD: But all your shots of the Angels in the film show them as totally menacing.

AM: That's right.

wwD: And I take it that they didn't like Mick Jagger at all? It certainly seems that way in the film.

AM: Yeah, yeah, there was that, right.

wwD: So, when were you aware that the concert was really going to get bad?

AM: I don't know, but I'll tell you one thing. When we first arrived at Altamont, we were walking through the field, and we came across this fence, and somebody began to pull the fence down. And Keith Richards made the comment, "The first act of violence." We didn't pay much attention to it at the time. But in retrospect, that was really an incredible piece of prophecy. And then when I saw the footage in the cutting room and realized that it actually contained someone getting stabbed to death . . . it was terrible.

wwD: What about the scene where you're showing Mick how the film can be cut in various different ways?

AM: That actually happened; it wasn't a piece of staging. While we were filming those events, at some point the Stones said, "At some point we'd like to see some of the footage." And so, as Charlotte Zwerin was editing the film, it occurred to us, wouldn't it be great to have them watching this stuff? We

Albert Maysles, David Maysles, and Mick Jagger in the cutting room during the post-production of *Gimme Shelter* (1970). Courtesy Albert Maysles.

didn't have anything of their reaction to all of the events. And so, since they asked for it, let's go along with that and film them watching it. And that, of course, helped enormously in the structure of the film.

WWD: It just worked perfectly.

AM: But the minute the actual concert was over, we got in a helicopter and got the hell out of there.

WWD: Did you realize that you had made sort of a summing up of the sixties in a way? It sort of all fell apart that night, don't you think?

AM: Yeah. But I think it's important to note that when they made *Woodstock* [Michael Wadleigh, 1970], and everything seems to be coming up roses, that's just one way to look at it: "Isn't this a wonderful thing, the flower generation" and so forth, and all of those happy interviews that were in the film. But when you come to think of it, there were probably just as many people—and I'm talking about tens of thousands—who took bad drugs at Woodstock, took bad drugs at Altamont, and who are suffering from that right now. *Gimme Shelter* just brought that out.

WWD: I wanted to ask you about some other stuff in the sixties we haven't talked about. You shot a segment for Jean-Luc Godard of the multipart feature film *Paris vu par . . .* [1965], entitled *Montparnasse-Levallois.*

AM: That's right.

WWD: What was it like working with Godard?

AM: Well, I got to know a fellow by the name of Barbet Schroeder. He was a critic and then started directing films much later; but at this point, he was a producer. This was in 1963, and one day he said, "You know, I'm going back to Europe, but not for another week." I said, "Well, why don't you stay with me?" So he stayed in my apartment, and then one day he announced, "I'm making this film. It's going to be shot in 16mm because my purpose is to make a film that can get shown in theaters all over France, because all the theaters will have to put in 16mm projection systems."

WWD: Well, that's a noble ambition, but it didn't work out that way.

AM: No, the film had to be blown up to 35mm, of course. But he also wanted to have it directed by some of the hottest directors in the New Wave, because he was one of the writers for the *Cahiers du Cinéma*, and he knew them all personally: Godard, Eric Rohmer, Claude Chabrol, and the rest. So he contacted these guys, and he said, "Each one of you should do a Paris story in maybe fifteen or twenty minutes, and then we'll put them all together and have a feature film." One of these people was Godard, and one day it occurred to Barbet that it would be great if I did the cinematography for Godard's section. And so he called Godard and told him about me, and Godard said, "Yeah, come on over. Take the next flight because we're going to shoot it in a couple more days." So I went over to France. But Godard's idea during the actual shoot, which was brilliant, was that I wouldn't know anything about what was going on.

WWD: So you would just basically show up on the scene and try to record whatever you could?

AM: Right. It was really like making a documentary, because as things happened, I couldn't control them and didn't want to. But he had it all set up. And people would leave one location and go to another, and I'd just follow along, and shoot it as if it was actually happening. It was just a few days, but it was great. His stuff is just brilliant. That was released in 1965, but it took only two days to shoot, that's it.

WWD: You also worked as a cameraman on *Monterey Pop* [1968].

AM: That's right, but there were several cameramen: Ricky Leacock, me, Pennebaker, James Desmond, Barry Feinstein, and Roger Murphy.

WWD: What stuff did you shoot?

AM: I can't remember, but I know I did some of Ravi Shankar's section, and then a lot of the people in the crowd, you know, a lot of audience stuff.

WWD: What did you think of the finished film?

AM: I liked it very much.

WWD: We sort of skipped over *Meet Marlon Brando* [1966]. How did that happen?

AM: That happened, again, in its own way. We got a call one day from United Artists, and they said that Brando had just finished this film, *Morituri* [Bernhard Wicki, 1965]. Brando had agreed that he would do interviews when the film was finished. And so at the Hampton Hotel in New York the next day there was going to be a long session, lasting two or three hours, of people imported from all over the country—the local Jack Paar types—having their own interview session with Brando. So we showed up, and the idea was that we would film each one of these interviews and then make a little two-minute piece out of each one and send it off to Pittsburgh or wherever the reporter was from, so that they could have an "exclusive interview" with Brando.

WWD: Sort of the forerunner of the electronic press kit.

AM: Exactly.

WWD: What did Brando think of this?

AM: We shot maybe two or three of the interviews; and David and I looked at one another, and, without saying anything, we knew that later on we would put them all together and make a whole film of that. And that's what we did.

WWD: It's hilarious, because Brando really interviews the reporters, rather than the other way around. You once said, "Wouldn't it be great if we could see films like *Salesman* instead of the regular evening news, where 'news anchors' are lecturing you and telling you what to think?" Could you talk a little bit more about that?

AM: I think this would make such an important difference in the kinds of information that we get. What we need to know is other people's experiences. And what is unique about a movie camera or a video camera with good sound is that it can put you *exactly* where the action is. It can put you there, in the presence of what's going on, but without somebody telling you how to feel. If there was more stuff like that on television, that would be revolutionary.

WWD: From the beginning of your career, you and your brother seemed to have made this decision that you weren't going to make stuff that was in the traditional corporate mold. You wanted to create your own vision of the world and let the truth of the situation appear out of actual events, rather than manipulate things. So did you know, in a sense, that you were saying, "I'm going to be working from the outside in," all your life, in a way?

AM: Yeah.

WWD: And are you OK with that?

AM: Oh, yeah. Because what we need to know, more than anything else, is what's going on in the real world. That's more important than anything. And along with that, you begin to develop a common understanding that all of us are

Marlon Brando with a member of the press, from *Meet Marlon Brando* (1966). Courtesy Albert Maysles.

on common ground. And what better way to solve conflict situations? If an Israeli could see a film, for example, of what an average Palestinian is going through, and vice versa, it would be a real breakthrough. "Now," you can say, "I can understand better what this person is going through." We've got to do something about that.

WWD: You've done a lot of projects with the artist Christo [known for "wrapping" buildings and similar projects]. What's the connection there?

AM: Well, in 1962 there was a get-together sponsored by the French government in Lyon, France, for people who were on the fringes of the new developments in documentary filmmaking. But the French were doing something like that as well: *cinéma vérité*. So I met Jean Rouch and some other direct cinema filmmakers, but also a technician who was working on a new kind of lightweight 16mm sync-sound camera. So we started talking, and he asked, "Where are you going from here?" I said, "We're going to Paris." "Well, you've got to meet these two people I've been working with as chief engineer." And they were Jeanne-Claude and Christo. And he said, "I understand you're going to show your film *Showman* at the Anthropology Museum in Paris. So I'll invite them." So they see the film, and they're all excited because they see some kind of affinity between the way we're making our films and the way they do their projects. Christo makes the drawings, but that's only part of the whole project. The most important part of his project is getting all the legal permissions to create his works. And that interested us, and we started working together.

WWD: You've done five films with him: *Christo's Valley Curtain* [1974], *Running Fence* [1978], *Islands* [1987], *Christo in Paris* [1990], and *Umbrellas* [1994].

AM: Correct. So, for us, the attraction is that those projects are more than just a guy sitting and working on a canvas. It's all the social interaction to get it done. So the real story that develops out of this is what makes it an interesting documentary.

WWD: What about *Grey Gardens* [1975], another of your better-known works?

AM: Well, that again happened in its own way. We got a call one day from Lee Radziwill, who knew of us because her boyfriend at that time was Peter Beard, the photographer who became famous for his photographs of animals in Africa. Lee was thinking of doing something autobiographical, something from out of her childhood, maybe in writing, maybe in a film. So Peter said, "Well, if you're thinking of doing a film, then you should think of the Maysles brothers." So she called us up, and she had this whole list of forty or so items that she thought would be good for a documentary. And at first I thought, "Oh, she wants to do a childhood. That is not a documentary." But she said, "Well, I've got this list, so come over and we'll talk about it."

So we talked about it, and we found that there could be a film there, and she was going to pay for it anyway. And a few days after we got into filming, she got on the phone with Edie Beale and discovered that they were actually having some problems with the Board of Health—the plumbing wasn't right and this, that, and the other. So Lee went over there to help out and said, "Why don't you come along? And if you want to, I suppose, you should bring your camera." And I said, "Oh, yeah, we'll bring the camera." And we started filming. And then, maybe a week or two later, she said, "You know, we've done quite a bit of filming already. I'd like to maybe put together, maybe a half-hour, an hour, so I can take a look at it." Well, when she saw the Edie Beale part of it, she kind of lost interest in the project. And then some months later we thought, "Oh, we can't put this down; it's too interesting." So we decided to make a long film, and that's how it happened, through Lee introducing us to them. You have to understand that they are eccentric, but they never really realized their childhood dreams. The mother wanted to be a singer, had a beautiful voice. Her daughter wanted to be a dancer. But their families were

Albert Maysles (with camera) and David Maysles (with microphone) shooting *Christo's Valley Curtain* (1974). Courtesy Albert Maysles.

Edie Bouvier Beale in Albert and David Maysles's *Grey Gardens* (1975). Courtesy Photofest.

against it, thought it was beneath them. So they felt that if their families rejected them, they would live life alone, separate. But at the same time, if you examine the psychology, because they were rejected, they wanted to be accepted. And there's no better way to accept somebody than a good honest film of exactly who they are.

WWD: What did they think when they saw the finished film?

AM: Well, when the film was finished, we brought the projector and the film to Grey Gardens and showed it to them. And when it was all over, the daughter spoke up, and in a very loud, determined voice she said, "The Maysles have created a classic!" But then, later on when Edie was with her mother, and her mother, Edith Bouvier Beale, was dying, very near the end Edie said to her mother, "What more would you like to say?" And Edith said, "There's nothing more to say, it's all in the film." So we got that final confirmation that we had done it properly.

WWD: How do you feel about the shift from film to video?

AM: Oh, I think it's great, because when we went from 35mm to 16mm, we didn't regret losing the 35mm. It was clumsy and bulky. And in the same way, we're moving to video, and it's not quite as good technically, but does that really matter? In terms of the lightness of the equipment, the intimacy with the subjects . . . all that stuff is so much more important. I use a Sony PD-150, with a boom mike used separately. The tape runs for an hour, and it's only $10 a tape. Think about that, compared to the old four-hundred-foot loads of 16mm we used to shoot—heavy, bulky, constantly changing magazines. All of that is gone now.

WWD: What do you think will be the end format of future video projects?

AM: At some point, four or five years from now, so much of this stuff is going to be available, without any distribution problem, on the Internet. There are a lot of technical problems to be worked out, but it's going to happen. In the meantime, we can blow this stuff up to 35mm. I don't know whether streaming video is going to take over a market completely, but it's going to mean that so many of us, myself included, can get anything distributed. If I want to make a three-minute piece of poetry in film—

WWD: Right, you can just put it right online.

AM: Yeah, no one is going to stop me.

WWD: Do you think it will be sort of like the MP3 downloads, and people will pay for it?

AM: Yeah, I think so. It's the future; there's no question about it. But whatever happens, people are going to keep making these kinds of films, and they've got to find a way to reach their audiences. I think that the Internet is probably the future of film distribution in the twenty-first century.

Cult Visions

JACK HILL

As his Web site boasts, "legendary cult-film director, grunge auteur, notorious—these are some of the phrases used recently to describe writer-director Jack Hill. He has also been referred to as the man who initiated the women-in-prison genre of the seventies, and whose films helped define the so-called blaxploitation genre, as well as the man who discovered Pam Grier. Unlike most cult films, though, Hill's films were commercially extremely successful in their initial release, despite being generally snubbed by contemporary critics. But that situation has been remedied in recent years, as many of today's serious critics—perhaps inspired by the enthusiastic support of Quentin Tarantino, who gladly acknowledges the influence of Hill's films on his own work—have been taking a new look at some of Hill's films of the sixties and seventies and using terms like 'post-modern,' 'ahead of their time,' and 'feminist manifesto' to describe them." Throughout our conversation, I was not disappointed by the subject of this hyperbolic introduction. Jack Hill has crammed more into his career than most film industry insiders, and our conversation took a number of surprising turns, further illuminating the world of exploitational filmmaking in the early 1960s. Hill's best films have now been taken up by a whole new generation of critics and filmmakers, and he seemed eager to talk about such films as *Coffy* (1973), *Switchblade Sisters* (1975), and *The Big Doll House* (1971). I had the chance to talk to Jack Hill on January 20, 2004, and our conversation ranged over a wide variety of exploits, from his early years as a musician, to his career as a director, and to his future and current projects.

WHEELER WINSTON DIXON: I understand that your father was a designer for Disney and for Warner Bros. Could you tell me some more about your father's work?

JACK HILL: My father, Roland Hill, was a flyer in World War I in France. Then, after the war, he stayed to study art and architecture in Europe. When he came back to the States, after he got out of the army, he came to Hollywood, started working as an architect and designer, and very soon got into the movies. That was about 1925, at First National Studios, which later became Warner Bros. He worked as a set designer and then became an assistant art director and finally an art director on Warner Bros. shorts [such as *Let's Sing an Old Time Song* (1947), *So You Want to Hold Your Wife* (1947), *Let's Sing a Song of the West* (1947), *So You Want to Be in Pictures* (1947), *So You're Going*

A portrait of director Jack Hill in 2006. Courtesy Jack Hill.

to Be a Father (1947), and *Desi Arnaz and His Orchestra* (1946)]. Then, a little after the breakup of the studio system, in the 1950s, he did some television and ended up with Disney, where he worked for quite a while.

WWD: What did he do for Disney?

JH: He worked on a lot of the feature films. He did all the interiors of Captain Nemo's submarine for *20,000 Leagues under the Sea* [Richard Fleischer, 1954; Roland Hill is not credited for his work].

WWD: Were you hanging around on the set with him when you were a kid?

JH: Very, very little. Once in a while, if there were special effects or miniatures or something like that, which he thought I'd be interested in, he would take me there on Saturday, but otherwise not really, no.

WWD: When did you figure out that you were interested in making movies?

JH: I studied in the cinema school at the University of California, Los Angeles. I had been doing a lot of photography when I was very young, and then I got an 8mm movie camera and made films, edited them, put together things with my friends, and stuff like that, but not to a great extent. Mostly, in my younger days, I was a musician.

WWD: In fact, you majored in music composition at UCLA.

JH: Yeah. I got my B.A. in 1960.

WWD: With your father so involved in film, why were you more attracted to music?

JH: Well, my mother was a music teacher, and I started on violin and piano when I was five years old, and I was playing professionally when I was a teenager. Then later, I learned how to play the Hungarian cymbalom, which is a very difficult instrument. I started doing a lot of recording for films, television, and records.

WWD: What kind of films did you work for?

JH: I did all the films with Eastern European music. I did a lot of episodes of the television series *Mission Impossible*. I played on the soundtracks of *Dr. Zhivago* [David Lean, 1965], *The Brothers Karamazov* [Richard Brooks, 1958], *Taras Bulba* [J. Lee Thompson, 1962], *King Rat* [Bryan Forbes, 1965], *Dead Heat on a Merry-Go-Round* [Bernard Girard, 1966], *The Professionals* [Richard Brooks, 1966], a lot of projects. I don't remember all of them.

WWD: Who were your favorite composers when you were growing up?

JH: I went through a Rimsky-Korsakov phase, a Debussy phase, and a Wagner phase. It changed from time to time. Right now my favorite is, I guess, Schumann. I had the good fortune, when I was very young, to see Wagner's *Die Meistersinger von Nürnberg* at Bayreuth.

WWD: Where were you going to school?

JH: Hollywood High School. After Hollywood High, I went to Chapman College, which at that time was a small college in Los Angeles (it later moved to

Orange County), because they had a special system. Instead of taking a full curriculum, you could take just one subject and concentrate on that for six weeks at a time. So I took an entire music course there. Then I went to UCLA for a little while, and then I dropped out and worked as a musician for a long time. I did everything from little concerts, to playing Gypsy music in a Hungarian restaurant on the Sunset Strip, to playing electric piano in a rock group on the road in the late fifties. And then after *that*, I decided I wanted to go back to school and finish my degree in music and learn how to score films.

WWD: So you went back to UCLA.

JH: Yeah, I wanted to learn how to score movies professionally. And, in fact, I did score a twenty-minute student film called *Cross-Country Runner*. It was directed by a guy named Mark McCarty. I don't know whatever happened to him. I don't think the film was ever finished. I got into the UCLA Cinema Department as a minor, and I took a writing course; and they encouraged me to do more scripts. So I ended up taking a directing class and directed a short film for my project. Then I got to do what they called at that time a "major production." They would choose two or three scripts a semester by competition. You'd have to submit your story or your script, and so I got to do that. It came out as a thirty-minute-long film called *The Host* [1960], which I directed and scripted.

It's a gangster Western. It was a guy on the run. We don't know what he's on the run from. An existential Western, you might say. I don't know if you know this, but *The Host* turned out to be the template for the third act of *Apocalypse Now* [Francis Ford Coppola, 1979]. Believe it or not, it's on *The Switchblade Sisters* DVD. Quentin Tarantino got Miramax to put up the money to finish *The Host*. We scored it, did sound effects and everything, and now it's there for everyone to see.

WWD: How did you move into the orbit of Roger Corman?

JH: Well, Francis Ford Coppola got to work for Roger because they were looking for somebody to write a script—this sounds really bizarre. Roger had purchased some Russian science fiction films, which had a lot of marvelous special effects. They had a studio in Moscow where they did these big, beautiful special effects. They were propagandizing their space efforts, I guess. Roger wanted to pull out the special effects scenes and get an actress to dress up in space suits that looked like the ones in the existing footage and have somebody write a script that he could do that with. That was called *Battle Beyond the Sun*.

WWD: How did you get hooked up with *The Playgirls and the Bellboy* [1962], and what on earth is it?

JH: That was actually before we worked for Roger Corman. That was another thing that Francis put together. He was a quite a promoter. Basically, it was a film that had a lot of nudity but didn't make a lot of sense. It's got June Wilkinson in it and Karin Dor. But the first one that he put together ended up being called *The Wide Open Spaces*, or *Tonight for Sure* [1962], which was sort of a soft-core Western, if you can believe it. It had different titles because it was put together in different ways. But anyway, having done that, Francis got this job to do *The Playgirls and the Bellboy*. It was originally a German film that these bottom-feeding producers had bought because it had some nude scenes in it. They had the idea that they could use this to make—and this is very bizarre, because it was a black-and-white film—they wanted to make a 3-D color film that they could intercut with it, with a lot of nudity. They got Francis to write a script, June Wilkinson to star in it, and Francis brought me in to edit the picture. I was on the set all the time, making notes for the editing, and then I cut the picture together. The result was very, very bizarre. When they projected the film in the theater, they had to put titles on the screen, "Now put on your glasses" and "Now take off your glasses," so that you could see the 3-D. But you know what? The picture was a huge success.

WWD: I also have you as an uncredited director on Roger Corman's *The Wasp Woman* [1960]? Is that true?

JH: Well, that is and it isn't. Roger Corman used to make these horror movies that were roughly sixty minutes in length for double features. Then, when he wanted to sell them to television, they were too short. So a couple of them he needed to have footage added to, and *The Wasp Woman* was my assignment. I had to add about twenty minutes to the movie, so he could sell it to television. I also directed some extra sequences for an early Francis Ford Coppola film, *Dementia 13* [1963], which Roger asked me to do.

WWD: Now, what is your involvement with Corman's film *The Terror* [1963]?

JH: It was a similar kind of thing. It was shot on leftover sets from Corman's film of *The Raven* [1963]. Roger got Francis to write additional scenes to fill it out to a full-length movie and direct them. I was participating on the crew, and I did the sound recording and other things. But then, after it was done, Francis went on to work for the major studios, with *You're a Big Boy Now* [1966], and that was the end of that. Francis had a lot of scenes in the script for *The Terror* that were supposed to be day-for-night, but he had neglected to tell the cameraman that. The whole thing was just a mess. Roger got me to salvage what I could and write a new script to do additional scenes, which Monte Hellman directed most of. I did a lot of bits and pieces that filled in, and then I supervised the editing. Oddly enough, it makes little sense, but it's a beautiful film. It's a really odd movie. Now you know why.

WWD: Now we come to *Spider Baby; or, The Maddest Story Ever Told* [made in 1964; released in 1968]. What possessed you to make this your next project?

JH: Basically, what happened is that I wrote this story idea down because people were looking for low-budget horror movies. A friend of mine who had been an actor, who was in *Tonight for Sure* [1962], named Karl Schanzer, ended up acting in *Spider Baby*. He'd been working as a private detective, and he had some clients who were in the real estate development business. They had been students at UCLA the same time I had been, in the theater department, and they wanted to produce a feature. In fact, they had gone into the building business in order to raise the money to make movies. So they wanted to start off with a low-budget horror movie, which was the most common way for people to get started. They had been reading and reading and reading scripts and didn't find anything they liked. So Karl told them about me, that I had been doing work for Roger Corman and might have a story. So they looked at my outline, and they thought it was so different from anything else they had been reading that they contracted with me to write the screenplay and direct the movie.

A typically warped scene at home with the "family" (including Lon Chaney Jr., extreme right) in Jack Hill's bizarre horror comedy *Spider Baby; or, The Maddest Story Ever Told* (1968). Courtesy Jerry Ohlinger Archives. Copyright © 1968, American General Pictures Corp.

wwd: And that has a very unusual cast, to say the least: Lon Chaney Jr., Carol Ohmart, Mantan Moreland. What was that like?

jh: Chaney was a chronic alcoholic, but he loved acting very much. He wanted so badly to do a good job on it, because nobody ever gave him a chance to do comedy. Carol Ohmart had been in *House on Haunted Hill* [William Castle, 1959]. I hadn't seen that movie at that time, but she was suggested as somebody who had a little bit of a sort of a familiar name, who might be available because she wasn't doing anything.

wwd: And what about Mantan Moreland? How did he wind up in the picture?

jh: Well, I just thought it would be an interesting idea to have him in the film. I always liked him, and the people that I was working with really liked him, too. They thought it was a terrific idea; so we called him, and he said, "Yeah, I'd like to do it."

wwd: How long was the shoot on that?

jh: Twelve days.

wwd: And the budget?

jh: $65,000. The cameraman was Alfred Taylor, who had shot *Tonight for Sure*, and he also shot all the footage that Francis did for *The Terror*.

wwd: Who distributed the film?

jh: Well, for a long time it was locked up in litigation because the building business collapsed around that time, and the producers were in bankruptcy. It took several years, but there was a distributor, David L. Hewitt, who had seen the picture when it was first finished. He kept his eye on it during this bankruptcy. Eventually he acquired the picture for distribution. He's the one who came up with the title *Spider Baby*. The original title was *Cannibal Orgy; or, The Maddest Story Ever Told*. There was a biblical movie out at that time called *The Greatest Story Ever Told* [George Stevens, 1965], so this was going to be *The Maddest Story Ever Told*.

wwd: Next comes *Portrait in Terror* [1965], which is a rather interesting and moody vampire film.

jh: That started out as a Yugoslavian movie, which Francis was over in Yugoslavia supposedly supervising, to make sure that it would be a horror movie. But when Roger got it back, it wasn't a horror movie at all. It was a murder mystery. So Roger told me to salvage whatever footage I could to make a horror movie out of it. We had Bill Campbell, who had been in the picture, and he was available; so we shot a lot of new stuff in Venice, California. In the meantime, Roger called Stephanie Rothman.

wwd: Now, what was your connection with Stephanie Rothman? I'm moving now to *Blood Bath* [1966].

jh: *Blood Bath* was my script. It was my title.

WWD: Right, but you get a co-direction credit with Stephanie Rothman for the film.

JH: Well, that's because, after I left, Roger decided that he didn't think that the Yugoslavian footage matched the footage that we had shot in Venice. You see, both *Portrait in Terror* and *Blood Bath* came out of this same footage. Roger got the idea that he could sell the original movie to television and have Stephanie Rothman pad out what I shot with further scenes to make another full-length movie—and wind up with *two* movies instead of one. This is the kind of nutso stuff that we went through there. So Stephanie wrote new scenes and shot them, and turned it into a vampire movie. It became sort of a vampire movie with flashbacks. But we had no connection at all. I never met her at that time; we were working separately.

WWD: What about *Mondo Keyhole* [1966]?

JH: Well, after *Spider Baby* was *not* released, I was kind of in a desperate situation. So I went to work with this guy named John Lamb, who made nudist films on 16mm film and distributed them by mail order, because at that time you couldn't show nudity on the screen. So we went out and shot some nudist films—it's a funny image in your mind if you can imagine me going out to a nudist camp. I had to wear a belt in order to hold the stuff for the camera. Other than that, we couldn't wear clothes. So that was really, really a funny part of my life. Then I edited the films we shot into a full-length movie called *The Raw Ones* [1965], which actually played in theaters. We were all standing around waiting to be arrested; it was the first movie to actually show full-length frontal nudity on a screen in a theater. But nothing happened.

WWD: But what about *Mondo Keyhole*?

JH: Well, the original title of that film was *The Worst Crime of All*, and basically, it was a movie that I shot for John Lamb. A lot of it was a script that he kind of dictated, and the rest of it was what I wrote and directed. We used non-actors. I did the photography and the directing, and then I dubbed in the actors' voices with professional actors' voices, so it came out looking pretty good, actually, and it cost practically nothing to make. *Mondo Keyhole* looked so good for the money we had spent, Roger Corman saw it and said, "If you can do that on a legitimate movie, we can make some money. Can you make a stock car racing movie?" And I said, "I don't wanna do *that*. I want to make an art film." Roger replied, "Well, make me an art film *about* stock car racing!" I needed the job, naturally, so I said yes.

I hated stock car racing, so I thought, "Oh, God, how am I gonna do this?" I didn't want anything to do with it, but then I got Brian Donlevy and Ellen Burstyn for the cast (it was one of Brian's last films, and one of Ellen's first). And so I wrote, directed, and edited *Pit Stop* [1967] for Roger as a result of that conversation. It was about figure-eight racing, which was new then, racing on a figure-eight track. I think it's one of my best films. The original title was *The Winner*, which I liked better; but just at that time, Universal was coming out with a big racing movie called *Winning* [James Goldstone, 1969], so Roger decided to change the title to *Pit Stop*.

After I had done that, I was approached by my attorney at that time, who was also the attorney for all the Mexican film production companies in Hollywood. He had a Mexican producer who had made an agreement with Boris Karloff to do four pictures back-to-back, which was absolutely insane. It was quite common in Mexico. But he didn't have any scripts. So he looked at my rough cut of *Pit Stop* and contracted with me to write four scripts for Boris Karloff and direct all of Boris's scenes in Hollywood. Because of his health, Karloff could not go to Mexico City. The Hollywood footage with Karloff was then going to be added to the rest of each of the four films, which were

An action scene from one of Jack Hill's favorite films as a director, *Pit Stop*. Made and released in 1967, the film was subsequently re-released as *The Winner* in 1969. Courtesy Jerry Ohlinger Archives. Copyright © 1969 by Rio Pinto Productions, Inc.

going to be shot in Mexico City. This is something you learn—you can *only* learn—from working for Roger Corman.

WWD: How many days did you have with Karloff?

JH: I had four weeks. He was a very, very nice man to work with. These were his last four films, and he had to be in a wheelchair because he had emphysema. He had to have oxygen there. So if he had to do an action scene, he would breathe his oxygen, and then he'd get up and do the scene, and then come back and sit down in his wheelchair and get the oxygen again. He was just, just wonderful about it. He enjoyed playing four different characters in four weeks.

WWD: OK. What about *I, a Groupie* [1970]?

JH: Right after I did *Pit Stop*, I went to Switzerland to produce a film for a Swiss producer named Erwin C. Dietrich, who was kind of notorious. Roger recommended me to do it. He was supposed to send me the script, and we had a contract that provided for many things, including a certain amount of prep time. The contract required that the picture be shot in English, so that it could be released by Roger in the States. I was supposed to go to Zurich, and the script hadn't come. I was calling Dietrich and saying, "Where's the script?" And he said, "Well, it isn't ready yet, but we'll have it for you when you get here."

So I got off the plane in Zurich. "Where's the script?" I asked him. "Well, we don't have a script," he said, smiling. There was no script. There was no *story*, just a *title*. If I had been in my right mind, I would have said good-bye and gone home, but I took it as a challenge. So I worked out a story. But we couldn't find an actress who could speak English and Dietrich would approve. We finally started shooting, but it didn't last long. To make the long story short, it came to a parting of the ways.

WWD: Is this when you went back to Roger, working for New World?

JH: Yeah, the next thing I directed was *Big Doll House* [1971]. That was Pam Grier's breakout movie and one of the first big hits New World had.

WWD: You are often credited with discovering Pam Grier. Is this correct?

JH: Well, if anybody can be said to discover anybody. She had never done anything before, other than a walk-on in the background in a Russ Meyer movie. I interviewed her for the film, and I was immediately struck when I interviewed her and had her read for me. I thought she could do it, and she was great. She's gone on to an incredible career; she was really easy to work with.

WWD: What was the budget on that film?

JH: Officially, the cost of *The Big Doll House* was about $125,000, and it was the most profitable independent movie ever made up to its time.

WWD: Then you went on to do *The Big Bird Cage* [1972], another women-in-prison film, again with Pam Grier in the lead role, as well as *Foxy Brown* [1974] and one of my favorites, *Coffy* [1973]. I love the tag line for that film: "*Nobody sleeps when they mess with Coffy.*" On all of these films, what was your shooting schedule like?

JH: Well, for *The Big Doll House*, in the Philippines, we just took whatever time we needed to do it, because time was our cheapest item! Nothing was ever ready on time. There was a hurricane that blew the roof off the soundstage, and it was just one thing after another. And of course, people got sick. So I wouldn't call it a schedule. We just took the time we needed. It was fun for me and for the players, because we got to write new scenes and shoot them on the spot. We were waiting for a set to be built, so we had to do *something* with our time. I hated the script. I thought it was just horrible. I did as much rewriting on it as I could and tried to make more of a comedy out of it.

Coffy was shot in Los Angeles. That was a very different experience. The script was locked down, and that was it. That was for American International Pictures. A very tight shoot, very professional, all union crew, eighteen days. *Coffy* was one of the biggest hits AIP ever had. It cost roughly $500,000 to

Mud wrestling in a women's penitentiary in Jack Hill's *The Big Bird Cage* (1972). Courtesy Jerry Ohlinger Archives. Copyright © 1972, New World Pictures Inc.

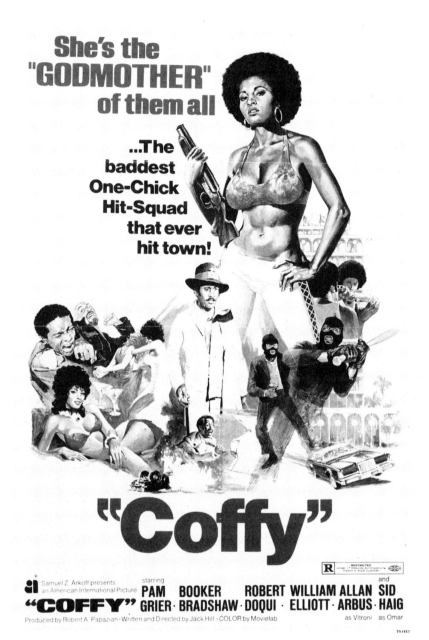

Jack Hill helped to pioneer the "blaxploitation" genre with such groundbreaking genre films as *Coffy* (1973). Courtesy Jerry Ohlinger Archives.

make. AIP had a standard fixed budget limit on the blaxploitation movies because they felt, at $500,000, they could—with almost anything—guarantee that the black audience would bring them out of it. But they didn't think that a black picture would cross over with a white audience. *Coffy* was one of the first movies to show that you could attract a large white audience.

WWD: Why did you direct *The Swinging Cheerleaders* [1974]?

JH: Well, it just came up. After *Foxy Brown*, AIP offered me another script, which I told them I would direct, but only if they gave me some time to fix it up. *Foxy Brown* and *Coffy* I wrote myself. I thought this new script needed a *lot* of work, and they didn't wanna hear that. I said, "Well, I don't wanna do it if I can't rewrite the script." So it was a standoff. Just then, another distributor said that with my name and the title *Swinging Cheerleaders*, we could get financing to do a movie. I did *Swinging Cheerleaders* because I had a nice percentage of it, and I felt that I could really, for the first time, actually make some money for myself, instead of making money for other people.

Pam Grier prepares to dispose of an opponent in Jack Hill's *Foxy Brown* (1974). Courtesy Jerry Ohlinger Archives.

wwd: *Switchblade Sisters* [1975] is the film that perhaps you're best remembered for. Quentin Tarantino has called it one of his favorite films. How did you two get together?

jh: I first met him at a screening. They had a screening of blaxploitation movies, and they were showing *Coffy* and *Foxy Brown* at a theater in Los Angeles. Quentin came with his arms full of posters and record albums he wanted me to autograph for him. I had heard of him, but I had not seen any of his films at that point. I had heard that he'd made a movie that won the Cannes Film Festival, and that's all I knew.

wwd: *Pulp Fiction* [1994], yeah.

jh: I was very, very impressed. Some time after that, I got a call from Miramax, asking me who owned the rights to *Switchblade Sisters*. I owned the rights, so we struck a deal, and the film was one of the first features distributed nationally by Rolling Thunder, Quentin's company that he set up to distribute underappreciated films.

wwd: Now after *Switchblade Sisters*, I have a long gap and then *Sorceress* [1982], which you directed as "Brian Stuart."

jh: Well, I didn't even have a manager or an agent. I just kind of fell into the business anyway, and I wasn't really taking it seriously. I didn't think of myself as a filmmaker or an *auteur* and all that kind of stuff. I just kind of went from one thing to another for the fun of it and took long vacations in between. But that's not the way you build a career in Hollywood. Then I got another call from Roger, saying, "Would you like to do a sword-and-sorcery movie?" He thought that might be a big genre. At that time, Roger had a special effects studio [at the New World Studios in Venice, California], which was doing really good work.

They had done some of the special effects work on *Escape from New York* [John Carpenter, 1981] and some other big pictures, and Corman owned the special effects unit himself, so he could do it for a low budget. So to me, it was an opportunity to make something that would look like a big movie, which I had never had an opportunity to do before. I thought this might get me back in business doing mainstream pictures. So I wrote the script, and he liked the script, but then things started to go wrong. There were all kinds of production problems, and by the time the film came out, I really didn't want to have anything to do with it.

wwd: Looking back on your work, what are the films that you feel the most satisfied with?

jh: In all seriousness, I think *Pit Stop* is actually a pretty good movie. And *Coffy* has a lot going for it. I really put a lot of effort into that film that's kind of between the lines, if you know what I mean. I feel that that movie was very, very successful, and I really felt I'd accomplished something because there was a lot of subtext there that people felt. Audience members talked back to the screen during the projection of the film; they identified with *Coffy*. I think I've done a lot of interesting work in film and some other stuff because I needed the money at the time. But all of my work is now coming out on DVD, and that's the final proof. These films last; audiences connect to them. That's the real test, if you ask me.

MONTE HELLMAN

One of the legendary figures of the American cinema, Monte Hellman is best known for directing *Two-Lane Blacktop* (1971), considered by many to be the definitive "road movie." But Hellman's career goes back to the 1950s and his work in the formative days of television. Later, he worked for maverick producer/director Roger Corman on a number of projects. He then branched out on his own as a director, while continuing his work as an editor for such luminaries as the late Sam Peckinpah. In recent years, he's been involved in various projects with Vincent Gallo, Quentin Tarantino, and numerous other contemporary filmmakers. Hellman has seldom spoken at length about his work in film. In this interview, conducted on January 19, 2004, he offers a number of insights into his long and varied career.

WHEELER WINSTON DIXON: You were born on July 12, 1932, in New York, New York. Could you tell me something about your early education and your family?

MONTE HELLMAN: I was born in New York by mistake. My parents were from St. Louis, Missouri, and they were traveling in New York, expecting that I wouldn't be born for a week or so, but I was born accidentally in New York.

WWD: What did your father and mother do for a living?

MH: My mother was a housewife until her kids were grown, at which point she worked in retail. She had a job as a salesperson at a clothing store, and then she sold real estate. She was also a bridge teacher.

WWD: And your father?

MH: My father was in small businesses, like grocery stores and gas stations. He ultimately sold real estate as well.

WWD: So your parents were on vacation in New York, and then they went back to St. Louis, and that's where your family was based?

James Taylor listens intently as Monte Hellman directs him in a scene from *Two-Lane Blacktop* (1971). Courtesy Photofest.

MH: No, actually they moved back to New York! [*Laughs.*] They moved to Brooklyn for about six months. Then they moved to Albany, New York, until I was about five years old, and then we all moved to California.

WWD: What kind of early education did you have, and did you know early on that you wanted to be a filmmaker?

MH: Well, I was exceedingly shy, and my parents thought they would bring me out by giving me drama lessons when I was about six years old. I guess they've regretted it, because I came out too much. [*Laughs.*]

WWD: What do you mean by that?

MH: I became interested in theater and directing. When I was ten years old, I went to a YMCA summer camp and wrote and directed a ten-minute play.

WWD: Which schools did you go to?

MH: I went to John Burroughs Junior High and Los Angeles High, which by coincidence coincided with Dustin Hoffman's education, I just found out.

WWD: When did you realize that you wanted to be involved in movies?

MH: I think I always wanted to be involved in movies, but I thought that, not having a family in the business, the theater was a more realistic ambition. So I really expected that I would work in regional theater, which I had an opportunity to do; but I did graduate work in film at the University of California, Los Angeles, after I finished theater studies at Stanford. I must have had some kind of hope in the back of my mind that I could make films.

WWD: When did you graduate from UCLA?

MH: I didn't graduate. I didn't finish my graduate studies.

WWD: Like lots of other great people.

MH: I was in the Class of 1951 at Stanford, and I finished at UCLA in 1953.

WWD: What was your first film experience?

MH: I was an apprentice editor on the television series *Medic*, with Richard Boone, the lovely old drunk.

WWD: How did you get that?

MH: After I had done three years of summer stock, one of the members of my stock company was offered a job in the editing department at ABC TV. He wasn't interested, so he turned me on to it. I applied, and my first job was cleaning out the film vaults at the ABC studios. I was actually an apprentice editor, my duties being to synchronize dailies and do hot splicing and things like that, but I unofficially moved up to assistant. I can't remember what the reason was. The assistant must have been busy doing something else, so I was working as an assistant.

WWD: How did you move on from there?

MH: The Film Editors Guild had a rule that you had to put in eight years in the Guild before you could edit. I was a member, and as long as I was a member, the clock was running. It didn't matter whether you were working as an actual editor or not. So I decided to put in my eight years doing something else, because I got tired of being an apprentice editor. I quit and started my own theater company in Los Angeles.

WWD: What was the name of that?

MH: It was originally called the Playgoers Company, and then we were sued because the magazine that was handed out in all the theaters in Los Angeles was called *Playgoers*, so they handed us an injunction. We had to change our name to the Theatergoers Company. It wasn't a stock company, so we didn't have a group of players. We did a season of plays with different casts in each one.

WWD: How did this get you back into film?

MH: Well, Roger Corman was one of the investors in my theater company, and we lasted a year, at which point we got evicted because they decided to convert the theater to a movie theater. By the way, the theater was a beautiful facility, which had been built by the Actor's Lab, with a revolving stage. So we got evicted in 1958.

WWD: And what kind of plays did you do?

MH: The first play we put on, which I also directed, was *Waiting for Godot*.

WWD: Good choice.

MH: That was the first Los Angeles production of the play, and the fifth production in the world at that time.

WWD: Roger Corman was actually a backer of this?

MH: Roger was actually one of the backers. He wasn't a major player. I think he invested $1,000, but you know—

WWD: That's something for him.

MH: Yes. So when we got thrown out, Roger said, "OK, the theater is being converted into a movie theater, and you should take that as a sign. You should direct a movie." So my first movie was *Beast from Haunted Cave* [released in 1960]. You know, I just was looking to do anything. Roger hired me because he thought he was getting a bargain.

WWD: Was that a Filmgroup production?

MH: Yes, it was.

WWD: And how many days did you have?

MH: We had thirteen days, and the reason he thought he was getting a bargain was that he hired me as a writer, director, and editor.

WWD: What was the budget?

MH: I think the budget was about $13,000 or something like that.

WWD: $13,000?

MH: Yes, about that.

WWD: Did you shoot in 35mm?

MH: Yes, we did.

WWD: That's a very low budget.

MH: It was very low. Gene Corman was actually the producer on the film. We were shooting the film on location in South Dakota, and Gene told everybody that we were from UCLA doing a student film! So he made a deal with the hotel for a dollar a day per room, and he put two people in a room. We had cold Velveeta sandwiches for lunch or sometimes salami. This is ten below

The poster for Monte Hellman's first film as a director, *Beast from Haunted Cave* (1959), produced by Roger Corman. Courtesy Jerry Ohlinger Archives.

zero, mind you, so not even a cup of hot soup. So it was very low budget from every point of view.

WWD: So you wrote that, you directed that, and you edited that?

MH: Leo Gordon started the script, then Chuck Griffith finished it, and then I supervised some rewrites that Chuck did. And it's funny. Roger didn't get me as an editor either, because it wasn't a union production. So my union [the Editor's Guild] wouldn't let me edit it.

WWD: Yes, Anthony Carras wound up cutting it. That's amazing.

MH: Roger really got screwed. He paid me $1,000 for three jobs, and I only did one.

WWD: How did you get involved in Corman's film *Ski Troop Attack* [1960]?

MH: Well, Corman shot *Ski Troop Attack* back-to-back with *Beast from Haunted Cave*. Then a couple of years later, when he sold everything to television, he sold a number of films that were made as companion features, B movies for a double bill, and they were all sixty-minute movies. For television, they needed to be at least seventy minutes. So he hired me to expand four of his old pictures for television. One was my own picture, *Beast from Haunted Cave*, one was *Ski Troop Attack*, which he had shot back-to-back, and then the two pictures that he shot at Puerto Rico, *Last Woman on Earth* [1960] and *Creature from the Haunted Sea* [1961].

WWD: Robert Towne stars in *The Last Woman on Earth* under the pseudonym of Edward Wain, in addition to writing the script—another Corman economy. And, of course, Towne went on to write many more films of his own after that, including Roman Polanski's *Chinatown* [1974].

MH: That's right. So I shot additional scenes for all these films, just to make the sale to television.

WWD: Then you went to work on Corman's multidirector film, *The Terror* [1963].

MH: There were actually only three directors. Roger directed two days on a set he had left over from *The Raven* [1963], because he had Boris Karloff and Jack Nicholson, both of whom were in *The Raven*, and he'd finished that film ahead of schedule. So he shot two days, and then he shut the film down. Then Francis Ford Coppola and I shot all the rest of the stuff. Coppola did all the stuff that was down at Big Sur. [Other sources contend that Jack Hill and Jack Nicholson also shot some material for *The Terror*, but Hellman disputes this claim.] I shot all the exteriors that Coppola didn't do; Coppola shot most of the scenes with Dorothy Neumann, who played the witch, Katrina, in the film.

WWD: Now I have an interesting credit here: Harvey Hart's film *Bus Riley's Back in Town* [1965], based on a play by William Inge, who refused the screen credit; he used "Walter Gage" as a pseudonym. You worked on that film as an assistant editor. Were you on the set at all?

MH: A little bit. Not very much.

wwd: Do you like that film as much as I do?

mh: You know, I can't remember if I ever saw the final cut.

wwd: Michael Parks played the lead.

mh: Yes, Michael was great. That was cut by a great old editor, Folmar Blang-sted. He was very, very demanding of assistant editors. An assistant has a lot of work to do on his own, syncing up dailies and so forth. But Folmar de-manded that the assistant do all this work after hours and that during the day the assistant would stand by Folmar, just to hold a piece of film that he might need in the cutting—the next scene, whatever.

wwd: Like a human trim bin.

mh: Exactly. So it was demanding, but he was great. I learned a lot from him. But then I was offered two pictures in the Philippines to direct, *Back Door to Hell* and *Flight to Fury* [both 1964]. So I told Folmar that I had this terrific opportunity, and I was going to go to the Philippines and direct these two films. And he was furious! How dare I desert him in the middle of a film? So that was unfortunate. But I did go to the Philippines and shot those two films back-to-back for Roger.

wwd: Before we get to that, I want to talk about *The Wild Ride* [1960]. What was your involvement in that?

mh: *The Wild Ride* was a picture for Corman directed by Harvey Berman, who was one of the people in my summer stock company. Roger wanted me to go up there to make sure everything went OK. It was a teenage rebel movie. That was really when I got to know Jack Nicholson, who was the star of the movie.

wwd: Now back to *Flight to Fury* and *Back Door to Hell*. These are both in the Philippines. These were your first real serious directorial credits?

mh: Yes, I think they were the first films I did that I felt were real movies. They were back-to-back, but I was upset about *Back Door to Hell* because it was the only film that I had done that I wasn't the sole editor on. I was shooting *Flight to Fury* while somebody else [Fely Crisostomo] was cutting *Back Door to Hell*, which I didn't like at all. And then I got really deathly ill, and I was in the hospital for a long time, and nobody could figure out what it was. It was some strange tropical disease; they never did figure it out. They gave me all kinds of tests, and finally Jack Nicholson came to the hospital and put his hand on my head and said, "Be well."

wwd: You're healed.

mh: And believe it or not, the next day I was out of the hospital scouting loca-tions. I was not completely 100 percent but nearly 100 percent better! So they put *Back Door to Hell* together while I was in the hospital. I came out. I was horrified, so I recut it while shooting *Flight to Fury*. So my schedule was some-thing like this: I would get up at five in the morning, have breakfast, leave for the set at six, sleep in the car until we got to the set at seven, shoot until 6 p.m., drive back to the house from six to seven at night, sleep in the car during that time, have dinner, and then go to the cutting room to recut *Back Door to Hell*, work until two in the morning, then sleep from 2 a.m. to 5 a.m., and then repeat the same process the next day. So I fought for that one. It's really hard to recut a picture once somebody has done the first rough cut. You haven't seen the original dailies, you can't pick the takes. That just doesn't work for me.

WWD: I agree.

MH: I never was really happy with the way *Back Door to Hell* came out, even though I put a lot of effort into it—like years later, when I was brought in to recut some of *The Killer Elite* [1975] for Sam Peckinpah.

WWD: Yes, I was going to ask you about that.

MH: From my previous experience, I just knew that I couldn't do it. I said, "Listen, I can't recut somebody else's cut. I'll have to order all these dailies over again and start from scratch." And he said, "Fine." And so that's what I did. You just can't do it any other way.

WWD: What was your relationship with Peckinpah?

MH: He was a wonderful, sweet guy who was also impossible to deal with. He was a wild man. Some friends of mine made a movie about insanity called *Fit to Be Untied* [1975]. And that's him.

WWD: What were the schedules and budgets on *Flight to Fury* and *Back Door to Hell*?

MH: I had eighteen days and something like $35,000 on one, and $50,000 on the other.

WWD: Would it be fair to say that you and Jack Nicholson became good friends on *Flight to Fury*? At this point in your career, he's in all your films, and now he starts writing scripts with *Ride in the Whirlwind* [1965].

MH: Well, he also wrote *Flight to Fury*. As I said, we had gotten to be friends on *The Wild Ride*. So we wrote a script together, which was never produced. And when we came back from the Philippines, we went to Roger, who had basically promised to give us the money for the script. But he'd changed his mind, and so that's how we did *Ride in the Whirlwind* and *The Shooting*, two Westerns shot back-to-back [both films were shot in 1965; *Ride* was released in 1965, and *The Shooting* in 1967]. Corman said, "I'm sorry, but I don't want to make this picture. But if you want to make a Western, I'll back that. And as long as you're making one, you might as well make two." So Jack went away and wrote *Ride in the Whirlwind*, and Carol Eastman wrote *The Shooting*.

WWD: What was *The Shooting* like?

MH: Well, Cameron Mitchell was crazy. We were shooting during the television hiatus period, when all the series were shut down, so we got all of our costumes from Western Costume [a famous costume rental company]. A lot of it was stuff that was used regularly on some television series or other, *Rawhide* or something. So he had these beautiful chaps that we'd rented for him, and behind my back Cameron took a pair of scissors and cut holes in them because he wanted them to look rough and weather-beaten. So now I had to explain this to Western Costume, and ultimately I had to buy his costume because he'd ruined it. I didn't believe what he was doing.

WWD: Millie Perkins is in *Ride in the Whirlwind*, as is Harry Dean Stanton. Is this another example of Corman's ability to pick out actors early in their careers?

MH: Millie Perkins was my next-door neighbor. But I tried to cast *Ride in the Whirlwind* in a normal way. I thought about Sterling Hayden and Donna Winters for the shooting. But then I was in a bookstore in Beverly Hills called Martindale's, a great bookstore. And I remember I had just kind of a flash, a light bulb that suddenly appeared above my head.

WWD: And the light bulb said?

A very young Jack Nicholson in Monte Hellman's existential Western *Ride in the Whirlwind* (1965). Courtesy Jerry Ohlinger Archives.

MH: And the light bulb said, "Millie Perkins, Warren Oates, and Will Hutchins. These are your actors." Now, Jack was a given. Jack was part of the deal, he was my partner. But I just had a flash of the three of them all together as a unit. I was so excited by it that I called Jack right away, and he was equally excited. He knew Warren Oates a little bit. I don't know if either of us knew Will Hutchins.

WWD: Will Hutchins was in the early television Western *Sugarfoot* [1957].

MH: Yes. And Will was actually the kind of catalyst that made *Ride in the Whirlwind* happen, because he was the best known of anybody.

WWD: Where did you shoot them?

MH: Jack and I did a road trip of every known Western location, trying to find one location that would work for both pictures. The pictures are vastly different, and there were key scenes that had specific locations, and I didn't want to compromise. So we traveled around, searching. We went to Lone Pine, we went to Arizona south of Flagstaff, and we went to Monument Valley, John

Warren Oates (standing) and Jack Nicholson (on horse) come upon a fallen gunfighter in Monte Hellman's atmospheric *The Shooting*. The film was shot back-to-back with *Ride in the Whirlwind* in 1965 but not released until 1967. Courtesy Jerry Ohlinger Archives.

Ford's home territory—all over the place. Then we went to Kanab, Utah, and Kanab was the only place where we thought we could shoot both pictures in the same locale without having to move the company. It worked out very well; they both came in on time and on budget.

WWD: And what did you do after this?

MH: I edited *The Wild Angels* [1966], the Hell's Angels film Roger directed with Peter Fonda.

WWD: How did *Ride in the Whirlwind* and *The Shooting* get released?

MH: Well, that's the sad part. They were both shot in 1965, and they actually were never released. I think they had a very brief theatrical release in 1971, for something like three days in Texas.

WWD: So how did they make money?

MH: Television.

WWD: Straight to television?

MH: Straight to television. That horrified both Jack and me. Roger made the deal. He sold them both to a company named Walter Reade Sterling. They had a mess of theaters, and we thought, "Wow, we'll get theater distribution all over the country!" But all they wanted the pictures for was a television package. So they went direct to television, and that was it. After you do that, there's never really a chance to do a theatrical release.

WWD: The next credit I have is *Two-Lane Blacktop* [1971], so there's quite a gap of time in here. What did you do in between?

MH: I was under contract at Universal. Then I developed another picture for Corman, and I was a dialogue coach on Roger's film *The St. Valentine's Day Massacre* [1967], which he shot over at 20th, his first big studio picture. I also did some editing for Roger on a film thing called *Target: Harry*, which finally came out in 1969. And then I was set to direct a picture for Corman about a black sheriff in the South called *Explosion*. We cast it, rehearsed it, and we were set to shoot the following week.

WWD: And what happened?

MH: And for the first time Sam Arkoff [co-founder of American International Pictures, where Corman got his start] decided to read the script. So this is the Friday before the shoot. And Arkoff tells me, "I grew up in Kansas, and we didn't have any racial tension."

WWD: Of course not. Right.

MH: I said, "How many blacks were there in your town?" He said, "Well, we had one. Everybody liked him."

WWD: Oh, my God.

MH: So that was it. He canceled the picture at the last minute.

WWD: Was that pretty much the end of you and AIP and Corman?

MH: Not totally. I did another picture for Corman in 1974, called *Cockfighter*, for which I ultimately didn't get any credit.

WWD: Tell me about *Two-Lane Blacktop*. What's the genesis of the film? What do you think when people compare your work to [directors] Robert Bresson or Yasujiro Ozu? Does this seem ridiculous to you, or does it make sense?

MH: Well, I was familiar with Bresson, because I was part of a film society, and I think the first picture we showed was *A Man Escaped* [1956].

WWD: Yes, a beautiful film.

MH: But I don't think I had ever seen an Ozu film until years later. But it's flattering. I think Bresson and Ozu are great filmmakers, so I have to be flattered by that.

WWD: How did your directorial style evolve into the almost trancelike state of *Two-Lane Blacktop*, which is really about the locations and about the road trip more than anything else?

MH: I would have to credit one person with my philosophy and my approach to theater and film. I'm teaching now at the University of Southern California,

Left to right: Warren Oates, Dennis Wilson, Laurie Bird (back to camera), and James Taylor in Monte Hellman's most famous film as a director, *Two-Lane Blacktop* (1971). Courtesy Jerry Ohlinger Archives. Copyright © 1971, Universal Pictures.

and basically what I teach is the approach that Arthur Hopkins used in all his work in the theater. Arthur Hopkins was a producer/director in the twenties, thirties, and forties in New York. He had a tremendous amount to do with discovering some of the greatest people in the business. He didn't really discover John Barrymore, but he directed Barrymore's Broadway stage production of *Hamlet* in 1923, which really made his reputation. I think he was the first to cast Katharine Hepburn and Spencer Tracy on the stage. He was casting the original Broadway production of *The Petrified Forest* in 1935, and he was having a hard time finding the right person to play Duke Mantee. But by a stroke of luck, he walked into another theater where a play was in rehearsal and heard this dry, tired voice that belonged to Humphrey Bogart, who up until that time had only played juveniles on the stage. Bogart didn't want to do the role, but Hopkins insisted, and the role ultimately made Bogart a star.

Arthur Hopkins taught selflessness. He believed that anyone—whether actor, director, designer, whoever—who called attention to himself did so at the expense of the production. Everyone must be a servant to the work he's creating. He also taught simplicity, the elimination of everything that isn't necessary. And he agreed with the adage that you can't serve two masters. If you do a play because you're sure it'll be a success, and it fails, you have nothing. If you do something you're passionate about, and it fails, you've created something you love.

WWD: So did you work with him as a teacher?

MH: No, unfortunately. I read a collection of his lectures that he gave at Cornell University. And his approach turned me around and gave me a kind of a vision of what I wanted to do. This leads to the approach with the actors I used in *Two-Lane Blacktop*. That film came about because I had been in Italy preparing a picture from Patricia Highsmith's book *The Two Faces of January*. Mark Damon was the producer, and he was going to star in it. He brought me over to Rome, and I wrote the script; but he was not able to raise the money.

So I came back to Los Angeles, and my agent, Mike Medavoy, brought me into his office and introduced me to [producer] Michael Laughlin and said, "Michael has a picture that he is interested in having you direct." Michael actually offered me two pictures, *Two-Lane Blacktop* and *The Christian Licorice Store* [both 1971; James Frawley ultimately directed the latter]. I really was not interested in *The Christian Licorice Store* at all, but I liked the idea of *Two-Lane Blacktop*. The idea intrigued me. I think the reason that I was interested is that my father was a professional gambler and a bookmaker, besides selling real estate. So I was naturally interested in the subject of gambling, and that's what turned me on to *Two-Lane Blacktop*.

wwd: When you came on board, what input did you have? Warren Oates, Harry Dean Stanton, James Taylor, and former Beach Boy Dennis Wilson are all in the cast. How much did you have to do with this?

mh: The picture was already pretty far along in pre-production. It was not only cast, but they had paid $100,000 for a script, which I threw away. So I was looking for somebody to write a new script, not rewrite the old one, and I found Rudy Wurlitzer [Wurlitzer's later credits included the screenplays for *Pat Garrett and Billy the Kid* (Sam Peckinpah, 1973), *Shadow of the Wolf* (Jacques Dorfmann, 1992), and *Little Buddha* (Bernardo Bertolucci, 1993)]. I gave Rudy the original script to read, and he read about five pages and said, "I can't read this." I said, "That's OK. We have the basic idea, a cross country race, and we can work from that." So Rudy took the names of two of the characters from the original script, which were The Driver and The Mechanic, and rewrote the whole thing.

wwd: Who wrote the original script?

mh: The guy who wrote the original script was Will Corry, who gets a co-screenplay credit and credit for the original story on the film. Corry wrote the script, which we threw away, and he got paid $100,000 for it and bought a yacht. He had been recently divorced. He had a two-year-old daughter, so he took her on a trip around the world, just the two of them, on this yacht.

wwd: Where did you shoot the film?

mh: We shot it on the road from Los Angeles to North Carolina, driving in a caravan, just shooting a little bit, driving a little bit, and then doing the same thing again the next day. We drove and shot every day.

wwd: Are you happy with *Two-Lane Blacktop*?

mh: I'm never totally happy with anything. But you know, it's not my taste. I really like a lot of plot.

wwd: That's funny. *Two-Lane Blacktop* is nearly plotless, as you said, and for many people it's your signature film.

mh: You're right. A film with no plot was a little bit weird for me to get involved with, but it was a terrific experience making it, and I felt we had tremendous freedom. I think it's the only time I have had final cut on a movie. Getting the film funded, though, was something of a hassle. Originally the picture was set up at Cinema Center, but nobody read it until we were ready to start shooting; and when they did, they canceled the movie at the last minute. We were in turnaround, and we took the script of *Two-Lane Blacktop* to every studio. We took it to Columbia, MGM, Warners, and everybody said, "You know what it's going to cost?" And we would say, "A million one [$1.1 million]," and they would say, "It's not possible, you can't make it for that." So the next studio we go to, we would say, "A million three," and they said,

"Impossible, you can't make it for that." Nobody believed that we could do it for that small a budget. And finally we took it to Universal and—

WWD: So what are you up to now, $2 million?

MH: We went back to a million one. [*Laughs.*] And they said, "If you can make it for $900,000, we'll finance it." Actually, it wound up costing $850,000.

WWD: Of course, those figures today are just utterly impossible.

MH: I know.

WWD: What about *Cockfighter* [1974]?

MH: It's a long story. I went to Hong Kong to set up production on a picture called *In a Dream of Passion*, but it never got made, because the producer bailed on us at the last minute. Then I went back to Hong Kong a year later to do *Shatter* [1974], and I got fired in the middle of the picture.

WWD: Wasn't that a Hammer movie?

MH: Yes, that was for Hammer.

WWD: Who fired you?

MH: Michael Carreras [Hammer producer and sometime director].

WWD: Why did he do that?

MH: Well, I think that Michael really wanted to direct it from the beginning. We just fought a lot on the set. I didn't like the way he was treating a black actor [Yemi Ajibade] in the film. I thought it was demeaning, the things that he wanted me to make him do, so we had a lot of fights. And I just finally said, "There is some shit I will not eat."

WWD: What was it like working with Peter Cushing and Anton Diffring—British colonialist actors to the core?

MH: All the stuff of them in *Shatter* is mine. Michael waited until all the English actors were finished before he fired me. Stuart Whitman is in the whole picture, so Michael shot some stuff with him, but I did all the stuff with Cushing and Diffring, who were very professional to work with. But we were way over schedule, because he had made a deal with the Shaw Brothers.

WWD: Yes, [producers] Run Run Shaw and Run Me Shaw.

MH: Right. Run Run basically had his crews working twenty-four hours around the clock in three shifts. But because we were not a real Shaw Brothers picture, rather a Hammer co-production, like a facilities deal, we would get on the set at 6 a.m., and our crew wouldn't show up until noon.

WWD: Not a good situation.

MH: So at the end of three weeks, I was only halfway through the picture, and I think it was supposed to be a four-week picture. Then Michael Carreras said, "All right, I'm taking it from here." He spent four months doing the other half of the film, and of what he shot, only a tiny portion made it into the final cut. Basically, the film is two-thirds mine, even though I only shot half of it.

WWD: What about *Cockfighter*?

MH: I came back from Hong Kong, having been fired, and I got a call from Roger Corman. This was completely out of the blue. Roger just called me up and said, "I've got this film set up. Will you do the picture?" Again, I did a total rewrite on the script; but since this was Roger's baby, he got very upset and anxious. After two weeks he put a stop to it and said, "OK, that's as much as you can do. Whatever you've got now, you have to work with."

WWD: This is for Corman's own company, New World?

MH: That's right.

WWD: But once again, the cast seems awfully familiar. You have Warren Oates, Harry Dean Stanton, Millie Perkins, all actors you'd worked with before.

MH: Well, because I couldn't really get the script that I wanted, it's my least favorite of my movies, with the exception of *Beast from Haunted Cave*. But I like the authenticity of that kind of milieu; I think as a documentary about the "sport" of cockfighting, it works fairly well.

WWD: Where was that shot?

MH: It was shot in Atlanta. But I was never really happy with it; it just didn't work for me, basically because of the script.

WWD: What about [the television series] *Baretta* [1975], with Robert Blake? What was your involvement with that?

MH: You're really trying to hurt a guy, aren't you? [*Laughs.*]

WWD: No, I'm just being a completist here.

MH: That's the other case where I was fired, but I still get residuals.

WWD: How many did you direct?

MH: I directed just half of one *Baretta*. Bobby [Blake] had been an old acquaintance of mine. We had known a lot of the same people. But he was just hostile from the moment I walked on the set. He kept saying, "I know you're a feature director, but this is television. We do things differently here," and that kind of stuff. Every time I tried to do something, he would say, "No, we don't do it that way." So it was impossible. I directed just half of one episode, and that was it.

WWD: What about *The Greatest* [1977], the Muhammad Ali biopic that you took over from Tom Gries?

MH: I've had a small secondary career taking over for deceased directors on films. [*Laughs.*] I also took over for Mark Robson on *Avalanche Express*. Tom had died, the film wasn't completed, and they brought me in to finish it. I'm kind of like the kiss of death.

WWD: Well, I don't think so.

MH: But all these experiences were interesting. On *The Greatest*, I had a lot of ideas that couldn't be realized because of budgetary problems. Since we had Muhammad Ali starring in it, I wanted to open the picture with stock footage of his Olympics fight. But the Olympics committee just wanted so much money for the stock footage that Columbia wouldn't pay it.

WWD: Now what can you tell me about *China 9, Liberty 37* [1978]? It's a really unusual project. Sam Peckinpah appears in it as an actor, along with Warren Oates and Jenny Agutter. It's a very peculiar Western. It seems to have also gone through a lot of different titles, including *Amore, piombo e furore, Clayton & Catherine, Gunfire*, and *Love, Bullets and Frenzy* [1978]. And who is Tony Brandt, who gets a director's credit on some prints of the film?

MH: It's a long story. The titles are the result of different versions that the producers put together, one of the things that was very frustrating. I think it's the best experience I ever had in a movie, the most fun shooting a movie I have ever had. [Director of cinematography] Giuseppe Rotunno and his crew were fantastic to work with. We had taken over this hotel in Al Maria, Spain. The camera crew would go into the kitchen at night and cook pasta. We would have caviar and chilled vodka every Saturday night.

I got involved in the film through [producer] Elliott Kastner. Elliott and I had been tossing around ideas for a movie for a couple of years, and then he found a script he wanted to produce, and I got a call from him just before Christmas in 1976. He called me up and said, "I'm over in Rome. I want you to fly over right away to talk about doing this script with me." And I said, "You know, Elliott, the script is really not very good. I don't know if I want to do it." He said, "Maybe you can do a little work on the ending. You'll put it in shape, don't worry about it." I said, "Well, it's Christmas, I can't fly over now. I got to spend some time with my family." But he kept after me and finally asked me point blank, "Well, when can you be here?" I said, "Give me ten days."

Well, in ten days I flew to Rome with a new script written by Jerry Harvey. Jerry just took the original script and rewrote it. So I came over with the new script under my arm, and Elliott hated it. But the Italian producers loved it. So Elliott left me in the lion's den with the Italian producers. We did the picture, it was a lot of fun, a lot of fights, but nothing that made it too unpleasant, and we had a great time. The picture was invited to the Cannes Film Festival. It was basically a Western, and I thought it turned out well. I had made a deal that I would take my name off the picture in Italy as director and that Tony Brandt, who was my assistant, would be listed as the director. In exchange for that, everywhere else in the world I would be listed not only as director but also as one of the producers. So that was a trade.

WWD: And you also edited the film?

MH: I edit all my movies, no matter whose name is on them. Anyway, the producers apparently were having trouble with their subsidy [funding], which was based on the fact that Tony Brandt was the director of record, because there was all this publicity about me during Cannes actually being the director. And so the producers withdrew *China 9, Liberty 37* from the festival; it made the front page of *Variety*. Gilles Jacob [director of the Cannes festival] was outraged. Everybody in the world knew that I directed the movie. So it was a terrible situation, and I was very disappointed, because obviously I wanted my picture in the Cannes Film Festival. So it turned out that it played in the Cannes Festival market, out of competition, in a terrible theater where they had two projectors that were mismatched. One was so dark you couldn't even see the screen. And then they started recutting the picture—which is my fate on a lot of my movies—changing the title, and doing all of that stuff.

WWD: On *Avalanche Express*, you took over from Mark Robson. How much did you direct of that?

MH: I would say I directed maybe 10 percent of the principal photography, and I worked a year on the picture. I did all the special effects—all the avalanches, all the miniatures of the train, and so forth. I did work with Lee Marvin and—

WWD: Robert Shaw?

MH: Not Robert Shaw. He had already died.

WWD: Maximilian Schell?

MH: I worked with Max Schell because I had to reloop him through the whole picture. We had to replace Robert Shaw's voice with another actor. I directed a lot of the interiors on the planes and some of the action sequences.

WWD: How did you wind up being the person who inherits all these pictures?

MH: I don't know, I think I'm just lucky! [*Laughs.*]

WWD: What about *Iguana* [1988]?

MH: This was another one of these strange Italian deals where I was very uneasy about the whole thing. We had literally the worst script I had ever read. It was taken from a novel by Alberto Vázquez Figueroa, and the entire script was, much like the novel, written as a diary. So the whole thing was voice-over; there is no dialogue. It was just unbelievable, so unprofessional you can't believe it. Again I was allowed to hire not one but two writers, and I was the third writer.

WWD: You hired Steven Gaydos and David M. Zehr as additional writers?

MH: Yes. I wound up being the third writer because I went to Cannes again; and while I was there, David and Steve wrote essentially two different scripts. I kind of put them together and did a lot of writing of my own.

WWD: How did you get involved with the splatter film *Silent Night, Deadly Night 3: Better Watch Out!* [1989]? And is that your daughter in it?

MH: Yes, that's my daughter Melissa as Dr. Newbury's assistant. She was also in *Two-Lane Blacktop*, in a small role, when she was much younger. One of my best friends was producing it, Arthur Gorson, and he asked me to do it, and

I said no. Once again, the script was no good. But finally I said, "Well, if we can throw the script out, I'll do it." And so we rewrote the script in, I guess, a week.

WWD: How long did you take to shoot it?

MH: It was a good schedule. We had twenty-three days and something like $800,000.

WWD: Genre films cost a lot more than they did in 1960.

MH: Hmm hmm.

WWD: You appeared as yourself in Wim Wenders's *Chambre 666* [1982], a film that Wenders made during the 1982 Cannes Film Festival, in which he asked a number of directors for their thoughts on the future of film. Quite a cast: Michelangelo Antonioni, Jonathan Demme, Rainer Werner Fassbinder, Jean-Luc Godard, Yilmaz Güney, Werner Herzog, Susan Seidelman, Steven Spielberg, and you, to name just a few of the many filmmakers who were interviewed. Wenders set up a camera in a hotel room and asked everybody where they thought the future of film was headed. Can you talk a little bit about that experience?

MH: Well, it was a *horrifying* experience. He turns the camera on, and then he leaves the room and leaves you sitting there, and you got to talk to a wall! It was terrible, just terrible.

WWD: Did you ever see the finished film?

MH: I don't think I did.

WWD: You know what Jean-Luc Godard did in the film? Wenders turned on the camera, as you know, and left the room. Godard talked for a while, stared at the camera for a bit more, then got up, walked toward the camera, and turned it off. And that was that.

MH: That's great. I should have done that.

WWD: How did you wind up working as second unit director on *RoboCop* [1987]?

MH: Well, Mike Medavoy, who was the head of the studio [Orion], wanted me to direct it; but Jon Davidson, who was an old friend of mine and a fan, felt that I was not an action director, and he wanted somebody else to do it. And then [Paul] Verhoeven was hired, and it got behind schedule; so, ironically, I was brought in to direct a lot of the action.

WWD: Even though you didn't want to direct *The Christian Licorice Store* [1971], you wound up appearing as an actor in the film, as Joseph, a very small part. Why did you do that?

MH: Oh—

WWD: Just a nice gesture?

MH: Yes, it was for the same producer, Michael Laughlin, and he asked me to do it. They had cast [legendary French director] Jean Renoir for the role.

WWD: Right.

MH: He did one of his two scenes, and then he became ill and wasn't able to finish it. So I was really playing the thin version of Jean Renoir! [*Laughs.*]

WWD: You're listed as executive producer on Quentin Tarantino's *Reservoir Dogs* [1992]. How did that come about?

MH: Again, I was asked to direct the picture, and they set up a meeting between me and Quentin, and we met. But the day that we met, Quentin sold his script for *True Romance* [made into a film by Tony Scott in 1993]. So he said, "Now I have the money to hold out to direct *Reservoir Dogs*, which is what I really want to do." Quentin said he was sorry that he had wasted my time; but by the time we finished our hot fudge sundaes, he asked me if I would help him get the picture made. So I sent the script of *Reservoir Dogs* to Richard Gladstein, who had been the executive at Live Entertainment when we did *Silent Night*. Richard loved it and agreed to do it if I would kind of stand behind Quentin and kind of guarantee that he would finish on time and on schedule. Which he did. He did a great job.

WWD: What about Vincent Gallo's *Buffalo '66*? You get a "thanks." [*Both laugh.*] Thanks, Monte!

MH: I know. I set it up for me to direct, and Vincent Gallo was unhappy with the deal, because the producers had this strange idea of wanting to wait for snow. And Vincent wanted to shoot the film on reversal [as opposed to negative] film, and the whole thing got very complicated.

WWD: The producers wanted to wait for it to *snow*?

MH: Yes. The studio wanted to wait for snow, and Vincent wanted to shoot right away, so he decided to direct it himself.

WWD: You edited *The Killing Box* [1993], which was directed by George Hickenlooper. This is a really odd movie, mixing voodoo with Confederate soldiers during the Civil War.

MH: I have the dubious distinction of having been the editor on it, yes.

WWD: But you had no real connection to the material?

MH: That's right.

WWD: What about the films that you didn't get to make, projects you wanted to get off the ground but never were able to?

MH: Well, I'm still working on most of them. One of them is a picture called *Dark Passion*, which Bert Schneider hired me to direct at Paramount about twenty years ago. *Dark Passion* has been called by Oliver Stone and a number of other people the best unproduced screenplay in Hollywood.

WWD: Could you briefly tell me what it's about?

MH: It's from a novel by Lionel White. Lionel White wrote the novel [*Clean Break*] that was the source material for Stanley Kubrick's *The Killing* [1956]. Lionel knew that Kubrick was doing *Lolita* [1962] and was campaigning to be the screenwriter. But Kubrick decided not to hire him as the screenwriter.

And so, as a kind of revenge, Lionel wrote this book, which was kind of his take on *Lolita.*

WWD: What do you think your chances are of getting this thing off the ground?

MH: Well, it's complicated, because there's about $3 million invested in it so far. Paramount owns the underlying rights now. So it's all dependent on casting. I have an idea of somebody I want to do it, and I'm talking to powers that be, trying to get it set up.

WWD: Looking back over your career, what do you think of your past work?

MH: Well, I think the thing that gives me the greatest satisfaction is the fact that there are some filmmakers who say, whether it's true or not, that they were inspired to make movies because of *Two-Lane Blacktop.* And so I really feel, as Peckinpah would say, "justified."

ROBERT DOWNEY SR.

On March 3, 2001, I had the opportunity to talk once again with Robert Downey Sr., a gifted filmmaker and the father of actor Robert Downey Jr. I first met Robert during the spring of 1969, when his film *Putney Swope* (1969) was a breakout hit and he was finishing up post-production on *Pound* (1970), a film that unhappily never received the attention or distribution it deserved. I was working as a writer for *Life* magazine at the time, covering what was then dubiously termed "underground cinema." Unlike some other filmmakers I interviewed, Downey welcomed me into his cutting room with true generosity of spirit, and we spoke for at least two hours of his plans for the future, which at that point were pretty much up in the air. Now, some thirty years later, Downey has amassed a deeply personal body of work, despite a hiatus of nearly ten years, when, by his own admission, he was unable to work due to a combination of drugs and alcohol. Clean since 1982, Downey has come back with such superb films as the memorably hallucinatory and yet still profoundly human *Hugo Pool* (1997).

Although we hadn't spoken in some three decades, Bob Downey was immediately "there" for me and answered my questions directly and honestly, without any pretension or evasiveness. In addition, Downey has fully embraced the new digital filmmaking technology and seems equally at home using both conventional and cutting-edge methods of production. In 2005 he directed the elegiac and deeply moving documentary feature film *Rittenhouse Square*, which chronicles one year in the life of an urban Philadelphia park and was shot entirely on video. The film is quiet, gentle, and a complete change from the "sawed-off shotgun" approach of his earlier films. During a follow-up phone call on August 28, 2006, Downey told me he has another new project in the works: a sequel to *Putney Swope*, with a several A list stars attached. So it seems he hasn't abandoned his renegade past altogether. One can only wish the best for Robert Downey Sr. He is a true survivor and a true independent, one of the last of the sixties mavericks who continues to redefine the American cinema.

For this interview, Downey spoke with me by telephone from his home in Manhattan.

WHEELER WINSTON DIXON: Hello, Bob, it's me.

ROBERT DOWNEY SR.: Hey man, how you doing?

WWD: I hope I'm not *too* punctual.

RD: No, you are. That's good. What do you want to know?

WWD: Well, for a start, when and where were you born, and what can you remember about your early life?

RD: I was born June 24, 1936, in New York City. My mother was a model for magazines and stuff; she was one of the twelve Powers [a famous modeling agency] models in the beginning. She was quite famous. My father did a lot of things, mainly motel management, restaurant management. My main interest when I was a kid was baseball. That's it. Boxing.

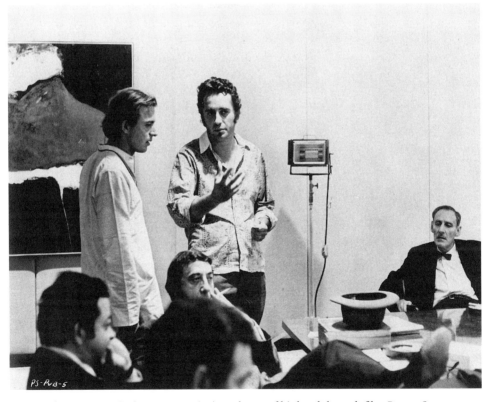

Robert Downey Sr. (center, gesturing) on the set of his breakthrough film *Putney Swope* (1969). Courtesy Jerry Ohlinger Archives.

WWD: Was it during this period that you acquired what I might call the "cheerfully nihilistic" view of such films as *Putney Swope* [1969] and *Greaser's Palace* [1972]?

RD: I can't analyze that. I don't know the answer to that, when, or if . . . I don't look at my stuff that way.

WWD: Well, how do you look at it?

RD: Most of it, I'm bored by. You know what I'm saying? So how can I even go try to figure it out if I'm bored by it?

WWD: Been there, done that?

RD: No, I'm just changing the way I do things and my writing, and leaning more toward documentaries. That's the new stuff I'm doing now.

WWD: You dropped out of high school. Why'd you do that?

RD: Well, let me see. I think I ran into geometry or something. And I just knew that it was something I wasn't interested in and that you had to pay attention, so I was happy to get out. And I joined the army.

WWD: What did you do in the army?

RD: Served a lot of time in the stockade for being a drunk.

WWD (*laughs*): So did you get an honorable or a dishonorable discharge?

RD (*laughs*): Bad conduct, three years later. Then for one summer I was a pitcher in semi-pro baseball. It was in Pennsylvania. I forget the name of the team, but it was in Brookline, Pennsylvania, near Pittsburgh.

WWD: Were you any good?

RD: Yeah!

WWD: You still like to do that from time to time, just go out and pitch a few balls?

RD (*laughs*): Well, I just went to the gym the other day for the first time in forty years, and I'm still hurting. So I guess that's behind me.

WWD: What drew you into filmmaking from this background?

RD: Well, my first inspiration . . . When I was in the army, I was in the stockade, and one of the guys who ran the stockade gave me a notebook and a pen and said, "When you have nothing to do, maybe you can amuse yourself." So I started writing. And when I got out, I wrote a little bit, and I was an off-off-off Broadway playwright. And when one of my plays was done, this fellow I was working with said, "Look, we can make a movie." I said, "How can we do that?" And he said, "I have a camera and you have a script, so let's just do it." Simple.

WWD: What was the play you were doing?

RD: It was called something like *What Else Is There?* The actors played missiles, in silos, ready to go off. It was kinda wild, pretty ahead of its time. The guy with the camera was William Waering, who later photographed *Babo 73* [1964] for me.

WWD: I almost hate to ask this question, but when you started making films, did you have any idols, anyone you admired as a filmmaker out there?

RD: Well, I was beginning to pay attention to [Federico] Fellini, and Bill [Waering] turned me on to Preston Sturges. Those were my two main influences at that point.

WWD: Was this first film *Balls Bluff* [1963]?

RD: Yeah. It was silent, about thirty minutes long. It was about a Union Civil War soldier who wakes up in the twentieth century in New York City. I had to play the soldier, because the actor kept quitting. It was OK for a first film.

WWD: And then *Babo 73* came out of that.

RD: Yeah. Taylor Mead [the legendary underground film actor] was our leading guy. He played the President of the United Status. And Tom O'Horgan, who later went on to do *Hair*, did the music. That was shot in 16mm, and we just basically went down to the White House and started shooting, with no press passes, permits, anything like that. Kennedy was in Europe, so nobody was too tight with the security. We were outside the White House mainly, ran around. We actually threw Taylor in with some real generals, and they of course were appalled by what we were trying to do. It was an hour long; the budget was about $3,000.

WWD: And then you jump straight into sexploitation with *The Sweet Smell of Sex* [1965], which was pretty much a Forty-second Street type of movie, which you directed for someone else.

RD: Yeah. Barnard L. Sackett offered me that. He produced it, and I directed it. I needed a payday to do what was considered kind of a porno film, but it really wasn't. We made a film that was a satire of that; it was funny. It was fun to do. I had to write, direct, and deliver the film in a week. But when Sackett saw it, he wasn't too happy. It wasn't porno enough for him. It was shot on 16mm and then blown up to 35mm. And it played on Forty-second Street and places like that. I actually did *Sweet Smell of Sex* to pay for the birth of my son [actor Robert Downey Jr.], because when my daughter was born, it was tough, in Bellevue; because of the film, I was able to put his mother [Elsie Downey] in a decent hospital, and that's what that was really about. I didn't mind doing it fast, either.

WWD: Now we come to *Chafed Elbows* [1966], which was your first substantial underground hit. That played at the Gate Theatre for months and got reviews in the *New York Post*, the *Times* . . . even Bosley Crowther liked it.

RD: Yeah, that was kind of amazing. We shot it in 16mm and 35mm for $25,000, and my first wife, Elsie, played all the women characters in the film. The live action I shot in 16mm. But it was mostly stills, and we photographed the stills on an Oxberry Animation bench in 35mm. The whole thing was in black and white; but just like *Babo*, there was one color sequence when the lead character, Walter Dinsmore [George Morgan], goes to heaven. Then we blew the whole thing up to 35mm. It was about a guy who married his mother, and then they go on welfare. It was kind of a musical.

wwd: I remember the last line: "I don't want to spend the rest of my life on welfare . . . but it's a start." Great stuff.

rd (*laughs*): Yeah, we had a lot of fun making that film. Anything seemed possible back then.

wwd: Were you consciously trying to break away from the "underground" film scene and go into commercial theatricals at this point?

rd: Not really. I never really analyzed it that way. I mean, I was happy to have anything shown.

wwd: *No More Excuses* (1968) follows this. You used sections of *Balls Bluff* in that film, am I right?

rd: Well, actually what I did was take five little shorts that I'd worked on, five little things, and intercut them all.

wwd: That seemed pretty much designed to come up with some product quickly. I remember it had a guy in it, Alan Abel, who was pretty much a

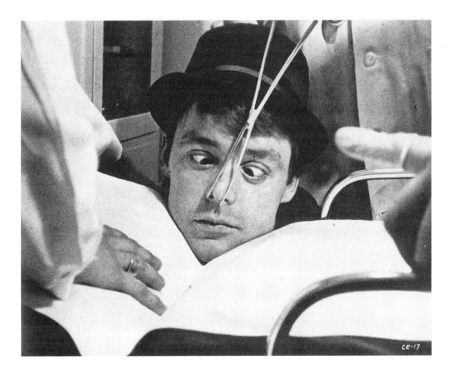

George Morgan as the hapless sad sack Walter Dinsmore in Robert Downey Sr.'s black comedy *Chafed Elbows* (1966). Courtesy Jerry Ohlinger Archives.

professional prankster, posing as an outraged citizen, protesting that all animals should wear clothing, otherwise it was indecent exposure.

RD: That's right. [*Pause.*] How do you *know* all this?

WWD: Well, actually, one of the times we met was at Douglass College in New
Jersey in the late 1960s, when I ran the film for a student group and you were
the guest speaker. At first you tried to pass him off as "a very sick guy" to play
along with gag, but later you copped to it.

RD: You've got a good memory.

WWD: Now we get to *Putney Swope*.

RD: That was my first film in 35mm. That was put together by a company called
Cinema V. The budget was $250,000. It was the first time I had a shot at
something that was really going to get major distribution. Donald Rugoff
put the whole thing together.

WWD: The plot revolves around Putney Swope, the "token African American"
on the board of directors of a huge New York advertising agency, who is
accidentally elected the new head of the agency when the chairman dies of

Robert Downey Sr. (extreme left, foreground) sets up a shot with Laura Greene (hands
on hips) on location for *Putney Swope* (1969). Courtesy Jerry Ohlinger Archives.

Arnold Johnson (extreme left) confronts a foul-mouthed young critic of his advertising methods in Robert Downey Sr.'s *Putney Swope* (1969), as a nun (Marie Claire) looks on. Courtesy Jerry Ohlinger Archives.

a stroke in the middle of a pitch meeting. What interested me in that film is that everyone is corrupt. As soon as Putney is voted in, he begins stealing everyone's ideas, starting with using Nathan [Stan Gottlieb], the token white guy, to pitch an advertising idea for the "Get Outa Here Mousetrap" to electronics mogul Wing Soney, and then immediately firing Nathan when the pitch is successful. By the end of the film, Putney is completely selling out, pushing war toys, the Borman Six [a huge gas-guzzling car], and even marrying a woman he doesn't like just to get ideas from her for ads. Are you saying that everyone is equally rotten and on the take?

RD: I should hope so! [*Laughs.*] That's what I was saying. How else could it be?

WWD: You dubbed Putney's voice yourself. Why?

RD: Arnold [Johnson, the actor who played Putney] never learned his lines. He couldn't. He just didn't, he couldn't. So the cameraman [Gerald Cotts] one night said to me . . . he knew I was upset . . . I said, "Jesus, I can't make any fucking sense out of this," and he said, "Well, look through here." And I looked through the viewfinder. He said, "You see that beard moving?" I said, "Yeah." And he said, "You can put *anything* in there. Including what you *wrote*. But you gotta do it later. Don't waste your energy now getting upset." So I would come in every night—we shot most of the film at night—and [Arnold] would say, "I've got the lines." And I would say, "Oh, good." And then I knew he didn't. He would get pieces of it. But we just kept shooting after that, and then I dubbed the whole thing in later. But it was my voice all the way through. It had to be. It sounded like it was coming from Canada [because it was so obviously dubbed in].

WWD: Where did you get into what I call "repetition humor" in your films? You take certain gags and use them over and over again, essentially running them

A leather-clad advertising specialist addresses the advertising agency's board of directors in *Putney Swope* (1969). Courtesy Jerry Ohlinger Archives.

into the ground, until they stop being funny; and then, after a while, the gags start being funny again because they simply won't quit. When the ad agency executive in *Putney Swope* dies of a stuttering stroke in mid-sentence, the other board members at first think he's playing charades; and even after he's clearly dead, one of his acolytes [Joe Madden] keeps shouting endlessly, "How many syllables, Mario?" Later in the film, when Putney is trying to come up with an angle for the Borman Six ads, one of his assistants repeatedly admonishes the other staff members that "Putney says the Borman Six girl has got to have *soul*!" And in *Greaser's Palace*, Allan Arbus's Christ character continually asks, "What's going *down* here?" for no discernible reason at all. So what *is* going down here?

RD: I don't even think about it as repetition humor. It was just the moment. I just wanted to hang on to the moment and stretch it out as long as possible. But that's a good name for it.

WWD: Another example in *Greaser's Palace* is the card sharp [Ronald Nealy] who tells Vernon Greaser [James Antonio] to "pick a card, any card . . . don't show it to me . . . now put it back in the deck. Is this the card?" Greaser replies, "No." "Is this the card?" "No." And on and on and on, all during a long tracking shot in the desert, for at least five minutes.

RD: Well, that's based on a real thing that happened, where somebody did a real card trick and kept asking, "Is this the card?" and it was always the wrong card. I was with the guy who ended up doing that; he was the line producer of the movie. So we put a coat on him and said, "Let's do it again." The thing was, he kept trying that trick on us, and he never *could* find the fucking card. [*Laughs.*]

WWD: You used a lot of dwarfs in your early films, like President Mimeo and the First Lady in *Putney Swope* [Pepi and Ruth Hermine] and Hervé Ville-chaize in *Greaser's Palace*. Why?

RD: First of all, in *Putney Swope*, it was written that the President of the United States *should* be a midget, for obvious reasons. The tough part was, this one guy showed up with five midgets—it was a family of them, and he was their manager. And we had to pick the husband and wife, so we picked them, and then they turned out to be brother and sister. So it made it twice as funny. But they were lovely people.

WWD: When *Putney Swope* opened in New York at the Cinema II theater, I remember that the guy who played a flasher in the film would appear in the lobby at the end of each performance, clad only in a raincoat and shoes, pre-tending to flash the exiting patrons.

RD: That was a great piece of street theater. That was Rugoff's idea.

WWD: *Putney Swope* was your biggest hit to date and really broke through for you nationally. At that point, it seemed like you could get funded for anything.

RD: You're right. *Chafed Elbows* never left New York, except for one time it played in Boston and got banned. It was playing on a double bill with *Scorpio Rising* [Kenneth Anger, 1964]. *Putney Swope* got real distribution; it was a big hit, particularly when you consider how little it cost.

WWD: But you followed up *Putney Swope* with *Pound* [1970], which is essentially about a bunch of dogs, played by human beings without any makeup, waiting in the pound to be either adopted or put to sleep. Not exactly an upbeat subject.

RD: Well, the irony of that one is that, when I turned it in to United Artists, the head of the studio said, "I thought this was gonna be animated."

WWD: Oh, no!

RD: Oh, yeah, which I though was hilarious. Then they finally put it out on the

Left to right: Ruth Hermine (as First Lady Mimeo, back to camera), Lawrence Wolf (as Mr. Borman Six), and Pepi Hermine (as President Mimeo of the United States) plot to undermine the U.S. economy in Robert Downey Sr.'s *Putney Swope* (1969). Courtesy Jerry Ohlinger Archives.

bottom half of a double bill with *Satyricon* [Fellini, 1969], which was all right with me. That's good company, at least.

WWD: That's where I first met you, in the cutting rooms on Fifty-fifth Street, I think, in New York, [producer] Floyd Peterson's place, when you were cutting *Pound*. I remember you explained the whole idea to me, and it was very clear what you were doing.

RD: Yeah, but they didn't pay attention; nobody read anything. The same thing happened with *Sticks and Bones* [1972], when I did that with Joe Papp [Downey's adaptation with theater producer Papp of David Rabe's antiwar stage play as a television movie for CBS]. Nobody paid attention to the script.

WWD: With *Pound, Putney, Chafed Elbows*, you're still pretty much working with New York actors, the whole New York theater group, right?

RD: Yeah, absolutely.

WWD: And *Pound* was Robert Jr.'s debut as an actor.

RD: That's right; it was his first film.

WWD: How did *Greaser's Palace* come about? With *Greaser's Palace*, you had a much larger budget. Where was it shot?

RD: It cost about $800,000; it was shot in New Mexico.

WWD: So what made you want to tackle a Western?

RD: Cyma Rubin came to me and said, "What do you want to do next?" And I said, "Well, I have this thought about Christ coming back in a Western." And she said, "I'll finance that," and she did, the whole budget. When the film was completed, she gave it to Cinema V to distribute; [Donald Rugoff, head of Cinema V] didn't give her any money for it, but he took it over and put it in theaters and ran this huge ad in the *Village Voice* for the film, with one letter per full page, spelling out G R E A S E R S P A L A C E. Pretty amazing. You couldn't miss that.

WWD: *Greaser's Palace* deals with the exploits of Jessy [Alan Arbus], who appears in the wilderness as Christ, and his interactions with Vernon Greaser [James Antonio], a corrupt land baron, and his band of cutthroats, who hold court at Greaser's Palace, a local saloon. Vernon runs the town with an iron hand; anyone who commits even the most minor infraction is shot to death by Vernon or his hired guns. The entire film takes place in a desolate wasteland, punctuated only by the small town where Vernon reigns as a virtual king. The film opens up with Vernon's wife, Cholero Greaser [Luana Anders], singing a dirgelike song praising virginity and condemning adultery, which her husband, Vernon Greaser, loudly applauds. What's up there?

RD: I did that basically to show that she can do whatever she wants. She's the only woman for a hundred miles, other than the Indian Girl [Toni Basil]. And that's what she does every day: she sings that song, and these same guys [Greaser's henchmen] applaud her every day. And she sings the same song the next day, and the whole thing keeps repeating itself. That's what I get out of it.

WWD: Jessy does a few pathetic miracle—walking on water, healing people with the phrase "if you feel, you're healed"—but then wants to avoid his ultimate crucifixion. He also keeps telling everyone he's working for "the Agent Morris." Christ is just a confused showman? When he finally does his song-and-dance routine for Vernon and his boys, dressed in a zoot suit, no one is impressed until he displays stigmata on his hands. Do you see Christ as a confused showman?

RD: That's absolutely right.

WWD: The Holy Ghost [Ronald Nealy, who also plays the ineffectual cardsharp described earlier] is shown as a guy in a derby and a white sheet; and poor old Lamy "Homo" Greaser, Vernon's son [Michael Sullivan], keeps getting killed over and over again. What's going on there?

RD: Well, Lamy's also, in a way, the son of God. He gets raised from the dead again and again, only to be killed by his father over and over. And then there's the final father-and-son bonding scene, where Vernon finally accepts Lamy and tells him, "You're not a homo; you're a Greaser." It's their big moment.

WWD: A particularly sick running gag in the film involves a family crossing the desert so that the wife [Elsie Downey] can audition as a dance hall singer for Vernon Greaser. When her husband and son [Robert Downey Jr.] get killed, she has to bury the two corpses on her own. Then, for the rest of the film, we keep cutting back to her "progress" as she continues toward her dubious goal, despite getting blasted with a shotgun and hit with a bow and arrow *twice* in the same place on her body. Does this mean that life is going to kick you in the teeth no matter what?

RD: Absolutely. She's Job. It's all pretty straightforward.

WWD: How long did it take to shoot *Greaser's Palace*?

RD: It took six, seven weeks to shoot, and it was a lot of fun to do, because I'd never been outdoors that much before, with such beautiful light for shooting. We shot a lot of it with natural light, and we used as much of the desert as we could. It was a whole new experience for me. Yeah, it was a lot of fun to shoot.

WWD: But it wasn't a hit.

RD: I don't think so. But through the years it's become quite a cult favorite. And Joe Papp saw it, liked it, and that led to my next job.

WWD: Tell me about *Sticks and Bones* [1972], your next project. This was a change, because it was made for television.

RD: Joe Papp saw *Greaser's Palace* and offered me *Sticks and Bones*. It was based on David Rabe's play [about a young disabled Vietnam veteran], which I really liked, and I said, "Sure, I'll do it." We shot it on two-inch tape, which was then the standard. But we transferred the whole thing to film, cut it on film, and then transferred it back to tape for broadcast, so we could cut it in a way that was more fun than just having to wade through those rolls of tape. Two-inch was completely primitive at the time, so we used a KEM [a European flatbed film editor] to cut the thing and then conformed it back to two-inch. And we mixed on film, too.

wwd: Were you happy with the end quality?

rd: Yeah! I liked it. And I liked that there were no commercials for two hours. It was on CBS, and when they first saw it, they panicked. They couldn't get anybody to buy any commercials, so it went out commercial-free. It was great. I was happy to work with Joe Papp, have some fun, and make David Rabe happy, because I'd never been able to do anybody else's stuff, then or since then, you know? I always do my own scripts better. David was always there, on the set, and we didn't change any of his stuff; we just took an hour out of the play. We had a pretty good schedule for that: five weeks. CBS financed it because they thought, "If it's Joe Papp, it's gonna be Shakespeare." [Papp was famous for his "Shakespeare in the Park" series in New York's Central Park each summer.] And they didn't even bother to read the thing. They didn't know what it was. And then when they saw it, they panicked.

wwd: Then there's a huge gap in your filmography, between 1972 and 1980. Other than writing for *The Gong Show Movie* [1980], what did you do?

rd: I worked on something called *Jive* [never completed], which was a black-and-white film that went to Telluride, and I was a mess on drugs. In the seventies, I was a mess. Not heroin, but a lot of coke and pot. It was a disaster. Coke is such a waste of time.

wwd: And so when we get to *Up the Academy* [1980], a rather lame satire on militaristic boarding schools, that doesn't seem like it's you at all.

rd: No, it's not. I was called in to do that, and I said, "The best way to do that is to have these kids be nine and ten years old." They said, "We can't do that." I said, "Why?" They said, "You can't work kids all day." And I said, "Well, then, work them *half* a day. But don't use fifteen- and sixteen-year-olds, because it's not going to work." And they basically said, "If you don't like it, you can get the fuck out of here." No, I'm not really involved in the film at all . . . you're right about that.

wwd: You did some *Twilight Zone* episodes in the 1980s, when the show was briefly revived on CBS.

rd: Yeah, I rather enjoyed those. One was called "Tooth and Consequences." It was about a paranoid Jewish dentist who has a visit from the tooth fairy, and he can't believe it. It winds up with the dentist on a train to nowhere with a lot of other dentists; it's kinda weird. "Children's Zoo" was about a little girl who was so tired of her parents she wound up putting them in a zoo. These were short pieces, very short; one was ten minutes, and the other was maybe twelve. Then about 1980 I began to climb out of the whole drug thing, and I got sober in 1982, and I've been that way ever since.

WWD: The next credit I have for you is *America* [shot in the early 1980s; released in 1986]. It had a great cast—Zack Norman, Tammy Grimes, Michael J. Pollard, Richard Belzer, and a lot of other ensemble actors—and centered on the crew of a wacky cable television station in New York that accidentally bounces its signal off the moon, thus gaining international fame. But it didn't really work, I don't think.

RD: It was shot and shelved for a long time. That was horrible. It was the end of the drugs. It wasn't a failure on every level, and there were some good things in it, but it never really focused.

WWD: *Rented Lips* followed in 1988. Again, an enormous cast: Martin Mull, Dick Shawn, Jennifer Tilly, Robert Downey Jr., June Lockhart, Eileen Brennan, Shelley Berman, a host of others. It's a remarkably twisted film about two industrial filmmakers [Mull and Shawn] who get tricked into directing a porn film by their crooked boss [Berman]. The two hapless filmmakers go from producing such films as *Aluminum, Our Shiny Friend* to making Nazi-themed porn films for hire. Were you happy with this movie?

RD: That was Martin Mull's film, really. I was just the filmmaker on it. It was all right; it had a couple of moments. But it was always fun to work with Robert on any project. When we work together, he more or less comes up with characterizations, and then we kick it around a bit, and then we shoot it. That's it.

WWD: *Too Much Sun* [1991] was another ensemble film with a huge cast: Allan Arbus, Howard Duff, Eric Idle, Ralph Macchio, James Hong, and Andrea Martin, to name just a few. The plot is typically twisted: a brother and sister compete to see who can have a child first in order to inherit a fortune from their father. However, the son is gay, and the daughter is lesbian, so this complicates matters. Are you happy with the film?

RD: That was kinda fun. That was somebody else's script, which I wrote a screenplay out of. It was OK, and it was fun to work with Eric Idle and James Hong. It was all right; it didn't really come together as a whole.

WWD: *Hugo Pool* [1997] is your most recent feature to date, a very beautiful film, with an unusually relaxed and mellow feel to it. The plot is more straightforward than some of your films of the late eighties and early nineties: a young woman, Hugo Dugay [Alyssa Milano], has to clean forty-five pools in one day while putting up with her coked-out, alcoholic father [Malcolm McDowell] and her gambling addict mother [Cathy Moriarty]. It's a day-in-the-life film. There are the usual star-studded cameos: Robert Downey Jr., Sean Penn, Chuck Barris, Michael Lewis, Ann Magnuson, and many others.

But the real focus of the film is the relationship between Hugo and Floyd Gaylen [Patrick Dempsey], who is afflicted with ALS [amyotrophic lateral sclerosis]. What's going on with this film, which seems more about human relationships than your previous work?

RD: *Hugo Pool* came out of a real experience, because my second wife, Laura Ernst, had ALS, and she died of it. We wrote that while she was ill. Actually, I'm doing some ALS films now, which I enjoy, documentaries and films for patients.

WWD: How did you get the funding for such a personal film, not to mention the services of Sean Penn as an actor, who would much rather direct these days?

RD: Sean Penn was very easy to work with. When Hal Ashby, who was my best friend, was dying, a friend of both of ours gave Sean a couple of my films; and I guess he liked them, because when I called and asked him to do this, he said, "Let me read it." And then he called up and said, "I like this little part. I'll be there." It was because of him it got [funded]. He worked on it for a week, mostly with Malcolm McDowell, as a hitchhiker who's obsessed with his shoes. He was an absolute gentleman to work with.

WWD: The thing that stays with me is that the film seems less narrative-focused than people-focused. It's not so much interested in what will happen next, as 99 percent of Hollywood movies are today, but rather how people will interact with each other.

RD: Well, I wouldn't know a narrative if I saw one. And that's a good thing. You know a film I saw recently that's really good, a really good relationship film? *Last Resort* [Paul Pavlikovsky, 2000]. I also liked *Croupier* [Mike Hodges, 1999]. I just saw *Last Resort* yesterday; it's refreshing to see a good film. There are really so few good films these days; it used to be there were always one or two.

WWD: In the meantime, you've also carved out a second career for yourself as an actor, in such films as *The Family Man* [2000], *Magnolia* [1999], *Boogie Nights* [1997], *To Live and Die in L.A.* [1985], and other films. How did this come about? What do you think of your work as an actor?

RD: I'm not really an actor. It's just that guys like Paul Thomas Anderson and Brett Ratner like films and want me to show up. But I can't learn lines or anything; this is all just improvisational stuff. I just show up, do it, and I'm gone.

WWD: When you look back on all the work you did in 16mm and 35mm, the technology probably seems very clumsy compared with the digital stuff you're doing now. You've told me that you embrace the new digital technology. Why, and what kind of work are you doing with it? How is it a departure from your earlier work?

RD: What I like about the digital technology is that people, especially if you're doing documentary stuff, don't even know you're there, even though you're with them. They don't think of it as a movie, so they're totally real. We use a Sony digital camera for a lot of stuff, and we just helped out a guy in Philadelphia who was shooting some stuff on high-def [high definition] of the Mummers on New Year's Day. Even high-def technology is still so unobtrusive. The key to digital filmmaking is, you gotta pay attention to the sound; you can't use that mike that sticks out of the camera. You either gotta get a boom man, with a DAT [digital audio tape] recorder, or at least stick the plug into the camera and just hold up a mike! I just use the mike in the camera as a second mike, to pick up background. But most people think, when they start out, you can just use the mike on the camera.

WWD: What's next?

RD: Well, I'm doing a lot of the ALS stuff, and I'm working on a new script, which I'm very happy with. It's just about done, and Jonathan Demme is going to produce it. It's called *Forest Hills Bob*. I don't want to tell you about it, except that I'm very happy with it, and Philip Seymour Hoffman and Blythe Danner have both agreed to be in it. This is my favorite one, because it's totally real. I don't have a dime yet, though. I've just had two readings, and Jonathan and his partner are trying to get me the money; but I'm about a month away from finishing the next draft. On this one I'm going through a *lot* of drafts. In the past, I've been a little bit lazy, I think. But this one is really good. As Godard said, "A film has a beginning, a middle, and an end, but not necessarily in that order." And I've finally figured out the order on this thing, and I'm really excited about a project for the first time in years.

WWD: I love Philip Seymour Hoffman. He was the best thing in *The Talented Mr. Ripley* [Anthony Minghella, 1999], the rather indifferent remake of *Purple Noon* [René Clément, 1960].

RD: You know, I wanted to do that ten years ago with Robert Jr. I took the book around, and people said, "Are you crazy?" And they didn't do it right. It was supposed to be really frightening, and they made it too cute. Philip Seymour Hoffman is also a wonderful stage director, you know. I've seen two plays he's done in the last year, and they're both great.

WWD: Speaking of digital movies, have you seen *Celebration* [Thomas Vinterberg, 1998]?

RD: Of course! I love it.

WWD: What did you think of James Toback's *Black and White* [2000]?

RD: It was all right. I thought the scenes with my kid and Mike Tyson were great.

WWD: When you look back on your body of work as a whole, what do you think?

RD: They're OK. It's odd, thinking about them. I have to lecture tomorrow at the School of Visual Arts, and I've had to put together a clip reel to illustrate my talk. I used some ALS clips and a little piece from every film that I could find on tape, and the one that surprised me the most in being better than I thought was *Hugo Pool*. At the time, it didn't have any good distribution. In fact, *Putney Swope*'s the only film of mine that ever had any real distribution. But that's all right. I love the idea of getting them done but not worrying about what happens to them later.

WWD: Let me ask you one final question. You don't have to answer if you don't want to. How do you feel about your son's continuing problems?

RD: He's gonna be fine now. He's on psychiatric medicines for the first time. No, he's gonna be OK now, but it's been scary. When we were kidding around with cocaine in the sixties, nobody thought it was dangerous. There was no shame, and we just did it anywhere, But then when the literature started coming out saying it could kill you . . . my God!

WWD: Well, that about does it for me. Is there anything else you'd like to add?

RD: No, but I just want to say that I think there's hope so long as people keep trying to make good films. The one thing nobody's talking about—and it's easy for me to say because I'm happy with my new script—is that everybody keeps talking about this new technology and that new technology, but nobody talks about whether anything's any good or not, or says anything, in terms of the writing or content. It doesn't matter whether you cut it on an AVID [digital editor] or a Steenbeck [analog editor], or shoot it in film or digital; those are just tools. Without ideas, you're dead. Why not try and do something good instead of trying to get to Hollywood? *Celebration*, for example, is a wonderful movie, and what I like about it is that it's also a wonderful script. I don't know anything about computers, but my third wife, Rosemary, knows all about this stuff, and so I know the stuff is out there. Good films are getting made, but they're just not getting distributed. And that's OK, because then they'll end up on cable.

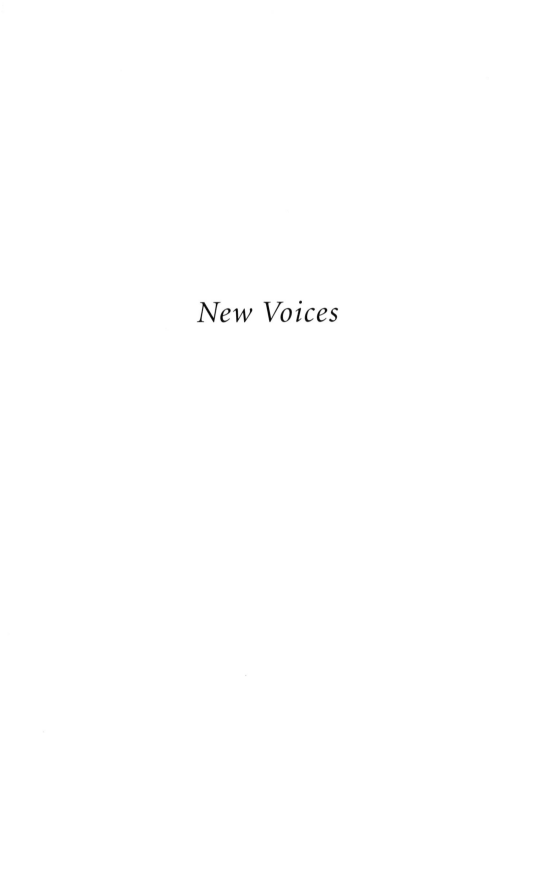

New Voices

TAKASHI SHIMIZU

In the spring of 2004, I traveled to New York to deliver a lecture at Columbia University, visit some old friends, and generally catch up on life in the city where I spent the sixties and seventies, deeply immersed in the culture of the cinema. As luck would have it, the Walter Reade Theatre was screening Takashi Shimizu's supernatural thriller *The Grudge* (2003), the first 35mm version of a project that Shimizu had seen through two previous video incarnations and one additional 35mm version. (It has now been remade as an English-language film, financed by Sam Raimi and distributed through Columbia Pictures.) I had long wanted to see the film, and *The Grudge* surprised me in nearly every way. Although it is a genuinely suspenseful and unnerving exploration into the realm of the supernatural, most of its effects are achieved entirely through suggestion, camera movement, and intercutting for suspense, much like the classic Val Lewton films for RKO in the forties, with appropriate hints of Yasujiro Ozu and Kenji Mizoguchi.

I was deeply curious about the aesthetic that informed the creation of the film. Through a series of friends and intermediaries, and the kindness of Columbia's production offices in Los Angeles, I was able to contact Shimizu. Because he does not speak English, my written questions were translated by members of his staff. Shimizu responded to my queries by dictating his answers into a tape recorder during the production and post-production of the 2004 English-language version of *The Grudge*, which stars Sarah Michelle Gellar, Bill Pullman, and Clea DuVall. Shoichi Gregory Kamei then translated the responses into English to create this completed interview. I want to thank Natalie Johnson, Marisa McGrath, Ian Shive, and most especially Stephanie Phillips of Sony Columbia Pictures for their help in making this interview possible.

As Kamei notes about his translation, "This is not a literal translation of Mr. Shimizu's speech. The goal was to capture the content of what he said and to be as faithful as possible with the spirit in which those words were spoken. However, replicating the tone of someone's speech, especially across languages and cultures, is a very subjective matter. These characteristics should be taken into consideration when reading the translation." Because so little is known about Shimizu's work in the West, I started with some questions about his childhood and family life.

WHEELER WINSTON DIXON: You were born on July 27, 1972, in Maebashi City, Gunma Prefecture, Japan. What do you remember of your childhood life?

TAKASHI SHIMIZU: I was born as the eldest son of a fourth-generation *tatami* [Japanese mat] maker. When I was a child, I watched my father work. I thought the work was interesting, and I intended to succeed him as the fifth generation of my family's business. Then I saw Steven Spielberg's *E.T.* [1982] when I was in the fourth grade, and I was completely captivated. I decided that I wanted a career in filmmaking. I wanted to make my own movies. Until

Takashi Shimizu on the set of his American version of *The Grudge* (2004). Courtesy Columbia Tri-Star.

junior high school, I hardly saw any horror films. I liked reading ghost stories, but I was scared of watching horror films. So I never thought of watching them, even when others recommended them, when I was a child. I was a big coward. I couldn't sleep when the trees rustled or the wind whistled outside my window. I can't believe how nervous and sensitive I was back then.

However, I was very mischievous. I would hide in the closet from my younger brother and sister, then jump out to startle them. I think my interest in making horror films came from the joy I felt in startling or frightening people. When I was in junior high school in the eighties, the splatter horror movie boom hit Japan. A friend of mine invited me to see a movie. At first, I didn't want to go see it, but eventually I went. When I actually saw it, it had some shocking moments, but it wasn't as "scary" as I had imagined. "So, this is what a horror movie is like," I thought. "This might be interesting." I was able to go see many horror films after that. I saw the then-popular films, such as those in the *Nightmare on Elm Street* series and the *Friday the 13th* series. But at that time I couldn't have imagined that I would be making horror films as an adult. Even now I'm surprised.

WWD: What was your home life like?

TS: My family got along very well. This is just as true now. In Japan and in the United States, families sometimes experience divorce or some dark cloud, but my family environment was very cheerful and warm. I am very grateful to my parents for that. They allowed me to pursue my interests. Of course, my father sometimes scolded us or told us to "cut it out," but no more than he would any other child. I had a really good relationship with my siblings and my parents. Even now, when my movies debut, my family, relatives, cousins, siblings, all come to see them. I was reared in a very good family environment. Someday, I would like to make a comedy, family drama, or love story that my family would enjoy.

I mentioned this before, but my father is a *tatami* craftsman. After I saw *E.T.*, I told my younger brother that I had decided on pursuing a career in filmmaking, so I couldn't succeed our father. I asked my brother to succeed our father over and over again when we were young, as if I was trying to brainwash him. He finally succeeded my father in my place as the fifth generation and has carried on the tradition of the Shimizu Tatami Store, which has been in business for over a hundred years now. I am very grateful to him. I am able to do what I like and make movies because he succeeded my father and carried on our family tradition. My mother is very kind, a Japanese mother, a wonderful person. I respect her. If I were ever to have children, I would like to marry a woman who could be a mother like her.

WWD: What schools did you go to as a child? What were your major interests in grade school?

TS: I went to a regular elementary school. I was smaller and shorter than average. I was a bit brash and created a lot of mischief among the kids. My favorite subject in elementary school was art. Throughout elementary school, I got fives [the highest grade] in art. In elementary school and junior high school, my art teachers would ask whether I was interested in pursuing a career in art as a designer or an artist. Later, I learned that this was discussed with my parents at the same time without my knowledge. I was interested in and good at art, whether it was sculpting with clay, carving, or drawing. I enjoyed many movies and books, so I would make up my own stories. There wasn't a class for that. It was my hobby.

I would make my own drawings, create my own stories, and put them together to create my own books when I was a child. I think this distinguished me from others. I would make clay figures of the characters I created and move them around to act out my stories. This may appear gloomy, but I enjoyed my time alone like this. Of course, I played with my friends, and I was a bit cheeky and sometimes a bit rough. Although I was small, I was the boss of the kids. Although I sometimes caused trouble in school, throughout elementary and junior high school I was elected homeroom president each year. I would call everyone together and chair the homeroom meetings. It wasn't that I wanted to be president, but everyone elected me each time. I did it out of obligation at first, but I began to enjoy it and liked getting everyone to work together and follow my lead. It may be that I did not dislike taking leadership. This could be one reason why I like directing.

When I was ten, in the fourth grade, a relative took me to see *E.T.* At first, I didn't know what kind of movie it was. I had heard that a space alien appears in it, so I thought that it might be a scary movie. I was completely captivated and touched by it. I think the way Spielberg was able to "see" and tell a story from the perspective of a ten-year-old boy allowed me to be completely absorbed in the movie. To be able to make a movie like that is my dream, even now. My life in film began with *E.T.* I wondered who wrote this story, who was responsible for making this film. I wanted to be in the position where I could write my own story, shoot the way I wanted, select the actors who fit my vision, supervise it the way I wanted, and be able to say that it was my film. In Japanese movie theaters, a small pamphlet that describes the movie and lists the cast and crew is sold. When I went to see *E.T.*, I received one as a gift. It had "Director, Stephen Spielberg" written on it. I thought, "He's the one, he's the one who made the film. I want to have a job like his." I became attracted to the job of "movie director," and I began thinking about what I needed to do and learn to become one someday. I learned the specific details when I became an adult.

But first, I needed a video camera. I heard that the father of a friend of mine from a wealthy family had bought a video camera. This was during the era when home video cameras first appeared. I asked to borrow it, then shot footage of almost anything, while taking care not to damage the camera. Then I started to wonder why the image quality in movies differed so much. I figured out that movies looked different because they were shot with film. My grandfather had an 8mm film camera. I asked if I could use it. It came out of storage covered in dust. Some parts were broken, but I didn't have the money to fix it. So I jury-rigged some things and got it to work. In this way, I was able to shoot with film. I found I liked the film look much better.

I didn't come into filmmaking thinking that I wanted to make horror films or that it was the only genre I wanted to work in. I think horror films incorporate that aspect of thrills and suspense that attracts and grips the audience. Once I was able to view horror films, I realized that it was quite a difficult task to frighten people. However, what I find interesting is that I never planned to make a horror movie. The opportunity for me to become a director arose when a short horror film assignment attracted the attention of Kyoshi Kurosawa, who's called "the second Kurosawa" in Europe, and Hiroshi Takahashi, the screenwriter of *Ringu* [Hideo Nakata, 1998], who saw it and liked it. I like making horror movies, but I'm reluctant to be called a specialist in the horror genre. I know that some people are too scared to see a horror movie, because I was like that as a child. I would like to make movies that anyone can see and everyone will love, and know that my ability is not limited to making just horror films.

WWD: Who are your favorite horror directors? People like Mario Bava, Lucio Fulci, Masaki Kobayashi? Who was your biggest influence starting out?

TS: This may sound like empty flattery, but the *Evil Dead* [1981] by Sam Raimi, who is the producer of [the newest version of] *The Grudge* [2004], had a strong impact on me. I've probably seen it twenty to thirty times. Others would be George Romero's *Dawn of the Dead* series, Dario Argento's *Suspiria* [1977], and Tobe Hooper's *Texas Chainsaw Massacre* [1974]. The works of many directors, just in the horror genre alone, have influenced me. After a while, I got bored with watching splatter or shock-based horror films, so I sought out Japanese and other horror films that worked in a more subtle way. The first works that captivated me were Stanley Kubrick's *The Shining* [1980] and the remake of *Nosferatu* [1979] directed by Werner Herzog. After that, I started watching classic Japanese horror movies like Toyoda Shirô's *Yotsuya Kaidan* [1966] and those directed by Hideo Nakata and Masaki Kobayashi. I started to watch the films made by my predecessors in the horror genre as classics of the field when I was in college. I studied and came to realize that the culture of Japanese art, ghost stories, and horror stories was different and had its own aesthetic.

While I was doing odd jobs in the filmmaking industry, I saw Nakata's *Ringu* and thought that someone had beaten me to what I wanted to do. I was disappointed. *Ringu* was a big hit, really scary, and a wonderful piece of work. I realized that the same thing wouldn't work or have the same impact again, so I thought about what I should do. I started to work as a director during the height of the popularity of *Ringu*. Taka Ichise, who is one of the producers of *The Grudge*, told me to come up with anything so long as it was scary. I brainstormed and put together ideas that I had. What I ended up with was the video version of *Juon* [the first version of *The Grudge*], which was shot in 2000. For the video version, I only had nine days to shoot both *Juon* and *Juon 2*. The budget was very small. It was a difficult task. In comparison, I had more time with *The Grudge* [2003], which was funded by Americans. However, there were a few cultural differences that presented challenges. In light of all this, I believe that I have been blessed with many opportunities.

WWD: You have stated that you liked the *Friday the 13th* and *Nightmare on Elm Street* films. Yet your own work is so much more sophisticated and subtle than splatter filmmaking. How do you account for this?

TS: It's not that I particularly liked *Friday the 13th* and *Nightmare on Elm Street*, but they were popular when I was in junior high school. I saw many of the movies that were then popular over and over again. It's not that the movies in these series were my all-time favorites. Of course, they influenced me. I wondered why such horror "heroes" [like Freddie Krueger and Jason Voorhees] didn't appear in Japanese films. I was attracted by the characters and was impressed that so many films could be made in those series. If I were to make them, I think that I could make them scarier. This is what I thought, frankly.

WWD: When you're working on the writing of a film, do you have a specific target audience in mind, or are you trying to please yourself?

TS: Both, I think. I want to make movies that I want to see, that I think would be fun to watch. That's always in my mind when I shoot a film. When I'm editing, I think about what kind of audience would want to see it and what kind of audience should see it. I like movies that are made to entertain. Of course, commercial considerations come into play when making movies designed primarily to entertain, because you want as many people as possible to come see the film. So I think about which generation would most want to see this movie. That's in my mind. Plus, there's what I want to do on film. I can't say which I put before the other. Both are in my mind.

WWD: Film is an art and a business, but you seem to have made a success making the films that you like, and they still make money. Did you ever think of making a film for yourself alone?

TS: Frankly, I've never thought of making movies for myself alone. One of the reasons I was attracted to filmmaking was that I wanted to make movies that a lot of people would want to see. When I saw *E.T.*, I thought that everyone would love the film and would want to see it. In that regard, I know that there are those who are afraid to see a horror movie, and I'm now making horror movies. That's a bit disappointing. Without restricting myself to the horror genre, in the future I would like to make movies that more and more people can see.

WWD: What was your first job in the film industry? I have you working in 1998 as an assistant director on film and video productions. But what did you do before that? What were some of your very earliest jobs in film?

TS: I've heard that in the American filmmaking industry there is a distinct position called "assistant director," and the assistant director that I met on the American version of *The Grudge* is such a person. But in Japan, *jokantoku*, assistant director, is a position for someone who is working toward becoming a director. I wanted to become a director, so I tried to get a position as an assistant director and was introduced to people in the industry in that way. However, at first, I couldn't get a position as an assistant director, so I started out in props.

I left college because I wanted to work in film. I went to a film studio in Kyoto on my own and asked if there was any work available. I was told that they had enough people. However, they told me that there was a part-time job at a movie theater associated with the studio. I thought that if it was related to the movies in some way, that would be OK. I took tickets, worked at the refreshment counter, sold movie pamphlets, sold popcorn, did all sorts of things as a part-timer. I did that for a while; I felt comfortable on the job and made many friends. However, I realized that this wasn't what I wanted to do. What I wanted to do was to make movies.

At that time, I heard that [director] Oguri Kôhei, who was born and grew up in Maebashi, Gunma Prefecture, which is also my hometown, was making an art film there. I read in a newspaper article that he was recruiting locals to work as cast and crew on the film. I called and told him that I would do anything he wanted me to do without pay, because I wanted to work on a film. I started doing miscellaneous tasks. I met a lot of people, was introduced to people, and made contacts. I came to Tokyo and worked on props, while telling people that I wanted to work as an assistant director. That opportunity finally came. I worked as an assistant director for three or four years. I was fortunate to become a director in such a short time.

WWD: How did you make the jump to director? I understand that *The Grudge* is really a compilation of a bunch of small three-minute scripts you did for a film class. Can you tell me how this came about?

TS: I worked as an assistant director for a while, and I thought that if I continued working as an assistant director in this way, with the Japanese system being the way it is, I wouldn't ever become a director. I thought about what I needed to do to become a director, and what I needed to grasp and understand in order to make the kinds of movies that I wanted to make. I heard about a seminar being taught by director Kiyoshi Kurosawa and screenwriter Hiroshi Takahashi, whom I've mentioned earlier. It was a ten-month seminar, taught in the evenings. It was attended by a wide variety of people: older ladies and gentlemen, students, as well as many television directors, who sat in on the seminar secretly. I went to this *eiga gijutsu bigaku kouza* [film technique and aesthetics seminar] while working as an assistant director. There were various assignments. For one, I was told to write a script for a three-minute video. For the final assignment, from the script I had written, I was to select a scene that I most wanted people to see and to gather all the equipment, crew, and cast on my own and shoot it. This included sound, editing, everything.

There was a limit to the equipment I had available to me; so I asked around and borrowed equipment. I asked actors who I thought would fit my piece to participate. Kiyoshi Kurosawa and the other instructors who saw it introduced me to others and gave me opportunities to work in the field. That was my break in becoming a director. The actress who played the ghost in that three-minute assignment was Fuji Takako, who plays Kayako in [the 35mm version of] *The Grudge*. I first saw her in a play that an actress friend of mine was performing in. After I saw her, I knew that I wanted her to play the ghost in my film. When I think of it, there are many coincidences between us. Much later, when I read her profile, I learned that we were born in the same year and have the same birthday. The coincidence was almost frightening. Sometimes, I think that fate may have been playing some role in having us meet and work together.

That three-minute assignment was originally a psychological thriller, not a horror piece. Hiroshi Takahashi commented that it was about as good as a late-night [television] drama [or television serial]. I was really disappointed. I didn't want to throw away the idea; I really wanted to work on it and make it better. After much thinking, I came up with the idea of having the mother who was supposed to be dead come back to life, and wondered how that would change the story. I changed that part of the script, and from there, things developed, and I came up with the story that is the basis for [all the films in] *The Grudge* [series]. This is how the basic story of the mother and child ghosts who come back came about.

I didn't have the equipment or the technical know-how to make this three-minute video assignment. I used two home video recording machines at my house to put this film together. The image quality wasn't that great, and noise would get into the audio track. I repeated this process many times to edit this piece. I never imagined that this would provide the opportunity for me to make well-received movies and an American movie, so I feel that I was very lucky.

WWD: Your films use extremely elegant and smooth camera work, and are more interested in the psychology of fear than gore effects. Were you influenced at all, or do you know about, the 1940s RKO films by producer Val Lewton, such as *The Cat People* [1942], *I Walked with a Zombie* [1943], and other moody horror films that seem much like your own work?

TS: I've seen the classic *Cat People* and [Paul Schrader's 1982] remake, which starred Nastassja Kinski, but I don't think they influenced me. I've probably seen them only once. However, I am grateful to be compared with classic films made by my predecessors. As for my "elegant camera work," I'm not sure about that myself since I'm looking at it from my own perspective. Of course, I think many films have influenced me. As for how to make something scary even scarier, when I was a child playing hide and seek, I thought about where to hide and with what timing and what motions I should come out to scare someone. I was fascinated by this and paid a lot of attention to such things from that time on.

WWD: Did Hammer horror films in the 1950s and 1960s, like Terence Fisher's *Horror of Dracula* [1958], Don Sharp's *Kiss of the Vampire* [1963], and other films with Christopher Lee and Peter Cushing, by directors such as Fisher, John Gilling, and Freddie Francis, have an influence on your work?

TS: I viewed these films after I became a director. I heard a lot about how terrific these films were from Hiroshi Takahashi, who recommended me as a director, and Kiyoshi Kurosawa. I got a lot from seeing them, but they haven't influenced directly how I make films.

WWD: What American films being made today do you especially like? Which American directors do you admire most?

TS: Frankly, there are so many that it's hard to choose. What comes immediately to mind is *Jaws* [Spielberg, 1975]. Even now, I think how human drama, fear, thrills, and entertainment all came together so perfectly in that film. Movies like that don't come around often. There are so many good movies and directors. If I praise them all, I'll sound insincere. However, when budgets are considered, frankly, sometimes I wonder why so much money and energy were spent on some productions. But I also make movies, so I understand the power and thought behind making movies. So, frankly, I can't criticize. The American film industry, like those in Europe and Japan, brings in directors from all over the world. Of course, I admired American films, but recently the material is a little wanting. I feel it's the same here. A lot of remakes. Of course, I shouldn't be the one to talk about that!

wwd: Do you admire John Carpenter's film of *The Thing* [1982] or his early
    films, like *Halloween* [1978] and *Assault on Precinct 13* [1976]?

ts: Yes, absolutely. I haven't seen all of John Carpenter's work, but I like very
    much those that I've seen. *The Thing* is wonderful. To take a remake in a new
    direction and have it still come out so well is a real achievement. *Halloween*
    is an American "bloodthirsty killer" film with a horror-hero, isn't it? It cre-
    ated the foundation for this genre. Just the music by itself is great. The most
    prominent feature for me is the scene where the main character, Laurie
    [Strode, played by Jamie Lee Curtis], is looking out from the window of the
    house. When she glances out the window, she catches the starlit shadow of
    Michael Myers, but when she looks again, it's gone. That captures the essence
    of contemporary Japanese horror films, where just the suggestion of the pres-
    ence of a ghost is frightening. American films of that time were the most
    frightening for me.

wwd: What separates your films from the work of many other Asian film-
    makers is your slow, deliberate pace, which seems reminiscent of Ozu, Mizo-
    guchi, or the French filmmaker Robert Bresson. Are any of these filmmakers
    an influence on you?

ts: I think this is a matter of "sense." I like the works of directors Ozu and
    Mizoguchi. I've seen many of them. I believe there is a reason they are con-
    sidered representative of Japanese directors. A deliberate pace is more fright-
    ening; a deliberate pace is more interesting. Simply, I just think that way,
    and I have to believe in it. I have to convey that to the crew and the actors,
    and have them do it that way. I need to get them to trust me, because I
    believe that is the best way. Of course, the works of these directors have influ-
    enced me, but perhaps that happens unconsciously. I like the works of Robert
    Bresson. Whether I should film at a deliberate pace or at a quick pace, I have
    to trust my own sense of that. That is just the way I work. It's difficult to say
    precisely who or what has influenced me.

wwd: Much other Asian filmmaking is extremely violent, using bodily spec-
    tacle to hook the audience or enormous amounts of violence, as in the films
    of Takeshi "Beat" Kitano or the nonstop action of Jackie Chan. This isn't
    your style at all. How did you develop it?

ts (*laughs*): This is a difficult one. Takeshi Kitano's movies—only he can make
    them. I've admired Jackie Chan's action movies since I was in elementary
    school. I was attracted to the idea of becoming a strong, cool man like him
    and making movies like that. I often pretended to be Jackie Chan when I
    was little. As for how my style developed, it is hard to give an objective reply
    when talking about myself. Probably, from when I was young, I was inter-
    ested in many things. As I saw, listened to, and read many things, over time,
    those things became integrated into my "sense" of things.

WWD: When you write a script, how do you go about creating the camera work to illustrate the ideas? Do you wait until you get on the set to block it out? Or do you storyboard everything?

TS: When I am writing the script, I have an idea of the pace and camera work in my mind. When I don't have that, there are times when I can't write. Of course, that is not always the case. An important aspect of the psychology of a professional who works with fear is a sense of the pace and how to reveal things—when and how to reveal things, when to use slow timing, when to use a quick pace, and how these decisions will affect how the film will be received by the audience. I think about these things when writing a script. Some scenes are thought out and written beforehand, but some of those that aren't are thought out on the set. Even with those scenes that are written, based on the mood on the set, the spirit of the crew, the performance and thoughts of the actors at that particular moment, I might convey to everyone how I envision and want the scene enacted, or I might get an inspiration for something different and use it. There is a limit to what I can come up with, so I like to choose the course I take after hearing the thoughts and opinions of the actors and the crew.

WWD: What do you think of Martin Scorsese's work? Do you have a favorite film of his, one that you like especially?

TS: I haven't seen all of Martin Scorsese's work, but I like most of what I have seen. I like *Taxi Driver* [1976] in particular. That's a masterpiece, I believe. It may be rude of me to say it in this way, but I don't believe Scorsese could make the same movie if he were to try to make it again. A film like that comes only once or twice in each director's career. Tobe Hooper with *The Texas Chainsaw Massacre* is another example. The youthfulness, energy, and boldness of the time come out strongly. Such works only emerge at a particular time, when you're young and starting out. *Taxi Driver* exemplifies this.

WWD: Your first film credit as director seems to be *Gakkô no kaidan G* [1998], roughly translated as *School Ghost Story G*, a television movie for which you directed the segments "Katasumi" and "444 . . . 444." What can you tell me about this?

TS: After I completed the *eiga gijutu bigaku kouza* [film technique and aesthetics seminar], Kiyoshi Kurosawa and Hiroshi Takahashi recommended me. Kiyoshi Kurosawa told me that he was directing one of the segments, asked if I wanted to direct one, and introduced me to the producer. From the point of view of the producer, it was a brash request, because I had never worked as an assistant director or director of a commercial film. Kiyoshi Kurosawa told the producer that if I were given a thirty-minute segment to direct, it would come out well. The producer looked at me with unease, but I can't say for certain what he thought. He probably thought that it wouldn't be such

a good idea to trust me with a thirty-minute segment. So, almost apologet-
ically, he asked me to make two three-minute segments instead.

I was really disappointed when I heard this, because I had already written
ten minutes of the thirty-minute segment that I thought I was going to make.
I thought all that work was going to go to waste. He told me that it couldn't
be helped, because it was my first job. So I tried to make something really
scary for those three minutes. I wrote about fifteen to twenty pieces that
could fit within three minutes, which comes out to three or four pages of
script. I selected a few to take to the producer and asked him to choose from
them, because I could make any of them scary. "Katasumi" and "444 . . . 444"
were the ones that were chosen and developed over a series of meetings.

For "Katasumi" and "444 . . . 444," the shooting schedule was one day for
both segments; we shot "Katasumi" in the morning and "444 . . . 444" in the
afternoon. When I think of it now, the producer took me lightly. That's not
polite Japanese, but it's true. I was the only one who had to use a consumer
model video camera. I didn't have any film to work with. Their attitude was
that I should shoot anything I wanted; since it was only a three-minute segment, it could be slipped anywhere into the television program. I was really
disappointed and upset. Frantically, I thought that I would make it as frightening as possible and show them. That may have been a good thing. It was
videotape, so the image quality was rough. I think of what may have been if
I had shot with film.

Kiyoshi Kurosawa, who directed a thirty-minute segment, and Hiroshi
Takahashi, who wrote the script for that segment, saw the completed three-
minute segments and praised them, saying that I had "stolen" the film with
those two segments. I was really pleased, but I didn't get steady work as a
director afterward. I still worked as an assistant director. A year later, when
the video came out, Hiroshi Takahashi told my current producer to look at
my work. He saw the two segments and said he wanted to meet me. We met,
and he said that he wanted to make a film with me. That's how I met my producer, Ichise Taka. Within the framework he presented, he told me to develop
anything I wanted, so long as it was scary. What I came up with were the
video versions of *Juon* and *Juon 2* [the first two versions of *The Grudge*].

wwd: Why did you shoot on video?

ts: Budgetary constraints! We didn't have the budget to shoot on film. This
work was to be part of a series for Toei V Cinema, a Japanese production
company, which was to be shot in video for the direct-to-video market.
However, I felt that a horror film shot on film is more frightening, so I used
film effects in editing to make it look more like it was shot with film. But the
image quality was quite rough, and the quality of the cuts still doesn't look
all that great.

As for the shooting schedule, it took ten days to shoot both films. This includes a rest day, so it was actually nine days of filming combined for both *Juon* and *Juon 2*. This happens frequently in Japan and is called *nihondori* ["two" shooting]. Both "1" and "2" were shot simultaneously; that was the plan for this project. So each film took an average of four and a half days to shoot. Even for Japan, this is very short—too short a time for shooting a really good film. People wonder how anything can be shot in such a short time. When I mention this to people, they are always surprised. However, there are "pink movies"— Japanese porno films—that are shot in three days. Since this was my first long work as a director, I decided to accomplish it under those conditions without complaining. As for the actors, most of them were ones whom the producer Ichise Taka had worked with. Those with less experience and others also came for auditions, but the selection process was mostly handled by the producer and the casting producer, who had ideas of whom to cast in certain roles.

The cursed house theme was inevitable. I had started and left uncompleted many short works and assignments from the film seminar, and there were many ideas that I wanted to do and develop. At that time, what came to mind was Krzysztof Kieslowski's *Dekalog* [1987]. I was really impressed by the setting and situation of different people—parents, couples, friends— who live in the same building, illustrating the theme of the bonds between people. I believed that the structure of *Dekalog* could be applied successfully to a horror film. If I used a house as the setting, the family that moves into the house, the family that previously lived in the house, and those, like the realtor, who come in contact with the house could all be connected together. As a result, the house becomes the center of the film. After making the video version of *Juon*, I was often asked if Quentin Tarantino's *Pulp Fiction* [1994] was the model for it. However, I didn't have it in mind when I made *Juon*. Of course, I like *Pulp Fiction* very much, but *Dekalog* was in mind when I came up with the structure of *Juon*.

WWD: When the first episode of *Juon* was such a hit, were you surprised that it made such a success with the public? What were the circumstances that led to the sequel?

TS: It wasn't a big hit when it was released. From about six months to a year after its release on video, it was talked up among horror fans on the Internet and gained wider recognition and popularity. Then the producer asked if I was interested in making a theatrical version. There were new techniques and things left undone that I wanted to do if I were to make a movie, so I decided to direct the film version. Even so, there are those who feel the video version is more frightening. A lot of its popularity spread on the Net, so I didn't directly experience the impression that it was "a hit" or "a big hit."

WWD: Which do you prefer more, film or video?

TS: Of course, I prefer 35mm film. It takes more time and effort to set up lighting, cameras, but it's worth it. At the present time, no matter how much
video has developed, film provides more depth. A real sense of depth and
darkness can be captured. I don't think this applies just to horror films. Film
is wonderful. No matter how close video gets to film quality, I hope that the
history and technology of film is preserved. As for the shooting schedule,
the film was shot in twenty days. We just barely got it all shot in that time.
We finished in the early morning hours of that next day. With the theatrical
version, we had some well-known actors, so it was difficult to fit them into
our schedule, and we faced many challenges. From Hollywood's perspective,
this would seem like a very short time. However, after shooting the two
video versions in nine days, twenty days felt like a luxurious amount of time
at the beginning. But with film, there are many things to consider, so it was
a tight schedule. The first day ran over, and the producer asked if there were
too many shots. I thought that there weren't too many shots and told him
that it would be OK and that we would get back on schedule. I remember
speaking to him on the phone and apologizing for making him worry.

WWD: Do you use a "video tap" on the set so you can see what you're doing?
And how closely do you work with your cameraman? Since you write the
films, is it fair to say that you supervise the editing, lighting, and other aspects,
including the digital effects, as well? How tight is your control on the look
of the finished film?

TS: We did use a "video tap" to see what we were doing, but we were often
pressed for time. So if I felt that a scene had been done well, then I went to
the next scene without checking. If the cameraman was satisfied with the shot
and I was satisfied with the shot, we would go ahead. I can't say for certain
that the cameraman understood or did what was in my mind. I believe that
I made myself clear so that no one could complain afterward. As for editing
and digital effects, I make suggestions at every opportunity. Perhaps due to
my lack of study in this area or my ignorance, I rely on the knowledge and
skills of professionals.

I try not to interject myself too much, but if the writing departs too much
from the vision I have in mind, then I express myself. This may sound rude,
but I had many disputes with the writer of the video versions. What he wrote
differed from my plan, and that wasn't conveyed clearly to me in the pre-
production phase. As a director, I don't want to pin any shortcomings on
the cast or crew. So I asked him to change some things. There was a lot of
rewriting done on the set. Writing is important to a horror film. If there are
compromises made or corners cut, just because one is making a horror film,
or there isn't a large budget or the director is new—whatever the reason—

I cannot forgive that sort of attitude. I draw the line and fight for matters like that. If there was someone more dedicated than myself, I would be disappointed in myself. But if it were clear that someone was not working to his or her level of ability, then I would become disappointed and begin having words with that person.

WWD: You made two video documentaries in 2000 entitled *Shin rei bideo V: Honto ni atta kowai hanashi—kyoufu shinrei shashinkan* (Ghost Video Number 5: The Real Story That Happened—The Photo Museum of Scary Ghosts) and *Shin rei bideo VI: Honto ni atta kowai hanashi—kyofu tarento taikendan* (Ghost Video Number 6: The Real Story That Happened—Discussion by Personalities of Scary Experiences). What can you tell me about them?

TS: *Shin rei bideo V* and *Shin rei bideo VI* were shot and produced simultaneously. I directed and wrote the screenplays for them. I attracted the attention of producer and director Norio Tsuruta, who has worked in the horror genre for a long time, when he saw the video version of *Juon*. He directed *Ringu o: Bâsudei* [2000, a "prequel" to *Ringu*]. He was the producer and supervising editor of the documentary series and asked me if I would like to make *Shin rei bideo V*. The subject was *shinrei shashin* [ghost photographs], where images of faces, an extra finger, or a vague, unidentifiable entity appear in photographs. That was the subject of this video. The other video, *Shin rei bideo VI*, was a collection of frightening episodes experienced by famous celebrities, recounted on video. I undertook these two projects, but I experienced difficulties unlike those associated with dramatic plays or films.

There is a monthly horror comic called *Honto ni atta kowai hanashi* [True Scary Stories] in Japan. Readers send in ghost photographs to the comic. I selected photographs that I thought were scary for the video. Regular people send these in. There were hundreds of them in a cardboard box. It took me three full days to select fifty photographs for the video. It was tremendous task. *Kyofu tarento taikendan* [frightening episodes] are also included in the comic. A comic writer turns celebrities' stories into *manga* [graphic novels]. Some of these experiences were selected, and the celebrities were interviewed for the video. I hadn't done a documentary until then, and it took more time and energy than I had envisioned. However, it was fun, although it took a few all-nighters to get it done. These were made and released as direct-to-video titles, so they have not been broadcast on television.

WWD: In 2001 you made *Tomie: Re-Birth* as a theatrical feature. How did you get involved in this, and how much input did you have in the film? Are you happy with it?

TS: Tomie is a Japanese woman's name. It's not a common name now, but was more common in my grandmother's generation. The film was made before the film version of *Juon*. Therefore, this is my first theatrical release. It was just released this May on DVD in the United States. This was the third film adaptation in the *Tomie* series, which is a *manga* series written by Junji Ito, who also wrote the *Uzumaki* [Spiral] series. There were a lot of challenges in adapting a *manga* to film, but I was satisfied with it. Frankly, it wasn't a hit. I was the director; but unlike *Juon*, someone else was the screenwriter. I was happy with the end result; but now that several years have passed, I think about what I might have done differently.

wwd: You seem interested not so much in plot, but more in incidents, coincidences, and what Freud would describe as "the uncanny"—things that happen when they're not supposed to and people or places that cause great unease in the viewer. How do you feel about very heavily plotted films? Does plot "get in the way," so to speak?

ts: No, I don't think so. It may look like there is no plot, but there is one. There is an overarching structure that the disparate parts are linked to, and the

Takashi Shimizu (center) working with Sarah Michelle Gellar on the set of *The Grudge* (2004). Courtesy Columbia Tri-Star.

different events and threads tie together. It may appear that only the parts
leading up to the scary sections or where strange events are encountered are
laid out, but the parts in between, the backgrounds and motivations of the
characters, are all planned. Plot is not a hindrance but something that is
very necessary. With horror films, especially those organized as a puzzle,
like this one, the most frightening things are those that could be encountered in the realm of ordinary day-to-day life.

WWD: Now you are making an Americanized episode of *The Grudge* (2004),
but you're shooting it in Japan with some American actors, like Sarah Michelle
Gellar, Bill Pullman, and Clea DuVall, as well as some of the actors you used
in the Japanese versions. How is this working out?

TS: We're in the process of editing now, so I can't say with certainty what I felt
at that time, but it came out well. There is only one actor who was in the
Japanese version, and the other Japanese actors are ones I had not previously

Actors Jason Behr and Sarah Michelle Gellar with director Takashi Shimizu on the set
of *The Grudge* (2004). Courtesy Columbia Tri-Star.

worked with. Some of the actors who were in the Japanese *Juon* films wanted to appear in this version and asked why they couldn't appear in the American version. This put me in a bind. But, frankly, I wanted to work with different actors and crew. Of course, there are many cultural differences in Japanese and U.S society; but also, the way in which movies are made in the United States and Japan is quite different. There were some misunderstandings and mistakes arising because of that, and the original cast and crew felt some discontent and dissatisfaction. However, I believe it was limited to the extent that we had anticipated in pre-production. Sarah Michelle Gellar was a person of firm thoughts and clear understanding, and an actor of considerable ability. She starred in the popular television series *Buffy: The Vampire Slayer*, but she demonstrated the desire to grow even further as an actor through this role. I was most grateful for her professionalism. As for Bill Pullman, the Japanese crew saw him off at the airport and came back in tears. He is truly a wonderful person. Clea DuVall is so cool and mature that it is hard to imagine that she is much younger than I am. In that regard, the film was blessed with a cast of a very high character. If the opportunity ever presented itself, I would like to work with them again.

There are many challenges in making a movie, even with an all-Japanese cast and crew, but I think this experience went very well. This is what I think. Of course, there may be those who felt some dissatisfaction. I had heard some say that American actors are selfish or hard to work with, but making this movie was easier than I had anticipated. They offered their opinions and listened to mine. Of course, if any was the kind of actor who wouldn't listen to anyone, then I would have fired him or her immediately, I think. In that regard, I am prepared each time I make a movie to be fired if the decision is to fire the actor or the director. I think things went very well.

wwd: What is it like to direct American actors when you have to direct through an interpreter? Interesting, difficult, or both?

ts: Of course, it is both. There are difficulties in directing a movie through an interpreter, regardless of how good the interpreter is. The common language of the world is English, so I must improve my English-language ability. On this film, the people involved were good actors, so they showed an interest in Japanese culture and tried to accommodate me. So, for me, it was an interesting experience. I noticed that Americans are relaxed and loose in many ways, in terms of adhering to schedules and in other matters. I would like them to think not only of what is good for them personally. There are many Americans who consider the thoughts and feelings of others. But from the perspective of Japanese and people from other countries, when Americans think of themselves and their country as the best, this comes across as arrogance. Of course, having confidence and pride in oneself and one's country is important;

but it's also important to realize that others don't see things in the same way. Depending on the country and culture, the use of time and commitments to time are different. This is very important. To be loose with time or expectations of punctuality depends on the country, the people, the location, or the situation. I would like American cast and crew members to understand this. Naturally, the Japanese crew must, to some extent, accommodate the needs and rhythms of their American counterparts. If this can be accomplished smoothly, I think opportunities for joint production will appear, and many new and profitable movies that people will want to see will be created. This is something that I would like to say to the American film industry, which seems to be more and more dependent on series and remakes.

WWD: The house that is used in all of the *Grudge* films is not a set but a real house. How did you come to find this house, and are you shooting the new film in the same house?

TS: The first versions were shot in an old house that the producer and his partner found. That it was an old house, that filming could be completed in nine days, that there were old buildings around it where people had once lived were all conditions that had to be dealt with. The house in the original *Juon* was not the one that I had envisioned. However, that house isn't used in the new American version of *The Grudge*. It is a set made to look like the original house. Designer Iwao Saitô thought that it would be nice to display a range of Japanese colors on the set and worked very diligently on that. Attentive people will probably notice the differences. Frankly, I didn't think we would use a house with the same structure when I was coming up with the script for the new version. Stephen Susco, the screenwriter, enjoyed the original *Juon* and was drawn in that direction. He couldn't imagine the location of the rooms as anywhere but the places seen in the original. I left the organization of the story/house to him; so if he envisioned the story in that way, then I had the sets built to his specifications.

WWD: Do you find it more difficult to shoot on location, what with lighting, sound, and camera movement (tracking shots and the like)? Or is it more liberating because it's more real?

TS: That's a lot for one question. I'm not as familiar with filming on a set, because my previous works had low budgets; so that may be the reason I feel location shooting is easier. If there was a way to film on a set what can't be shot on location, then that would be best. Ideas that come while on location, different and/or better ideas than those developed in pre-production, ideas that come after principal shooting is completed, things that one would be hesitant to do on location—as much as possible, these could be shot on location. Then those that couldn't be done could be shot on a set. This would be an ideal arrangement. Of course, there are budget and scheduling considerations.

WWD: Do you think that your films, along with the films of the Pang brothers, Hideo Nakata, and other Asian horror directors are the beginning of a new style, a new wave of Gothic filmmaking that relies more on mood and atmosphere than violence? Do you socialize with these other directors and view each other's works? Do you have a favorite contemporary Asian director?

TS: I don't think that I'm on any "cutting edge." I think big Hollywood productions use and rely too much on extravagant editing, CGI [computer-generated imagery], and effects shots. Mood, atmosphere, and point of view aren't anything new; they are the essentials of filmmaking. Even great works that feature CGI and effects have mood and point of view fully established, I think. Therefore, I don't think that I'm on the forefront of any new Gothic moviemaking trend. Establishing mood, point of view, and atmosphere is a natural prerequisite for a horror film, a love story, a family movie, or an art movie, for that matter. Of course, I have contact with Hideo Nakata. It's nothing particularly special, but when we meet, he seems to make it a point to talk to me. I've seen most of his work. The Pang brothers are well known in Hollywood, but not to the same extent in Japan. However, I've seen their work. One thing that I would like to say is to stop looking at "Asian horror cinema" as one entity. This may sound impudent, but that is how I feel.

WWD: It's good to see that you are shooting the new episode of *The Grudge* in Japan. But can we expect that you will come to the United States and start making Hollywood films, as John Woo did? It seems to me that Woo's best films were his Hong Kong films, such as *Bullet to the Head* [1990]. His Hollywood stuff is less inspired, because it's cut off from his native culture. Now he's just another action director. If you do come to the United States, how do you plan to keep things fresh in a very different society?

TS: This is something that is left to others and the media. I don't think Woo is just another action director. This is what the American film industry wanted. They wanted him to exercise his skill and vision in American films. They invested a lot of money for him to direct Hollywood movies. I think this is what American producers and moviemakers intended. Whether he had this in mind or not is a separate matter, I think. This is what I feel as someone who makes movies. Of course, I have not met John Woo, so I can't say with certainty. As a Japanese and as someone reared in Japan, I have pride in that. I want to cherish that culture, but I also want to make a movie in America directed toward an American audience. This may sound rude, but if American pictures and people embraced a wider perspective, not just Americans, but people throughout the world, then more and more interesting films will emerge.

WWD: Do you see yourself primarily as an artist, a commercial artist, or a commercial filmmaker? In short, what sort of films do you want to do in the future? Do you want to stay with the horror genre or move on to something else? What do you think your future as a filmmaker will be?

TS: I don't see myself as an "artist," but that is how others may see me. No matter what I may say, I am human, so it is difficult to give a completely objective response. However, I think that I don't work just for the sake of making a profit. If my fee as a director can be called "profit," then I can say with certainty that I'm not in it for the sake of profit. I won't take a job just because there is a big budget or a big fee involved. I don't intend to restrict myself to the horror genre. There are many projects that I would like to develop outside the horror genre. However, I want to make films that entertain, for families or couples. I would like to build upon my experience in the horror genre to create films that entertain everyone.

Translated from the Japanese by Shoichi Gregory Kamei

JAMIE BABBIT

Jamie Babbit's *But I'm a Cheerleader* was one of the breakout independent film hits of the 1999–2000 season. Babbit, a surprisingly assured thirty-year-old from Cleveland, Ohio, came to filmmaking through amateur theater and went on to direct a series of short films, including *Frog Crossing* (1996) and *Sleeping Beauties* (1998), before making her debut as a feature director with *Cheerleader*.

Cheerleader tells the story of "femme" Megan (Natasha Lyonne), a young woman who doesn't realize that she's a lesbian until her parents stage an "intervention," which results in Megan being shipped off to True Directions, a "deprogramming" center where gays and lesbians are forced to become "straight." True Directions is run by the monstrously repressive Mary (Cathy Moriarty) and her in-denial gay son Rock (Eddie Cibrian), with the assistance of camp supervisor Mike (RuPaul Charles, in his first non-drag role). At True Directions, Megan meets and falls in love with the "butch" lesbian Graham (Clea DuVall). Despite all of Mary's threats and machinations, Megan and Graham's love triumphs over True Direction's worst efforts to make the two girls "straighten out."

Babbit staged *Cheerleader* as a "popped out" comedy, with bright colors and heavily stylized sets. At the same time, Babbit's experience with actors allowed her to handle a large ensemble cast seamlessly and with practiced efficiency. Babbit also works in television, where she directs the WB television series *Popular* and the MTV series *Undressed*. Honest and open about her work and her lifestyle, Jamie was pleased to have a chance to talk about *But I'm a Cheerleader* in detail during our interview on October 21, 2000. Since then, she has directed episodes of the televisions series *Alias, Gilmore Girls, Nip/Tuck, Malcolm in the Middle,* and *The Bernie Mac Show,* and has completed two other feature films, *The Quiet* (2005) and *Itty Bitty Titty Committee* (2007).

WHEELER WINSTON DIXON: How did you get started in the business, and what was your childhood like?

JAMIE BABBIT: I came to filmmaking through theater. I was born in Cleveland, Ohio, and I started at the Cleveland Playhouse when I was about seven years old, taking acting classes and then moving on to stage managing. There are a lot of elements of *Cheerleader* that are autobiographical. I never went to a homosexual "rehabilitation" camp, although such places do exist, like the Exodus Project; but my mother runs a treatment program for teenagers in Ohio called New Directions, which helps them beat alcohol and drug problems.

My father is more like the Bud Cort character in *Cheerleader*. He's really sweet and supportive. He doesn't really want to talk about my being lesbian, but he's always been there for me. He's a lawyer. So I'd always wanted to do a comedy about growing up in rehab and the absurdity of that atmosphere. But I didn't want to make fun of twelve-step programs for alcoholism and drugs, because they really help people; but when you turn it into Homosexuals Anonymous, then I felt that was a situation I could have fun with.

WWD: Did your parents support your work in the theater?

JB: My parents were very supportive, doing the car pool thing, taking me all around, so I continued all through high school doing a lot of acting. Even though we were in Ohio, it was a really avant-garde theater program; we were singing Leonard Cohen and Tom Waits songs, not the usual stuff. Gradually, I moved more into being a stage manager and doing lighting, which I enjoyed

Jamie Babbit directing on the set of her satirical lesbian comedy *But I'm a Cheerleader* (1999). Courtesy Jerry Ohlinger Archives.

more. Then I was lucky enough to go to college at Barnard. And when I was there, I did theater, and I started taking film classes. So I really came to film through acting and working with actors. I really think that's essential, and I love working with actors to this day.

wwd: How did you get involved in film? At Barnard?

jb: I didn't take the film classes at Barnard; I took them at New York University during the summer. I got a Centennial Scholarship, which basically gave me money to pursue something I was interested in. So I wound up taking film classes at NYU. My film teacher was named Boris; he was pretty tough on all of us. He'd look at my films and say, "Jamie, I don't like this at all. It's terrible. Make babies, not films." Pretty hardcore! [*Laughs.*] But he would do it to everyone. He was brutal, but really, really talented. He was a great teacher, and he really put me on the right track.

wwd: The importance of lesbian identity is a central issue in *But I'm a Cheerleader*. When did you come out yourself?

jb: I came out to myself as a lesbian in high school, but it was one of those things that you kind of know but you're not really sure, you know? I think I had lots of pictures of women in my locker at high school, just like the character of Megan in *Cheerleader*. Other people would say to me, "Hey, you're a lesbian," and I would think, "Hmm, you think so?" [*Laughs.*] And I was still thinking about it in college and then fully came out after college, when I was twenty-two. I was very lucky. My mother and father were very supportive of my decision, and so that made things much easier.

wwd: What were your first short films like?

jb: I made a lot of short films before *Cheerleader*. I made a bunch of short films for classes, just exercises. But there's one I'd still like to expand into a feature, which I made in college in Super 8mm, called *Discharge*. It was just two minutes long, the first thing I ever made in Super 8mm. It was simple: this woman is walking down the streets of New York, and some guy is harassing her, some construction worker type—played by my brother, incidentally. [*Laughs.*] And she gets really irritated and finally reaches under her skirt, pulls out her tampon, and throws it at him.

When I screened it in class, the instructor was somewhat taken aback by the film. I remember he asked me, "Do you think this is a *feminist* film?" [*Laughs.*] So then I did some other short films, which were awful, and then I made *Frog Crossing* in 1996 with a friend of mine, Ari Gold. It was a short film we made in San Francisco, about an animal rights activist who protects frogs as they hop across the highway. It was about twelve minutes, but it's very similar to *Cheerleader* in that it's very stylized, and there are only two colors in the whole movie. It's very constructed in every sense of the word. It's got a real pop feel to it.

WWD: How did you make the jump from college to working within the industry?

JB: When I graduated from Barnard in 1993, I needed a job. I had worked as an intern in the industry when I was in college, while I was making my own short films on the side, but I wanted to jump into a real film. My first job was as a production assistant in Martin Scorsese's office on *The Age of Innocence* [1993]. I actually never met him, because it was such a huge production. I would run errands, and his mom would knit booties for Steven Spielberg's new baby, and I would go over and pick them up. That was my job.

But it was a good office to work in, because Marty has such an encyclopedic knowledge of film and an enormous personal archive of films. He really knows film history inside and out. It was a good lesson for me, because I still had a lot to learn about the history of film and how valuable that can be in the day-to-day production process. Marty would phone the office from the set and ask me to get some Italian film from the 1940s from his archive and send it to the set so Daniel Day Lewis could look at it to help him work on his character. Marty's knowledge in this area is so vast, and I thought, "This is something I really have to get on with." That was $50 a day, but it was a start, and I was learning a lot.

WWD: That's a good entry point. What happened next?

JB: From there, I got a job with John Sayles on *The Secret of Roan Inish* [1994], also as a production assistant. It was a much smaller movie, and there were three people working in the office. One was Karen Kusama, who has just directed her first big hit, *Girlfight* [2000]; one was Jasmine Kosovic, who has produced a film called *The Adventures of Sebastian Cole* [1998]; and one was me! It was just the three of us working in this small office, and we were all saying, "We want to be filmmakers someday!" [*Laughs.*] Working with John Sayles is great; he's just a wonderful person. His whole philosophy is, if you're going to make a movie, just do it, you know? And that goes back to his first film, *The Return of the Secaucus Seven* [1980]. John is really down-to-earth, and working with him made me realize that I really wanted to get on the set, because I had been stuck in the office, and I really wanted to work with the actors and be part of the creative process. I knew I really needed to learn from directors working on the set, so I decided to lie my way into being a script supervisor. [*Laughs.*] And it worked.

WWD: In time-honored Hollywood tradition! Did anyone catch on?

JB: Well, my first job as script supervisor was with John Duigan on *The Journey of August King* [1995]. I love John's work, especially *Flirting* [1991], which is one my favorite films. The director of photography on *August King* was a great guy named Slavomir Idziak, who also photographed Krzysztof Kieslowski's *Blue* [1993] and a bunch of other projects, and he was wonderful to me. The assistant director, Skip Cosper, was an old pro who had worked on huge films like *Days of Heaven* [1978]. So everyone really knew what they were doing, and they helped me get away with it. I didn't know anything, but I pretended that I did, and they were so good; they didn't work me that much anyway, thank God! [*Laughs.*] And then from there I worked with Su Friedrich on her first narrative movie, *Hide and Seek* [1996].

WWD: That's quite a jump, from a more traditional narrative project to an experimental narrative feature.

JB: Well, I was taking what I could get! My next job, Nancy Savoca's television movie *If These Walls Could Talk* [1996], was actually my first job in Los Angeles. I fell in love with producer Andrea Sperling. I was going through a breakup, and Andrea lived in LA, so I went there and wound up working for Nancy on that film, which was an incredible experience. I actually worked on only one segment of the film, the "1974" sequence with Sissy Spacek, in which she plays a mother who decides not to get an abortion. After that, I went on to my first big-budget Hollywood movie, David Fincher's *The Game* [1997]. That was a fascinating experience, because I went from Nancy's movie, which was probably a $2 million, $3 million movie, to an $80 million movie, working with Michael Douglas, Sean Penn, and a real Hollywood crew.

WWD: What was that experience like?

JB: Intense. But David Fincher is so interesting; even though he's a Hollywood director, he's a real *auteur*. He really has a vision, and his command of the technical aspects of filmmaking is staggering. I learned a lot from him. And I was very lucky, because he was very supportive of my work.

WWD: That's surprising to me, because Fincher's films like *Se7en* [1995] and *Fight Club* [1999] are really dark movies, and your films are exactly the opposite.

JB: Well, *Fight Club* was meant to be a comedy, actually. [*Laughs.*] The whole time I was watching it, I was laughing, because I know him, and he just took the whole thing as a really, really dark comedy. It's not a typical Hollywood film at all. But it was David who actually gave me the chance to shoot *Sleeping Beauties*. We'd been talking about fairy tales on the set, and David was very interested in the project, so he wound up giving me some leftover film stock from *The Game*, about six thousand feet of 35mm film. That allowed me to shoot in 35mm, which made a big difference in the short. And also, David's editor for *The Game* gave me the use of the AVID [digital editing machine] for free; so it was a real break. And to top it off, I met Michael Douglas while we were making the movie, and he was kind enough to write a letter to Paramount saying, "Please give Jamie Babbit access to the costume and wardrobe department for her film," and so I basically had free rein at Paramount. *Sleeping Beauties* cost about $10,000, which is pretty cheap for a twelve-minute 35mm color film.

WWD: You're quite a hustler.

JB: Well, I had to be! I was desperate! [*Laughs.*] I wanted to make *Sleeping Beauties*, and I was going to do it any way I could. You have to do this sort of stuff when you're starting out, if you're ever going to get anything off the ground. You have to go for it, and that's what I did.

WWD: Tell me about *Sleeping Beauties.*

JB: *Sleeping Beauties* [1998] is a retelling of the fairy tale *Sleeping Beauty*, which in turn is inspired by the Disney version from the 1930s. *Sleeping Beauties* tells the story of a girl who works as a makeup artist at a funeral home; she is obsessed with unavailable women. And the metaphors for the unavailable women are the corpses that she paints.

WWD: Cheerful.

JB (*laughs*): Yeah. And then through her job, she ends up meeting a photographer at one of the funerals, played by Clea DuVall, who also plays the character of Graham in *Cheerleader*, and they wind up in a relationship, so it has a happy ending. It's only about twelve minutes long. The great thing about that film was working not only with Clea, but also with Radha Mitchell, who really broke through as the lead role in Lisa Cholodenko's *High Art* [1998]. I fell in love with Radha when I saw her in a film called *Love and Other Catastrophes*, when I was at Sundance with *Frog Crossing*. She was at Sundance promoting the film, and we met very briefly. Then I came back to Los Angeles, and Radha had just moved there, and I called her up and asked her to be in *Sleeping Beauties*, and she was great. Then, a couple of months later, Lisa Cholodenko called me and said, "I'm considering this actress Radha Mitchell for *High Art*. What do you think of her?" [*Laughs.*] And I said, "She's fabulous, you should definitely hire her!" So that's how that happened.

WWD: When and how did you decide to tackle a feature film?

JB: When I finished shooting *Sleeping Beauties*, I realized it was time to make the jump to a feature, so I wrote a three-page treatment for *Cheerleader* and met with a bunch of writers who were recommended to me by friends, who would basically write me a screenplay for free. *Sleeping Beauties* was still in post-production, and I had enough experience from *Frog Crossing* to know that when you screen something at a festival and people like it, they're immediately going to ask you, "What are you doing next?" So you have to have something new in the pipeline.

My girlfriend Andrea Sperling agreed to produce *Cheerleader*, and Brian Wayne Peterson came on board as the screenwriter. By this time, Andrea had produced a whole bunch of films, like *Desert Blue* [1998], *Fame Whore* [1997], and Gregg Araki's *Nowhere* [1997], *The Doom Generation* [1995], and *Totally Fucked Up* [1993]. So we said to Brian, "*Sleeping Beauties* will be done in four months, so you have four months to write the script. So let's do it, and we'll take the film and your script to Sundance and see if we can get it financed." By this time, Andrea had become friends with the financier Michael Burns, who is now the vice president of Lion's Gate Films; but at the time he was just financing movies out of his own bank account. We approached him and said, "We want to make this comedy about these two girls falling in love at a homosexual rehabilitation camp," and he said, "I love it, it's a great idea, I'd love to see the script." And so he ended up financing it himself.

WWD: What was your budget?

JB: The initial budget was $500,000, and when the film actually went into production, he agreed to give us $1 million.

WWD: How did you get your cast? It's really a superb ensemble: Natasha Lyonne, Clea DuVall, RuPaul Charles, Cathy Moriarty, Bud Cort, Richard Moll, Mink Stole . . . that's some pretty ambitious casting.

JB: Well, I simply pursued Cathy Moriarty. I simply wouldn't take no for an answer. You know, I'd pop out of the bushes with the script in hand. [*Laughs.*] And I just pursued her until I got her. I needed a really strong person to play Mary, the head of True Directions, a person who could utterly dominate the frame, and Cathy was the perfect choice. She works really hard in the film;

Natasha Lyonne as the troubled lead character, Megan Bloomfield, who is unsure of her sexuality in Jamie Babbit's *But I'm a Cheerleader* (1999). Courtesy Jerry Ohlinger Archives.

RuPaul Charles as a sexually conflicted camp counselor in Jamie Babbit's *But I'm a Cheerleader* (1999). Courtesy Jerry Ohlinger Archives.

she makes True Directions real and simultaneously over the top. For the rest of the cast, I started with Clea, because Clea worked at a coffee shop in an art house theater in Los Angeles, and Clea would give me free coffee for a while. [*Laughs.*] So we became friends. I showed her my first film, and then I wrote *Cheerleader* with her in mind for the part of Graham, the butch girl whom Megan, Natasha Lyonne's character, falls in love with. Clea was actually friends with Natasha, so that's how we got her in the film.

At this point, we got a really good casting director who had worked on Tamara Jenkins's *Slums of Beverly Hills* [1998], Sheila Jaffe. She does at least five movies a year at Sundance, works on *The Sopranos*, and so she had access to a lot of excellent actors. I loved Doug Spain from *Star Maps* [1997], so I knew I wanted him. RuPaul was really excited about it and really happy to do a role that wasn't in drag for a change. Mink Stole came in and auditioned. Sheila brought in Bud Cort. I love Bud in *Harold and Maude* [1971] and *Brewster McCloud* [1970]; *Brewster* is Natasha's favorite movie, so she was really pleased to be working with him.

WWD: What about Jules LaBarthe, your director of photography?

JB: Jules shot *Frog Crossing, Sleeping Beauties,* and *But I'm a Cheerleader.* He's done all my films. He went to NYU as a filmmaker, and he was someone I met at a coffee shop in Los Angeles. He'd shot some B features before he did *Cheerleader,* but this was his first real independent feature.

WWD: You meet a lot of people at coffee shops! [*Laughs.*]

JB: No, but it's true! Coffee culture, desperate filmmakers alone in Los Angeles—you make some really good connections there. You have to keep working to keep your skills up, and that's the reason I like directing television. I'm obviously still working on feature projects, but it takes a lot of time to put a feature project together, to put the financing in place and get a script ready. Since I'm developing my own material, it takes longer. Some people say, "I'm a director," but they haven't been on a set for five years! That's the nice thing about television shows like *Popular* and *Undressed,* because you're not responsible for anything except working with the actors. The directorial style's been established, the writers really have the power, and the producers do the casting, so you're just really working with the actors.

WWD: And you have to work really quickly to get it in the can.

JB: Yeah, but they asked me when I started working on *Popular* [a weekly, hour-long comedy series on WB] and *Undressed* [an MTV series] whether or not I'd be able to keep up the pace, and I said, "Look, I come from independent filmmaking, so I'm working as fast as I can all the time on the set anyway." It actually feels really luxurious. Eight days to shoot one hour of programming is fine. And it's not even really an hour. When you get rid of the main title, end title, and all the commercial breaks, it's really about forty-two minutes.

WWD: *Cheerleader* is very much interested in performativity, defining gender through tasks: the boys play football, fix cars, and chop wood, while the girls do household chores. It seems that the film is one enormous "drag" act, whether lesbian, heterosexual, or gay.

JB: Well, I definitely wanted to talk about gender roles, gender expectations, and the absurdity of them, and I think a lot of that came from my own life. When I was coming out as a lesbian, a lot of people made fun of me because I was bad at sports. I mean, I was terrible, an absolute sissy. I couldn't do anything. And one of the many bizarre gender expectations is that lesbians are supposed to be really good at sports. But I'm not; I'm femme, and that's it. I was doing an interview for *The Advocate* [the gay and lesbian magazine], and a lesbian reporter came over to my house. And the walls are pink, and there are Barbie dolls everywhere, and she was really upset. "Are these Barbies *yours*?" she demanded, and when I said "yes" she shot back, "I don't know any lesbians who have Barbie dolls!" So, maybe I was born as a gay man! [*Laughs.*]

   That's the kind of stuff I wanted to talk about in this film: how gender expectations define our lives, and how others see us. In some ways, that's where the title of the film came from. Because Megan is a cheerleader, she can't believe that she's a lesbian. But then, at the end of the film, Megan uses her cheerleading skills to affirm her lesbian desire, when she urges Graham not to buckle under to the True Directions manifesto and to come out as her lesbian lover. I didn't want it to be a film about a lesbian who comes out and then drives off on a motorcycle at the end. She was still a cheerleader at the end.

WWD: Why did you make the character of Graham, Megan's love interest, so "butch," the archetypal "bad girl," smoking cigarettes and dripping with macho attitude?

JB: I just wanted to make her the antithesis of Megan. Megan's such a good girl, and good girls always fall for bad girls—or maybe that's another autobiographical element of the film. [*Laughs.*] Clea DuVall just has such a kind of raw, natural sexiness to her that she was perfect for the part.

WWD: What about Eddie Cibrian, who played Rock, Mary's gay son who is supposedly straight? He doesn't do much, but he manages to get a lot of mileage fooling around with a chainsaw and stroking a rather phallic rake.

JB: Well, he's great to work with, and a lot of that stuff with the rake was just improvised on the set. He played the masseuse in *Living Out Loud* [1998], giving Holly Hunter massages throughout the film, playing a muscle-bound hunk who is basically a male prostitute.

WWD: When you run *Cheerleader* for a sympathetic audience, you're obviously going to get an enthusiastic response. But have you ever run the film for an audience that flat-out hated it because they were that homophobic? At several screenings I attended, when Megan and Graham finally kiss, a number of audience members simply got up and walked out, which astounded me. It's just two people kissing, but apparently that's too much for some narrow-minded spectators.

JB: Well, I've never had a bad response at any screenings in Los Angeles, where I live, although I have shown it to some "not as friendly" audiences elsewhere, so I know what you mean. But the most bizarre screening was—and I'm going to kill my girlfriend for doing this to me—when Andrea made me show it to her ninety-six-year-old grandmother! [*Laughs.*] She's really conservative, and I thought, "This is the most excruciating screening I've ever attended." She really didn't need to see the film, you know what I mean?

WWD: Why did she do that?

JB: Well, Andrea has produced a lot of really dark films, like Gregg Araki's *Doom Generation* and *Totally Fucked Up*—a lot of dark, very gay movies. And this was the lightest movie that she's ever made, so she thought, "Well, my grandmother can see this!" She didn't think she could screen the other films, but she thought that *Cheerleader* was a *happy* movie. And I said, "Yeah,

Clea DuVall in Jamie Babbit's *But I'm a Cheerleader* (1999). Courtesy Jerry Ohlinger Archives.

it's a happy movie, but there's lots of swear words, and there's girls kissing."
I think Andrea kind of forgot the kind of levels there.

WWD: How would you differentiate your film from such recent lesbian films as
Go Fish [1994], *The Incredibly True Adventure of Two Girls in Love* [1995], *The Watermelon Woman* [1996], and *Boys Don't Cry* [1999]?

JB: Well, they're told from the butch angle, and so they're films that I wouldn't make; but they're films that I like. In *Cheerleader*, I wanted to make a conscious choice to have a femme protagonist. In *Go Fish*, Max is the femme character, but she's the love interest of Ely, the lead character, who gets the buzz cut. And when you deconstruct the film, Max becomes more butch, and that's how she gets the girl. And in *Incredibly True Adventure*, we're given a tomboy girl who ends up going for the femme, the object of her affections. In *Cheerleader*, I wanted the femme to be the pursuer, not the pursued. Not only in movies, but also in a lot of lesbian fiction I've read, a lot of lesbian narratives are told from the butch perspective. And it was important to me not to tell that story again, because I wanted to show that a femme can be strong, and a femme can get what she wants.

At the same time, one of the things I've been most interested in in the art world is the concept of "constructed realities," like Cindy Sherman, Red Grooms, Barbara Kruger—people who create an entire alternative universe in which everything is hyperreal, popped out, colorful, and utterly plastic. So at the same time that I wanted to talk about gender constructs and the absurdity of gender constructs, I wanted to explore the artifice and unreality of a completely constructed world in which nothing is real. I really wanted the sets and the world that I created for the characters in the film to be something unreal, campy, and yet really colorful and vibrant—lots of pinks, blues, and very artificial. When I was going to Barnard, Red Grooms did an exhibit at Grand Central Station, which I really loved; I adored his papier-mâché cityscapes. As part of this Grand Central exhibit, Grooms created a fake subway car that you could really sit down in, and it was like living inside a cartoon. That's the look I wanted for the film. I'm also really fond of Derek Jarman's work, particularly *Caravaggio* [1986] and *Queer Edward II* [1991], in which all of his sets are transparently constructed in one location.

WWD: Were you at all influenced by the television series *Pee Wee's Playhouse*?

JB: Yes, I love *Pee Wee's Playhouse*, and I also love Tim Burton's work, which is pretty much the same thing—the creation of a safe or, in Burton's case, menacing alternative universe. Actually, I offered a part in the film to Paul Reubens [Pee Wee], but he was busy on another project, and he had to turn it down. But then, after the film came out, Bud Cort had a birthday party, and I ran into Pee Wee there. He came over to me and said, "I want you to know that

I loved the script, and thank you for thinking of me," which made me really happy, because I'd felt rejected. [*Laughs.*]

wwd: What about working with Richard Moll, who is probably most famous for his work on the television series *Night Court*?

jb: He was great because he's such a bear, and I wanted to cast him because he's such a huge, yet gentle guy. There was a scene that I wanted to do with him, though, that caused a big controversy on the set. Megan has just escaped from True Directions and finds safety in Lloyd [Wesley Mann] and Larry's [Richard Moll] house. I wanted Richard Moll's character to offer Megan a platter of dildos when she walked in and say, "Welcome to being a lesbian." [*Laughs.*] Richard and I had this big controversy on the set. Essentially, he said, "This is weird, Jamie. I don't want to do this." And then some other people on the set agreed with him, and Andrea said, "You know, I think there's something weird about coming out as a lesbian, and then someone hands you a bunch of plastic penises." Eventually, I agreed, and we just said forget it. I think Richard thought I'd gone off the deep end! [*Laughs.*]

wwd: How long was the shoot?

jb: Twenty-eight days.

wwd: Did anyone give you any grief because of your relative youth? I mean, you look *really* young.

jb: I know what you mean, and a lot of people say that, but I didn't have any real problems. Sometimes people would be a little shocked when they came in to audition. When RuPaul came in, he took one look at me and said, "You're twelve!" [*Laughs.*] But during the shoot everyone was fine. I think a lot of it was that I was working with a lot of people who were younger than me or slightly younger than me, so it all worked out.

wwd: Your film has a very childlike, innocent air, a place of safety and reassurance in which people can come out and be themselves. Is this the kind of world that your films try to construct in the real world, for real audiences?

jb: Well, in the film, True Directions is a really violent, horrible place, and I shot a lot of Cathy Moriarty's close-ups right in the camera, with a slight wide-angle lens to make her appear *really* scary. One of the things that I said to the production designer and the costume designer was that I wanted to be sure, as the film went on, that the materials for the sets and costumes became more artificial. So by the end, when all the kids at True Directions are "graduating" to the straight life in their plastic uniforms, I said, "I don't want cotton. I don't want polyester. I want pure plastic."

wwd: That "plastic" look is central to the film's overall vision and design.

jb: Absolutely. If you notice, in the beginning, Megan's clothing is cotton; in the middle, polyester; and at the end, everything is entirely plastic. I wanted the production design and the sets to follow the same pattern, because at the end of the film, when the kids all say that they're "straight," that's the most artificial that they are; they're denying their true selves. In fact, everything that Cathy Moriarty wore was plastic from the beginning of the film to the end; the costume designers originally put her in a polyester uniform, and I said, "No, let's give her a plastic lab coat." I thought that her character should be really paranoid about diseases—AIDS, germs—and so we made everything sanitized. When she's outside cleaning her flowers, they're not even real flowers, because she doesn't believe in real sexual urges. To Mary, gay desire is unnatural, so let's go to a completely artificial place with her character.

WWD: Do you think that American society has changed much over the past ten years or so? Can you come out without dealing with an enormous amount of free-floating hostility? What are the risks?

JB: I do think you can come out, and I do think it will be OK. I'm an optimist. I think it will be OK because at least you will have love. Megan and Graham really love each other, and that love will carry them through a world full of problems and conflicts. The outside world may be hideous and horrible, and it may be a fight to stay alive, but if you have love, you'll be OK no matter what happens.

WWD: A lot of people have compared *Cheerleader* to John Waters's films, sort of a camp aesthetic, but I don't see that at all.

JB: Nor do I. I like John's films. But to me, I'm doing something totally different, and the optimism of *Cheerleader* is one of the things that makes it something separate. Tim Burton and John Waters both go for the same kind of constructed hyperreality that I use in my films, but they both have a darker edge to their work, and I'm more interested in using the camp aesthetic to make a positive statement. Then there's the whole question of women doing camp, which I don't think has ever really been done before. I wasn't interested in doing a camp movie that was completely satirical. I wanted it to have emotion; and I'm a romantic, so I wanted it to have some heart. A lot of people got on the Internet and attacked me for it, saying in essence, "You wish you could be John Waters." But I'm not trying to do that. I think that misses the point. I love his work, especially *Serial Mom* [1994], but I'm doing something lighter, more romantic, and more positive.

WWD: What's next?

JB: Well, for the moment, more television and then a feature, but that takes so much time to get off the ground, as I've said. Sometimes you just have to work for money; but even then, you should always give it your best shot. I hope I can get a feature off the ground in the next couple of years, and obviously, all the critical and audience response to *But I'm a Cheerleader* really helps with your next project. We'll just have to see what happens next.

BENNETT MILLER

I first met Bennett Miller when we were both guests on National Public Radio's *Anthem* series, as part of a panel discussion on digital filmmaking with producer Peter Broderick in the spring of 1999. I had just finished my book *The Second Century of Cinema*, which explored the future of digital cinema in what was then the dawn of the twenty-first century, and Peter Broderick, as the CEO of Next Wave Films, had just produced Christopher Nolan's first film, *Following* (1998). When Bennett and I met, we immediately hit it off. He had just finished his first feature-length documentary, *The Cruise* (1998), a seventy-six-minute portrait of the eccentric New York tour guide Timothy Levitch. The film was the result of typically intense research by Bennett prior to shooting: after focusing on the figure of Levitch as his protagonist, Bennett shot some eighty hours of digital video as exploratory material, *before* he actually began shooting the film in earnest.

Before the NPR show, Bennett and I fell into a discussion of the about-to-be-released *Blair Witch Project* (1999), which was the hot topic at the time, and bantered about the future of film as a viable production medium. When we went on the air, we all talked about whether or not film would disappear entirely in the new millennium. I held out (reluctantly) for film's inevitable demise, simply as a matter of business economics that the industry could not ignore. Because *The Cruise* was a low-budget digital film, I was sure Bennett would agree with me that film's days were numbered. But to my surprise, he felt that, unlike the manner in which CDs had replaced vinyl records, film would remain the dominant standard within the industry. I'm pleased that he was right, and I've often thought about that conversation since.

Flash forward to 2006. With the release of *Capote* in 2005, Bennett at a single stroke had established himself as a major director. As I prepared to pick up my conversation with him, I wondered what he had been up to between that film and *The Cruise*. I knew he had gotten an agent, but seven years is a long gestation period for a film. Most directors, once they're hot, immediately strike out into features, accepting nearly any assignment. But Bennett had a much smarter strategy. Instead, his agent got him work directing high-profile television commercials, at which he became a master, putting together his own "shop" (with branches around the world) to create commercials, picking up valuable technical expertise and contacts, and making a nice chunk of change at the same time for his efforts.

The anonymity of the process also suited him. Because the commercials were unsigned, Bennett could work on them, forget them, and then move on to the next one, all the while keeping an eye out for his first major project. That opportunity finally came with *Capote*, featuring a screenplay by Bennett's longtime friend Dan Futterman and starring Bennett's other oldest friend, Philip Seymour Hoffman. This strategy seems to me a very practical and sensible one. Why make films you don't care about when you can work in commercials and save your real intensity for a project that deserves it? During our telephone conversation on March 20, 2006, Bennett talked about his childhood, his first forays into video and film production, the making of *Capote*, and his future as a director. He was at his apartment in New York, working on his next project.

Filmmaker Bennett Miller on the set of his film *Capote* (2005). Courtesy United Artists/Sony Pictures Classics.

WHEELER WINSTON DIXON: So how are you?

BENNETT MILLER: I'm great. A long time.

WWD: Tell me how you made the voyage from digital handheld to a full-scale theatrical work in 35mm. *Capote* is your first fiction piece. What pushed you away from the documentary approach and into a full-scale re-creation of an era?

BM: I was not pushed away from the documentary format at all; in fact, I fully intend on returning to it. But documentary was never my ambition. It's something I kind of discovered along the way. Since I was a kid, I've been aiming toward feature narratives.

WWD: That's funny, because I gathered from other interviews that after *Capote* your next project was going to be a documentary.

BM: It just might be. I kind of fell in love with the documentary form and really do hope to make a few more projects. I've got a couple right now that I'm kicking around.

WWD: But all your life you wanted to make a fiction feature.

BM: I wanted from the time I was twelve to make narrative features. And along the way, before that ever happened for me, I discovered some great subject matter that I wanted to turn into a documentary.

WWD: Timothy Levitch, the tour conductor in *The Cruise*. You basically follow him around during a typical series of workdays, as he shows off the Big Apple to out-of-town tourists from the front of a double-decker bus.

BM: Yes. I had the wherewithal to do *The Cruise* back then, but I didn't have a subject, or the money, to get a feature done at that time in my life.

WWD: What was the budget on *The Cruise*?

BM: *The Cruise* was a pinch more than $100,000 at the end of the day, after blowup to 35mm and prints and final sound mix. But to shoot it, it cost much less, maybe a couple of thousand, because the whole thing was digital video. It was inexpensive.

WWD: How do you feel about the difference between video and 35mm now? On that NPR show, I was predicting the immediate demise of 35mm, which obviously didn't happen, although I think it's still moving in that direction. But what was it like working in 35mm for the first time on *Capote*?

BM: Well, I wasn't working in 35mm for the first time. After *The Cruise*, I began doing television commercials—lots of them.

WWD: Back when we did the NPR show, I understood that you were going to do something with *This American Life*, the NPR radio show.

BM: Yes, I dabbled with them for a while, but then I got into television commercials, and I got in at a serious and high level.

WWD: Whom did you shoot ads for?

BM: You name it, I did it. Everybody from Verizon, to Cingular, to Kellogg's cereals, Lincoln Navigator . . . the list goes on. Commercials are a great way to learn more about the craft, and so I shot dozens and dozens of commercials.

WWD: In the wake of *The Cruise*, you were very hot, and I'm sure people were giving you scripts; but you made the decision to go to commercials. That's smart.

BM: Well, my goal is to make very special films. And you can't just knock one off after the next. I finished *The Cruise*, and there were lots of new opportunities. I got a great agent and began to read scripts, and also had this opportunity to direct commercials. The commercials were never a destination for me; they were never a goal. But they were a means to practice my craft. I needed that, because I'm a dropout. I never got to fully study the craft at New York University.

WWD: But you did graduate from Mamaroneck High School in 1985.

BM: I did.

WWD: Did you know that that's Norman Rockwell's alma mater?

BM: Indeed, I did.

WWD: Is this where you met [actor and *Capote* scenarist] Dan Futterman?

BM: I met Danny in junior high school actually, when we were twelve. We met in the library. We didn't really become friends until a few years later. I was a little bit of an exhibitionist, I think, at the time. I had some kind of little routine that I would do.

WWD: Some shtick.

BM: Some shtick, for which I was constantly getting kicked out of the library.

WWD: Did you work on any videos or other early projects when you were in junior high school?

BM: Yes, of course. Dan and I did a couple of little things together, but Danny is more into theater. Still, we had a great program at Mamaroneck High School, a great television and video program. The town's local cable station is actually *in* our high school, and we have a large high school of about two thousand students. So this was the local community cable television studio, right there for us to work in.

WWD: The public access station.

BM: Yes, the public access station was in our high school, and every morning it broadcast a new show. Every homeroom had a television, and you would watch the announcement. I was not so interested in the live news format that they did; but when I was a freshman, I immediately started making videos, shorts to be played during the morning announcements, and they would go out through the community. I did that throughout my high school career. Before that, my family had a little video camera, and I was just obsessed with it. So I was making videos early on.

WWD: I was just going to ask you about your parents. Can you tell me a little bit about what they did and whether they were supportive of your work? How did they feel about your interest in film and video?

BM: Well, my mother is a painter, really quite a good one, and my father is a builder, a contractor.

WWD: Were they supportive of your work?

BM: Not particularly. I think I had what was a fairly common *Ice Storm*-type upbringing [a reference to Ang Lee's 1997 film about growing up in 1970s affluent suburbia]. Actually, I grew up not that far from where *The Ice Storm* was shot. I had, thankfully, a complete absence of supervision. If parents today ask me, "How do you foster creativity in your children?" I always say, "Neglect, just neglect them." That's the best thing. Then they'll do something.

WWD: You met Philip Seymour Hoffman in 1984 in a summer theater program in Saratoga Springs, New York, correct?

BM: Right. Danny and I both met him there.

WWD: Tell me a little bit about that meeting, what brought you guys together, and how you clicked.

BM: The program was four weeks long. We were living at Skidmore College, in the dorms, for the program. At the end of four weeks, I had made a few friends from that place, and they became lasting friends. Dan and Phil were some of the main ones; there are a couple of other people. But Phil was the real one that came out of that. It was probably just a matter of weeks after the program was over when we started hanging out. He was living in upstate New York. I lived in Westchester, and so he came down to Westchester, and we took a trip into the city, and I started showing him around New York, New York, where I was born.

WWD: So you graduated from high school, and then you went to NYU. How long did you stay there, and why did you drop out?

BM: I was in the actual film school maybe a year and a half. I dropped out because I just have always been a bad student, and I hated it. I think Woody Allen dropped out, too.

WWD: And after that, you got *The Cruise* off the ground. So let's just move past *The Cruise* and past the commercials. How did you become interested in Capote as a person, and what drew you to the subject?

BM: Well, Danny Futterman was the one who got me involved. He conceived the project and sent me his first draft of it, while all the time he was working as an actor on *Judging Amy*, the television series.

WWD: How does he feel about that now? Does he seem more interested now in writing, or is he still interested in acting?

BM: I think he is going to continue to do both. And I hope he does.

WWD: The script is absolutely brilliant. How long did it take him to write it?

BM: I don't know. I really don't know. Years. We tinkered on it for a year and a half before we shot it; and then as we shot it, tinkering continued to happen. But from the time he gave me a draft to the final shooting script, it was about a year and a half.

wwd: What was the major key to Capote's personality for you and Dan?

bm: Well, I think that Capote was abandoned, and I don't think he ever really overcame that problem. I think, not to belittle or trivialize his art and his career, that there was always an element beneath everything that was this kind of free-floating neurosis and insecurity. I think that was born very, very early within him. He never really found a way out. No amount of success, no claim to fame was going to undo these feelings that he had. For me, it's so interesting that such a vocal, articulate, and eloquent person was not really expressing that.

wwd: Well, probably he was too close to it to even understand it.

bm: Absolutely.

wwd: So how did you get the film off the ground? You have the script, and Phil has agreed to do it. I gather that there was a very dramatic sit-down where you and Dan and Phil all met together with the producers to green light the film. Is that true?

bm: Well, I don't know how dramatic it was, but we did that numerous times with numerous different people, all of whom said no, until Danny Rosett of United Artists agreed to do it. He's really the one who got behind it and made it happen.

wwd: What kind of a budget did they give you, and what kind of a schedule? It was brutally short, wasn't it?

bm: They gave us $5.5 million to make it, and then our producing partner, Infinity Media, gave us another million something, and then Canada gave us a tax break. So we ended up having a budget of something like $7 million.

wwd: And the schedule?

bm: I think we shot the whole film in thirty-four days.

wwd: How many takes did you do on a given setup?

bm: Anywhere between two and twenty-five.

wwd: Wow! What was the one that took twenty-five takes?

bm: Do you remember the scene where Bob Balaban, as William Shawn, the editor of *The New Yorker*, calls Capote when Truman is in Spain?

wwd: Yes, right.

bm: It's one shot of Capote answering his phone. He's writing, he answers the phone, and he has this brief conversation with William Shawn. That took about twenty takes to get it right. We *had* to get it right.

wwd: How long did it take Phil to get into the character? It's such a tough character to play.

BM: It took about six months to learn.

WWD: Did he do it basically by watching archival footage of Capote at work and stuff like that? How did he prepare?

BM: Most of that work Phil did by himself alone in a room with a locked door. That's his craft.

WWD: Capote was a rather diminutive guy, and his body gestures were very close to the body, very controlled. Phil is a rather burly guy and rather tall. Did you use a lot of "apple boxes" to cheat the height of the other actors throughout the film?

BM: Absolutely.

WWD: I figured.

BM: We hired tall extras, and we elevated people and used lifts in footwear, and platforms, and stuff like that, but also camera angles and wardrobing. And Phil losing more than forty pounds really helped. Phil's performance is really the key to the whole thing, though. He really worked on it.

WWD: Where was most of it shot?

BM: Winnipeg. Almost all of it was shot in Winnipeg.

WWD: Was any of it shot in New York?

Philip Seymour Hoffman as Truman Capote in Bennett Miller's *Capote* (2005). Courtesy United Artists/Sony Pictures Classics.

BM: We did two days in New York.

WWD: What did you shoot in New York?

BM: Basically we did the party scene. The first party scene was shot up in Harlem, the one where Truman is talking about Jimmy Baldwin's novels.

WWD: Now I want to talk about Adam Kimmel, your director of photography. Did he work as a DP on your television ads?

BM: Yes, he did. He also shot *Jesus' Son* [Alison Maclean, 1998]. He's probably done around a dozen features.

WWD: How did you meet him originally?

BM: Well, Alison is a friend of mine, and I went to a rough-cut screening of *Jesus' Son*, and that's the first time I ever got to see his work, which was great.

WWD: He also played a cameo as Richard Avedon, the photographer, in *Capote*.

BM: Right.

WWD: Was that sort of an "in" joke?

BM: No, it's not a joke at all. He was just the best person for the part. He really just moves around beautifully in that scene. We shot in Winnipeg, and so we had to cast the thing out of Winnipeg, and I brought in a lot of people, but nobody really knew how to handle a still camera. I didn't want to do it myself,

Philip Seymour Hoffman as Truman Capote attends a New York literary party in Bennett Miller's *Capote* (2005). Courtesy United Artists/Sony Pictures Classics.

so I actually operated the camera on that scene, and Adam operated the still camera. He was just the perfect person for the scene.

WWD: How did Catherine Keener [who played Harper Lee] become involved in the project?

BM: She came on in the most conventional way. Everyone else was a friend, or somebody I had known from the past, or a colleague from the past. But in her case, the casting director just suggested her. I revisited her work; I've always been a fan. So I met her, talked to her, offered her the part. And she was really good in the role.

WWD: How did you do the research to get the correct period feel? Because I really think you nailed it completely.

BM: Care and attention to detail. I had a great crew to work with. It was really a labor of love.

WWD: But how did you get that period feel—the sets, the props, the music, the feel of the piece? The whole film just seems so seamlessly sixties.

BM: Well, we tried to not make the mistake that some films make, which is an effort to oversell the period.

WWD: Overdressing the set?

BM: That makes it really fake, you know? It's not hard to research that period at all—you just have to do it right. You don't have to scratch too deeply to unearth oceans of reference material. A few things were very helpful to us. One was a documentary made by Robert Drew called *Primary* [1960].

WWD: Right, that's a great film. That's one of the first 16mm documentaries shot with sync sound, way back in the day.

BM: If you look at the wardrobe in *Capote*, like the courthouse scene when the killers arrive and stuff like that, you know it's just taken from that documentary. And also *In Cold Blood* [1967], the Richard Brooks film, is also a very good reference, because it really captures the era completely. It was *shot* in the sixties.

WWD: Right.

BM: Shot just a few years later, in the actual house, in the actual courtroom, on the actual street, with some of the actual people and the actual jury. So that was a great reference for us. But mostly it's just not trying to sell the period, but just being truthful to it. And then within that, find the tones and colors and compositions you want, using true period elements to communicate what we wanted to, on a more tonal level.

WWD: Could you speak a little bit about Mychael Danna's music? Because it seems to me it's the perfect score for the film.

BM: I agree.

WWD: It's almost "not there."

BM: Right. When I first started thinking about the score, the guiding principle was that I wanted a score that was not specific to the period and not specific to the region—in fact, not specific to *any* period and not specific to *any* region. This is a period piece set in the middle of America, but I wanted the film to have more universal resonance. So I didn't want the music to be from the fifties and sixties, or from the middle of the country, or sort of jazzy New York, or anything like that. I wanted a score that would communicate on a narrow level. And I thought, "What score does that?" And then I thought of *The Ice Storm.* I kept coming back to that film.

WWD: Perfect, perfect.

BM: And you know who did *The Ice Storm*? Mychael Danna. So I spoke to Mychael, had a great conversation, and it was a no-brainer. He was my first choice.

WWD: And what about [editor] Christopher Tellefsen? His credits are all over the board. He cut Larry Clark's *Kids* [1995], Harmony Korine's *Gummo* [1997], and then Harold Ramis's *Analyze This* [1999] and Milos Forman's *The People vs. Larry Flynt* [1996] and *Man on the Moon* [1999], which are much more mainstream films. How did you pick him?

BM: *Kids* and *Gummo* were the two most attractive credits on his resume for me. But the fact that he was all over the map and worked with all sorts of different directors, plus the fact that he worked with Milos twice, made me realize that this guy is versatile and he gets along with people. So I spoke to him on the phone, and we had a great conversation. Our very first conversation was one of the great conversations about this movie. As a director— and I'll even say as a person—I find that my own ability to articulate is very influenced by the person I'm speaking to. I find that with some people my doors are just open, and I flow, and I'm articulate, and I'm connected to myself and what I'm talking about. But with other people I feel the doors slam shut, and my throat crunches up, so I just want to be around the people who allow me to be creative and feel safe doing it. I got on the phone with him, and I felt like I was being *received*, and I felt like he had great ideas. It was a total vibe decision. I hired him over the phone.

WWD: Did he do a rough assembly before you looked at it?

BM: He was in New York. We sent him the footage, and he was assembling the footage as we shot it. He was basically just putting it together. When I returned to New York for the editing, he had a two-and-one-half-hour rough assembly, and we both realized that we had our work cut out. But there couldn't have been a better collaboration. He was really there, all the time.

WWD: Well, the editing is razor sharp. Every scene is up there just exactly as long as it needs to be. Did you storyboard the whole movie?

BM: No. We shot-listed the whole thing, and if there was ever something that was somewhat confusing, I would just do my own little "chicken scratch" storyboards. But [the DP] Adam Kimmel and I sort of speak the same language, and we are really of the same mind. We can walk into a room and understand the problem. When somebody has the answer, we *know* it. It's in our minds. There's just no reason to draw it.

WWD: I've heard that you kept a really tight closed set on *Capote*, which I totally understand—nobody hanging around who isn't necessary.

BM: Yes.

WWD: Could you talk briefly about that decision?

BM: Phil is a very sensitive guy. I'm a very sensitive guy. Something that is very important when you make a film is to create the kind of *atmosphere* that is necessary for this sort of tender work to happen. I'm just very sensitive to people's vibes, and it's enormously distracting and irritating to have unnecessary people and thoughts in the room.

WWD: I absolutely agree. Because then you become a "host," so to speak, for the visitor. It's good to see that the film has done so well at the box office.

BM: Yes.

WWD: But it's not a "blockbuster film," even though I think it's perhaps the best film of the year, and your direction is really stunning. I'm just wondering,

Philip Seymour Hoffman and Bennett Miller on the set of *Capote* (2005). Courtesy United Artists/Sony Pictures Classics.

in the future, what kind of work you're going to do. I hope you won't turn out like Alfonso Cuarón, who directed one of the great films of the early twenty-first century, *Y tu mamá también* [2001], but then went on to make *Harry Potter and the Prisoner of Azkaban* [2004]. Or, the worst case scenario, somebody like Christopher Nolan. I don't know if you ever saw *Following* [1998], but that's a really interesting and original film; but then, after remaking, badly, Erik Skjoldbjærg's *Insomnia* [1997] in 2002 with Robin Williams and Al Pacino, he winds up directing the utterly ordinary action vehicle *Batman Begins* [2005]. Now he's in pre-production on a *sequel* to the *Batman* film. Do you see yourself headed in that direction?

BM: No, no. I would not have made either of those two movies, because those movies don't really speak to me, although I heard they both did very good jobs with those projects.

WWD: Well, they elevated them slightly. But there is still the source material to consider, which is distinctly limited.

BM: Right. I think it would be difficult for me to accept any assignment that I didn't feel passionate about.

WWD: How are you going to resist that, though, if somebody offers you millions and millions to do a highly commercial project?

BM: Well, I just ask myself this question: "Is this going to help me make peace with myself before I die or not?" It's that simple. And I also ask myself, "When I'm two years into this three-year commitment, am I going to feel good about it and myself, and is it going to be giving me energy back?" And if the answer is "No," I'll be an unhappy person with a big paycheck.

WWD: Right, exactly. All the publicity surrounding *Capote* has vaulted you into international prominence. But whenever I see you on television or doing an interview in *Time* or whatever, you always seem very quiet and controlled, as if you are sort of taking it all in and watching what happens.

BM: Yes.

WWD: Are you conscious of what you have to do to retain your artistic integrity in the face of all this publicity, to say nothing of maintaining a handle on reality?

BM: Yes, I think so. I hope so.

WWD: How are you approaching all of this? This is a life-changing experience.

BM: Right. I don't know, really. I just try to be honest about what I want and make sure that there is integrity in the work.

WWD: Do you and Dan and Phil keep each other grounded?

BM: Definitely, definitely. You know, both of those guys are very grounded and down-to-earth and care about the work. It was actually a very good experience going through the whole release process, the distribution and fanfare, with them, because whatever we did, they kept me grounded. Especially Phil and

I; Dan's got a family and wasn't on the road as much. Phil and I would be on the road pushing the film, and no matter what we would be doing, whatever the kind of publicity around the film was, it usually ended up with us hanging out in one or the other's hotel room late at night, ordering French fries and watching the news or sports programs. You know what I mean. None of us party or anything like that.

WWD: What are your thoughts on the continual struggle between commercial projects and the personal vision that constitutes the battlefield of film? Movies have got to make money, but at the same time you have to make films that you want to make, so that you respect yourself at the end of the day.

BM: Just try to find the overlap. It's there.

WWD: How do you approach the commercials you shoot in between?

BM: That's totally different. My name is not attached to those works. It's off the record of my life. I'm just there to make the car look good, so to speak. I'm not going to be making commercials for a handgun corporation. You know what I mean.

WWD: Will you be doing more commercials in the future?

BM: Well, part of the answer to your question on how to resist the temptation to do junk and to preserve my integrity in Hollywood is that I'm not dependent on feature film paychecks. I have a way to support myself comfortably if I'm not finding the exact right project to do. I enjoy shooting commercials, and I enjoy the people I do it with. I'm very fond of my production company, which is called Hungry Man Productions. They are like a family to me. I don't want to pooh-pooh commercials at all, you know, because it's a good way to keep food on the table, and there is also *some* amount of creativity.

WWD: Absolutely. Do you have any idea of how many movies you passed on before you did *Capote*?

BM: Actually, in my apartment right now, there's a big pile of scripts in one corner that I have yet to eliminate, all of which were pre-*Capote*. It's not like I was offered all these scripts. But they were sent to me, and I read them and passed on them, and there were dozens and dozens and dozens.

WWD: From our last conversation—and this goes back to what I was talking about earlier—what are your feelings about film versus digital? What do you think is going to happen there? I've talked to a lot of people about this, and the executives say they are going to do away with film. It's already happening, because it's just so much easier to shoot and edit video, and the studios are going to save so much money on prints and advertising. But yet, the film look of *Capote* is just so gorgeous, and film, as a medium, has got this certain quality to it that video will just never have. So what do you think?

BM: You're right. But I just visited with David Fincher on the set of *Zodiac* [2007] a few weeks ago, when he was wrapping that up, and he shot that on video.

So we'll see what happens. It's definitely an issue on many people's minds. I like to work in both mediums, so we'll see what the future holds.

wwd: Do you have any other fictional projects beyond this that are sort of like the Holy Grail for you?

bm: Yes, I do. And I'm happy to say that I'm developing it right now. It's going to take a while, but I'm optimistic that it's not going to take forever. I can't tell you anything about it until it's absolutely ready to go, but it's going to be something really special.

wwd: Thanks for talking with me. It's nice to see that you're doing so well.

bm: My pleasure, absolutely. See you soon.

KASI LEMMONS

Kasi Lemmons is one of the new generation of African American filmmakers who grew up in the business working as an actor in everything from
McDonald's commercials to series television and soap operas, and then moved
on smoothly to the big screen in such films as Jonathan Demme's *Silence of the
Lambs* (1991) and Bernard Rose's *Candyman* (1992). However, even while she
was absorbed in building her career as an actor, she also worked diligently as a
writer on her own unproduced projects and longed for a chance to direct her
own film. That moment finally came with *Eve's Bayou* in 1997, a touching portrait of African American family life that became a huge crossover hit with
mainstream audiences. The success of the film, which Lemmons wrote and
directed, effectively put her on the map as a talent to watch.

Most recently, Kasi has been shooting *Talk to Me* (2007), with Don Cheadle
and Cedric the Entertainer, and seems determined to continue to work as both
an actor and a director for the foreseeable future. Married to the actor/director
Vondie Curtis-Hall (*Waist Deep* [2006]), Kasi manages to balance the demands
of family life, an acting career, and her own personal projects as writer/director.
It seems that we have only just begun to hear from this immensely gifted woman.
This conversation took place on March 22, 2006, and offers a view into the life
of an artist who is constantly searching for the next project that will captivate
her interest, whether as writer, actor, or, as she makes clear she most prefers,
director.

WHEELER WINSTON DIXON: You were born as Karen Lemmons. Why did you
change your name to Kasi?

KASI LEMMONS: I never really changed it. Nobody ever called me Karen—a
couple of people, my father occasionally. My mother and my sister always
called me Kasi or Katie.

WWD: And so that just basically stuck?

Director Kasi Lemmons on the set of her film *The Caveman's Valentine* (2001). Courtesy Jerry Ohlinger Archives. Copyright © Universal Studios, Inc.

KL: Yes.

WWD: You were born in St. Louis, Missouri, on February 24, 1961, but you were raised in Boston, Massachusetts, after your parents divorced. Could you tell me a little bit about your early life, your mother and father, and what they did?

KL: My father was a biology teacher, and my mom a counselor, and then she became a psychologist. And she finally got her doctorate in education at Harvard, which is why we moved to Boston after they got divorced, because she wanted to go to Harvard.

WWD: Were your parents supportive of your early work?

KL: Well, my mom put me in drama school, but I think that the reason was to occupy my time. She didn't want me to get depressed about the divorce.

WWD: How old were you when they got divorced?

KL: I guess I was nine.

WWD: What effect did that have on you?

KL: Well, I'm not sure that they got along very well. As a matter of fact, I'm sure they didn't. There's always a question of whether it's more stressful to have kids in a marriage when the people involved clearly don't get along. So in some ways I was a little bit relieved. Also, I had an adventurous nature, and for me, going to Massachusetts was kind of an exciting thing. So I can't say it was all bad.

WWD: When did you first decide that you wanted to act?

KL: Well, it was really when my mom put me into acting school.

WWD: Was that the Boston Children's Theater?

KL: Even before the Boston Children's Theater. It was just a drama class, but I thought, "Wow, this is fun." So I kept at it. It was almost like a day care center where they played dramatic games.

WWD: What is the Boston Children's Theater like?

KL: Well, it was wonderful when I was a kid; they had several companies. There would be one company that would perform downtown in Boston at the big theaters. Then there was a touring company, which would go out on the road and do children's summer theater. We worked out of the back of a truck; it was very informal, but really fun. We had some very good actors, mostly between eight and sixteen. The older kids would get the great parts, and we would kind of shuffle around and do the smaller parts. But it also functioned for me almost like an agency, because I got my first professional acting job out of Boston Children's Theater.

WWD: How did that happen?

KL: They were looking for a kid, so they called up people that worked with children in the area. It was a courtroom drama called *You've Got a Right*. I played Catherine Cooper, the first black girl to integrate a white school. So it was a historic show.

WWD: What happened next?

KL: While I was still in high school, I was very academic, and I went to a super-difficult school called Commonwealth; and in the summer I went to the Circle in the Square Program, a theater program. I was about fifteen, and that was the next place that I was with kids who kind of wanted to be professional actors.

WWD: And what kinds of plays did you do?

KL: At that time I was probably doing a lot of Shakespeare.

WWD: Do you have a favorite Shakespeare play?

KL: Well, I had a lot of fun doing Lady Macbeth, and I had a lot of fun being Ariel in *The Tempest*. And of course I played Juliet in *Romeo and Juliet*. That was a given. Well, the Circle in the Square was in New York, of course, and that was part of New York University's School of Drama at the time. So you could go out and do your acting classes at different studios. I would go to Lee Strasberg's studio or Stella Adler's. So later, when I was at NYU, I opened with Circle in the Square. Then I transferred from NYU to the University of California, Los Angeles, and went back into academics.

WWD: And what did you plan to do?

KL: I just wanted to continue my education. I was already working professionally as an actor, doing commercials and stuff of that sort.

WWD: Do you recall what commercials you did?

KL: A lot of them. I made my living doing commercials for a long time. I guess one of the most famous ones I did was for Levi's 501 blue jeans. I did a *lot* of McDonald's commercials while I was going to UCLA. So I thought, "Well, I'll just finish up in subjects that I'm kind of interested in." So I did European history and became a sociology minor. But I didn't really hang out at UCLA too long either. I came back to New York and went to the New School for filmmaking classes.

KL: Your first film was *Fall from Grace*.

KL: Yes, I made that while I was at the New School, in 1987 or 1988.

WWD: But before that, when you were at UCLA, you got your first acting job in a movie, right?

KL: Yes, that was *The 11th Victim* [1979], directed by Jonathan Kaplan. I played a rape victim, and the film was based on the Hillside Strangler murders. It was my first real gig, so I think I was completely awful. I was terrified.

WWD: But you'd done all those commercials.

KL: It's different. This was more like acting—I got to scream and everything. It was exciting. The other stuff was just "look at this hamburger."

WWD: The next thing I have for you is a *Spenser: For Hire* episode in 1985, entitled "Resurrection."

KL: Yes, that was in New York. That's after I'd been working with the Steppenwolf

Theatre Company at the Minetta Lane Theatre in New York. John Malkovich was our director. Before that, I was getting "cute little girl" parts, but suddenly I was getting edgier material. For a while, that's what I wanted to do, and this helped me. A little bit tougher, a little bit edgier than the stuff that I had been doing. Then I got *Spenser: For Hire*, which was a series television episode, no more, no less.

WWD: Which led to an ABC Afterschool Special with Tempestt Bledsoe and Della Reese, *The Gift of Amazing Grace* [1986], in which you had one of the major roles, as Subaya. What did you learn out of that?

KL: I learned a lot about continuity. That was the first time that a continuity person ever came up to me and said, "Hey, I just wanted you to know, for your future as an actor, that you need to pay more attention to this." That was a wake-up call. There's lot of things you have to pay attention to.

WWD: Then you went on to some serious studio time with *As the World Turns* from 1986 to 1989 as Nella Franklin. What did all this work teach you? Was working on a soap good for your discipline and your ability to memorize and run lines quickly?

KL: Well, actually, it was very on and off—I mean *very* on and off. I wasn't on the soap every day; I reoccurred. I didn't even have a contract. It was more or less "we need you now, so come in." It's good for just teaching you to be natural and to be able to say anything naturally.

WWD: And also to get through it because you can't stop, right?

KL: Yes.

WWD: It's sort of like being on stage, because cutting the camera costs a fortune. They do it all live with multiple cameras, so you can't screw up.

KL: The big thing I learned with soaps is that when your camera is on, there's a red light on it. And it's not like talk shows: you can't look at the camera; you have to avoid it. Just look upstage, downstage, whatever; but don't look at the camera, even for a second. You have to pretend it isn't there. But it helped that I had been doing theater for a while.

WWD: You were in Spike Lee's *School Daze* [1988], which I thought was a very interesting film, in a small part. What was that like?

KL: Oh, it was wonderful. That was my first meeting with Spike. We got along great; he was fantastic. Oddly enough, I just saw Spike last night, at the premiere of his new film, *Inside Man* [2006].

WWD: What can you tell me about the experience? How long were you involved in the shoot?

KL: I was probably there a week. That was shot in Atlanta, on the Morehouse campus. The greatest thing about that film was working with Sam Jackson and Branford Marsalis. It was a big step up.

WWD: You continued to do a lot of television to pay the bills: a two-part episode of *The Cosby Show* entitled "The Birth" in 1988; an episode of *The Equalizer* entitled "Day of the Covenant," also in 1988; and an episode of *A Man Called Hawk* entitled "Life after Death" in 1989.

KL: I'm sorry, but I really can't remember anything about those shows. It was such a long time ago. But I remember it was work and put food on the table.

WWD: Then you appeared in this rather strange film, *Vampire's Kiss* [Robert Bierman, 1989], with a pretty amazing cast [Nicolas Cage, Maria Conchita Alonso, Jennifer Beals, and Elizabeth Ashley], in which literary agent Peter Loew [Cage] believes that he's becoming a vampire. You're billed fifth in this, as "Jackie." It's your first starring role. How did this happen?

KL: I love *Vampire's Kiss*. I auditioned for it, and I got it. It was a big coup for me. It was a really cool film, and I had a blast. It was so much fun. That was my first lead, and the cast and crew were really tight.

WWD: And then back to the soaps: "Jackie" in *Another World* from 1989 to 1990. What prompted the move back to daily television—lack of decent roles in other projects?

KL: Yes, yes. It was money.

WWD: But then you began appearing in some really solid theatrical films in rapid succession in the early 1990s, such as Larry Peerce's *The Court Martial of Jackie Robinson* [1990], a TNT television movie; Jonathan Demme's *Silence of the Lambs* [1991], which we all know about; and Robert Townsend's very sweet valentine to the history of rhythm and blues, *The Five Heartbeats* [1991], way down in the cast list but working with Diahann Carroll and the Nicholas Brothers. You also appeared in Larry Elikann's feature film *The Great Los Angeles Earthquake* [1991]. Was this a conscious decision to move away from television? What can you tell me about these projects?

KL: Well, Larry Peerce was great. At first I thought he was an intimidating guy, but it was just a first impression. He's a lovely, lovely guy, and we see each other.

WWD: And *The Silence of the Lambs*?

KL: Well, that was a huge moment in my life. Everybody who was associated with that film suddenly had enormous visibility; it was just a monster. It was huge in a lot of ways, and Jonathan [Demme] also took me under his wing a little bit on the press junkets and stuff like that. He thought it would be good for my education to participate as much as possible. He invited me to the Oscars; I was there when it won for Best Picture [in 1992, along with Best Director for Demme, Best Actress for Jodie Foster, Best Actor for Anthony Hopkins, and Best Adapted Screenplay for Ted Tally]. And so we became kind of quite close. I think it's easy when movies have, at least in one location, a contained cast. This was also true later of *Candyman* [Bernard Rose, 1992] and, before *The Silence of the Lambs*, on *Vampire's Kiss*. We were kind of a contained group, and so we got quite close. It's an extended family.

WWD: At this point you've been working with lots and lots of different directors. Is there anyone in particular from whom you are picking stuff up? Are you thinking about being a director at this point?

KL: I was starting to think about being a director. But when I was acting, I was very focused on acting; I was trying to be technically perfect. I can remember on *The Silence of the Lambs* not being able to hit a mark correctly that I had to get in a scene with Jodie, which was right before lunch. Of course, she could have hit it in her sleep. We had to come down some stairs and we're looking at a television, and for some reason we never quite got it—or I never got it—and I remember just kind of dwelling on that and how important it was to hit the marks *exactly*.

WWD: What about Robert Townsend's *The Five Heartbeats*?

KL: I love that. I loved working with Diahann Carroll and the Nicholas Brothers; it was a blast. By this time, I'm kind of cruising in my career; I've done a lot of work, and I'm very comfortable. These are my friends; I know a lot of them. So it was a lot of fun. That was a comfortable set.

WWD: *The Great Los Angeles Earthquake*?

KL: Oh, I had just come out to LA, and I took all the jobs. Why not?

WWD: Then suddenly you broke through in a very interesting horror film, Bernard Rose's *Candyman*, as "Bernadette Walsh." This was several cuts above the usual thriller; Tony Todd was fantastic in the lead role. How did you get involved in this?

KL: Bernard is very "imitable" as a director: most people who work with him can do an imitation of him. But he's lovely. We actually became quite close friends. I became friends with a lot of directors I worked with, and the producers.

WWD: Tony Todd was amazing in this movie as the Candyman, a sort of urban boogeyman, and the film was a major horror hit. Did you know that this was going to have such an impact when you were involved in it?

KL: No, I never did.

WWD: Is it like this with all your films? Do you ever know in advance how it's going to come out in the end?

KL: No, I never do.

WWD: Not even *The Silence of the Lambs*?

KL: No. It was just like, "Here we are, we're doing this movie, and that's that." So, yes, I was surprised when it broke through and became a cult favorite. You just never know when you're working on the set what it's going to be like when it's completed.

WWD: Then you were in the first U.S. film directed by John Woo, *Hard Target* [1993], a Jean-Claude Van Damme vehicle that was the victim of a lot of studio recutting, much to its detriment. But you were still working with good actors like Lance Henrickson, Wilford Brimley, and Arnold Vosloo. What was working on that project like?

KL: Well, I'm afraid I probably don't even know all the stories. John Woo and I became friendly, and I was good friends with Lance Henrickson. I was having a pretty good time. I usually had a really good time with people I was working with. I can't even remember that not being the case.

WWD: Some more television followed: an episode of *Murder, She Wrote* entitled "The Survivor" in 1993; and even a *Walker, Texas Ranger* episode, "Night of the Gladiator," also in 1993. Other than working with a nice ensemble cast in *Murder, She Wrote*, anything of interest here?

KL: It was series television, and I enjoyed it.

WWD: Then you did Rusty Cundieff's *Fear of a Black Hat* in 1994, which was a really interesting hip-hop comedy. How did you get hooked into that?

KL: Well, Penny Johnson [-Gerald], was supposed to do that; but at the last minute she got *The Larry Sanders Show*, so she couldn't do it. And so Rusty called me at the last minute and asked me if I would come in for that shoot. Now *that* was really funny. On that set, because I was working with comedians and kind of being the straight woman, I was thrown off balance a bit. So it was very challenging in a fun sort of way. I just laughed all the time.

WWD: Rusty Cundieff went on to score the next year with *Tales from the Hood* [1995], a very interesting social activism horror film; then he went on to do *Sprung* [1997], a romantic comedy. But then there's a big gap, and I'm shocked to see him reduced to directing *The New Adventures of Spin and Marty* for Disney in 2000. What happened?

KL: Well, I saw him last night, too, at the *Inside Man* premiere. Rusty has so much talent; he's really an enormously talented person, very prolific and relaxed about his style. He's done a lot of television, and I think he's really going to keep working in both features and television.

WWD: Which brings me to you. I keep hearing from your friends over and over again that basically you consider writing your real job, that you write all the time.

KL: It's true. I've been writing scripts all the time, pretty much every day for fourteen years. I write on the computer. I have to write scripts, because that's the only way I can write parts that will get a lot of people whom I really want to work with involved.

WWD: It seems to me that there's an enormous amount of talent in Hollywood, black and white, that gets wasted. When you think of people like David Alan Grier, Clarence Williams III, Tisha Campbell, Robert Townsend, and many others, they're just not getting the roles they should. Why do you think this is? And why are there so few African American films being made?

KL: In [feature] films I think it's really difficult, because there is still this concept that black movies don't sell overseas, which I don't believe. So it's still very, very difficult to get an African American film made. When there is one, what [the producers] want to know is, "Who can you put in it?" There is a very short list of people to choose from, so it makes breakout performances harder. They want A list stars to green light the film and to open it. Everybody is kind of looking for the star who is going to make their movie. So it makes it harder for new people.

    The other problem is that the films aren't getting green lit in the first place. At the studio level, we don't quite have the executives we need. And then, when they are in there, they have to do what they think is going to help them keep their job and what makes sense for their company. Studios feel that African American movies don't sell overseas, for whatever reason, and they feel that the black films will sell only to a certain segment of the population, and that's it. Once you go through that, there isn't going to be any crossover, especially with certain types of films. Which, of course, was one of the beautiful things about *Eve's Bayou* [1997]—we totally crossed over.

WWD: Yes, you absolutely did. Before you got into that, in 1994 you appeared in D. Clark Johnson's satire *D.R.O.P Squad* [an acronym for "deprogramming and restoration of pride"], which had Spike Lee as executive producer and a great cast: Eriq La Salle, Vondie Curtis-Hall, Ving Rhames, and Vanessa A. Williams, among others. Is this where you first met Vondie Curtis-Hall, your husband, whom you married in 1995?

KL: Oh no, no, we'd known each other for a long time. I met him in a dance class in New York when I was a kid.

WWD: So when did the sparks start to fly?

KL: We were friends for a while, for maybe a couple of years. I think I met him when I was twenty, and we were just friends for a couple of years. But by the time I was making this film in 1994, we were already an item. Shooting *D.R.O.P. Squad* was a lot of fun; we shot it in Atlanta.

WWD: So when did you start working on the screenplay for *Eve's Bayou*, which was something you'd been interested in for a long time, correct?

KL: Probably about 1992.

WWD: What's your working method?

KL: Well, I had written a couple of screenplays by then, and I was a member of the Writer's Guild, but I had always been writing with somebody else. I had never really written one by myself. So it was kind of a big thing for me to embark on. It took a while to get it down. I would tell people the whole story at a party, way before I wrote anything down.

WWD: So you had the whole thing in your head.

KL: I had the whole thing in my head, and then it was just a matter of the discipline of actually sitting down and writing it.

WWD: How do you start your workday?

KL: I usually wake up and procrastinate for a while, and sometimes I get some exercise. Then I sit down, and I try and basically be in that space for about four to six hours. Every so often, I get up and take breaks. But I try and do a stretch of writing every day, and I actually am very possessive of my time. I look forward to a day where I don't have to do anything else, don't have a meeting, or work, or anything, to have just hours in front of me to work on a script. I get excited about it.

WWD: When did you decide that you were going to direct it? Did you just wake up one morning and say, "Hey, if I'm going to do this, I'm going to do it myself"?

KL: I woke up one morning literally, and it was an epiphany.

WWD: But first you had to direct the short film *Dr. Hugo* [1998], based on a segment of your script for *Eve's Bayou*, starring Vondie in the lead role, in order to convince the studios that you could direct *Eve's Bayou*. Why was this necessary after all the work you'd done before and behind the camera? Short film to convince them?

Lynn Whitfield as Roz Batiste with her children (left to right: Meagan Good, Jake Smollett, and Jurnee Smollett) in Kasi Lemmons's domestic drama *Eve's Bayou* (1997). Courtesy Jerry Ohlinger Archives. Copyright © 1997 Trimark Pictures, Inc.

KL: Because I had just gone to film school and made these kind of semi-documentaries. I didn't have anything on film that resembled what was in my head.

WWD: Did you actually shoot film for *Dr. Hugo*, or did you shoot video?

KL: I shot film.

WWD: 35mm?

KL: Yes, 35mm. I mean, that was the whole point. It's kind of like, "OK, can you really do it, work with the cameras and a real crew and everything?" It took us about four days.

WWD: How did Samuel Jackson become involved?

KL: Well, Sam saw *Dr. Hugo*. Then he read the script, and at the time he was playing a lot of character roles. He hadn't really done a leading man, somebody who gets the girl. He saw that this was a really good part for him, and so he got behind the project.

WWD: How would you describe the shoot for *Eve's Bayou*?

KL: Stressful and interesting. It was about thirty-six days.

WWD: Wow, that's pretty short.

KL: Yes.

WWD: And what was your budget?

KL: $3.8 million. Not that much.

WWD: Wow. And what was your shooting ratio?

KL: Oh, maybe three to one, two to one, something along those lines. [For every foot in the finished film, only two or three feet were left over of any given scene; average mainstream features usually have a ten to one ratio or even higher.]

WWD: Well, it looks absolutely gorgeous. We should give Amy Vincent, your director of cinematography, total props for her work on the film.

KL: Absolutely.

WWD: How did you hook up with Amy?

KL: Well, when I was looking for somebody to shoot *Dr. Hugo*, I was really looking for somebody who could emotionally tell a story through film. I knew exactly what I was looking for, and the producer, Cottie [Caldecot] Chubb and I went to the American Film Institute and looked at some shorts to see if we could find someone. We saw this short film, and it was so very moody, and a lot of it took place in a house. It was very moody, shadowy, and emotional, and we thought, "This might the person for us to shoot the movie." So she was the director of photography on *Dr. Hugo*, and then she was the DP on *Eve's Bayou*.

WWD: This was her first job as a DP on a feature, right?

KL: It was.

WWD: Wow. So this is a lot of faith.

Samuel L. Jackson in Kasi Lemmons's *Eve's Bayou* (1997). Courtesy Photofest.

KL: It was a lot of faith on the producer's part; and he really insisted, after we shot the short film together, on keeping us together. So it was a lot of bravery and faith on his part.

WWD: How did you keep the whole thing together when you were shooting it, just basically moving like crazy?

KL: Moving like crazy. I had the entire film visually in my head. Amy and I developed a real rapport on *Dr. Hugo*, so we could talk in shorthand. I mean we could absolutely look at each other and communicate. She just got me. So we were able to kind of bring that to this film. Because we were trying for a look that we accomplished on *Dr. Hugo*, we kind of knew what we were going for. And then we prepped it out: we storyboarded it, we drew the whole movie.

WWD: So you storyboarded the whole thing?

KL: The whole thing.

WWD: That's a lot of work.

KL: So we were prepared. So when things got crazy, we had a fallback plan, and we knew with each shot exactly what we were going for. But it was still very, very, very crazy. It was a tough shoot.

WWD: How long was Sam Jackson actually on the picture?

KL: Sam was on most of the run.

WWD: How did you feel when you wrapped shooting?

KL: Well, when I finished *Eve's Bayou*, I realized what it was going to be, and I thought it worked beautifully. But you never know if something is going to work for audiences. But it worked for me. And once I realized *that*, I felt that I never had to do it again, in a way. I felt, "Oh, I've done this. I've accomplished something." I did much more than I ever thought I could. I brought something from my head to an audience, and it was a wonderful feeling. And when it worked for the audience, it was like having gone to heaven. It was just a magnificent thing. I guess as artists we really are searching for an audience, and you just want to communicate with them. So it was just really beautiful that the story found its way into other people's hearts. So in a sense I kind of felt, "OK, I don't have to direct again." And that lasted for about a minute. [*Laughs.*]

WWD: Who released *Eve's Bayou*?

KL: Trimark.

WWD: What was the relationship with Trimark like?

KL: Well, they did more for that film than I think almost anyone could have done, because they really put everything into it. They pushed it. I mean they really put a lot into it. And so it was very emotional from their point of view as well. It was a gamble.

WWD: Were you surprised by the massive critical acclaim that *Eve's Bayou* received? How did you handle all the attention? Suddenly you were a triple threat: an actor, a writer, and a director.

KL: It was great, even though some of it went by in a blur, I've got to tell you. There is a part of me that wishes I could remember every moment. The first time we screened it for a real audience, we got three standing ovations. It was one of those moments in life where everything is beautiful. We all burst into tears—all the producers, all the men, everyone. It was a very, very big moment for us, with our little film.

WWD: How do you and Vondie keep your life in balance, when both of you are actors and directors, and you have children to take care of as well? That's a lot to keep on top of. How do you keep the whole thing in balance?

KL: It works pretty well. We are each other's best support, so it's like having somebody who understands immediately where you're coming from. We take turns talking about the daily battles we have to go through with work and check in with each other during the day to find out what the status is. My first thought when you asked that question was that you should have seen this past summer. It got really crazy when Vondie was directing Hunter, our son, in his new movie, *Waist Deep* [2006]. That was really insane.

WWD: *The Caveman's Valentine*, which you directed in 2001, was an impressive and beautiful film, with another superb performance by Sam Jackson. But it just didn't click with the public, despite a larger budget and pretty good distribution.

KL: No, it didn't.

WWD: What do you think happened? Was the material too bleak? Or was it that people found it tough to identify with Sam's character, Romulus Ledbetter, an acclaimed concert pianist whose life has been derailed by severe mental illness?

KL: Well, I think that the script was always one of those that people either love or hate. And I think the movie kind of came out that way as well.

WWD: It was a much tougher picture to get into.

KL: Yes, it's not quite as accessible. I loved the character of Romulus and wanted to do it with Sam very badly. And I loved the script and the book [both by George Dawes Green], and I just thought it would all work out. But it was really the character that I fell in love with. And so, even though it didn't really hit, I'm glad I made it.

WWD: So how did you absorb going from heaven to purgatory, so to speak, when the film didn't hit?

KL: It was a reality check. But I think that we knew from the beginning that *Caveman's Valentine* was much, much riskier and that it really needed people that were in love with it behind it. And at a certain point there was kind of a regime change in the company that really didn't get it. So I think that, for whatever reason, it never really found its home. It's funny, because there are

Tamara Tunie as Shelia and Samuel L. Jackson as Romulus in Kasi Lemmons's *The Caveman's Valentine* (2001). Courtesy Jerry Ohlinger Archives. Copyright © Universal Studios, Inc.

    people out there who love it. But it never could find its way to those people who would probably be the right audience for it, and so it was genuinely hard.

WWD: Since then, you've done an episode of *ER*, "It's All in Your Head" in 2002, and you appeared in the documentary film *In the Company of Women* (2004), directed by Gini Reticker and Lesli Klainberg.

KL: Yes.

WWD: What was that like?

KL: It was great. I've done a few of those where I've been asked to talk about my work, and that was one of those projects that came out very well. But I'm never quite comfortable just talking.

WWD: About your work?

KL: About anything, actually. I don't like to verbalize too much. I think I'm better when I'm actually creating.

WWD: Do you prefer to direct, act, or write? What's your favorite part of the filmmaking process?

KL: I love directing.

WWD: You love it even more than acting now?

KL: Oh, yes. Acting was my first love, so it will always be my first love. But now I want to direct more films.

WWD: That's like Ida Lupino, the forties actress who went on to direct a bunch of very interesting movies in the fifties. Just before she died, she was asked which she preferred, acting or directing. She chose directing without hesitation.

KL: Yes, definitely, there is no contest.

WWD: Why do you think that is?

KL: You can control the entire vision, from the idea that's in your head to the finished project on the screen. And then the collaboration is so intimate. As an actor, of course, you are collaborating with the other actors and with the director, but that's still just a portion of the whole picture. There is something about the collaboration that I find deeply, deeply rewarding. When you put together a team, and everybody is there for the project, and everybody believes in it, and everybody is trying their hardest with very little money, it's magic to me. I like the collaborating. I like the people part of it. I like the sense of accomplishment you feel when you actually are able to present it.

WWD: So you get a real sense of being there in the moment with the actors, the crew, everyone?

KL: Oh, yes.

WWD: What are you working on now?

KL: Well, I'm just about to start shooting on *Talk to Me* [2007], the story of Washington, D.C., radio personality Ralph "Petey" Greene, an ex-con who became a popular talk show host and community activist in the sixties. It's just an incredible, incredible story, and I feel very passionate about it. I think it's going to be a fantastic movie. Don Cheadle and Cedric the Entertainer star in it. I really think it's going to be a great film.

WWD: What are your hopes for the future of cinema? Do you see the coming digitization of cinema as something that will be positive for independent filmmakers, or does the whole thing still rest on the issue of distribution? Where do you see yourself in your career in ten years? What is the primary work that you hope to accomplish as a filmmaker?

KL: Well, I think the whole thing rests on distribution.

WWD: I would agree.

KL: I think it's great when you can get stuff into the pipeline now with the Internet; and with all these new outlets, it's hard to say what's going to happen next. I guess I would like to change audience perceptions in a way, especially the way African American films are perceived. I would like to be a major influence in opening up the spectrum, and I would like to be an influence on a new generation of filmmakers. One thing we know for sure is that the medium is going to change. But I think that there will always be a future for celluloid and dark theaters.

INDEX

ABOUT THE AUTHOR

Wheeler Winston Dixon is the James Ryan Endowed Professor of Film Studies and Professor of English at the University of Nebraska, Lincoln. With Gwendolyn Audrey Foster, he is Editor-in-Chief of the *Quarterly Review of Film and Video*. His newest books as author or editor include *Visions of Paradise: Images of Eden in the Cinema*; *American Cinema of the 1940s: Themes and Variations*; *Lost in the Fifties: Recovering Phantom Hollywood*; *Film and Television after 9/11*; *Visions of the Apocalypse: Spectacles of Destruction in American Cinema*; *Straight: Constructions of Heterosexuality in the Cinema*; and *Experimental Cinema: The Film Reader*, co-edited with Gwendolyn Audrey Foster. On April 11–12, 2003, he was honored with a retrospective of his experimental films at the Museum of Modern Art in New York, and his films were acquired for the permanent collection of the museum in both print and original format.